Soviet Industry from Stalin to Gorbachev

STUDIES IN SOVIET HISTORY AND SOCIETY

edited by Joseph S. Berliner, Seweryn Bialer, *and* Sheila Fitzpatrick

---

Soviet Industry from Stalin to Gorbachev

Essays on Management and Innovation

JOSEPH S. BERLINER

Cornell University Press
Ithaca, New York

First published in 1988 by Cornell University Press.

Library of Congress Cataloging-in-Publication Data

Berliner, Joseph S.
  Soviet industry from Stalin to Gorbachev.
  (Studies in Soviet history and society)
  Includes index.
  1. Industrial management—Soviet Union—History—20th century. 2. Technological innovations—Soviet Union—History—20th century. 3. Soviet Union—Industries—History—20th century. 4. Soviet Union—Economic policy—1917–   . I. Title. II. Series: Studies in Soviet history and society (Ithaca, N.Y.)
  HD70.S63B425   1988   338.0947   87–47839

ISBN 0–8014–2170–5

Printed in Great Britain

Contents

38437

Foreword
Holland Hunter

These selected essays are both timeless and timely – offering wise perspective on Soviet experience and fundamental insights into the difficulties confronting M. S. Gorbachev. The managers who run Soviet enterprises are the key to Soviet economic performance. For over half a century they have operated under essentially unchanged institutional pressures, and for over three decades Professor Berliner has pioneered in analyzing their behaviour. These essays thus provide a deeply-informed background for appraising Gorbachev's efforts to revise the institutional pressures and alter Soviet managerial behaviour.

The papers, written from 1950 through 1987, also reflect the evolution of Western understanding of the Soviet economic system. Readers should be aware of two initial analytic complications. Soviet descriptions of economic practice in the 1930s were blandly prescriptive and over-optimistic. Western appraisals were coloured by a substantial literature offering or denouncing blueprints for a planned economy. Serious young students of the Soviet economy after the Second World War had to push through this misleading material and assemble primary evidence for an objective understanding of actual Soviet economic practice. Berliner's early essays were landmarks in this search.

Efforts to understand the Soviet economy in the 1940s and 1950s were also impeded by Soviet secrecy, so extreme that even the size of the total population was unreported. Moreover in the United States, during the worst cold war years, those who studied the USSR sometimes came under suspicion as possible sympathizers. In 1955, for example, because I was subscribing to several Soviet economic journals, Haverford College was asked by the UK Post Office whether it was aware of and approved the fact that 'communist propaganda', potentially 'non-mailable', was being received by a faculty member (letter from Solicitor Abe McGregor

vii

Goff to Gilbert F. White, president, 25 April 1955). Readers should appreciate Berliner's detached, objective approach, calmly ignoring the pressures that, on occasion, have played on Soviet studies in the West.

The analytic background for these essays has been marked by a trend in Western economic thought that has shifted emphasis from static equilibrium to output expansion and technological innovation. Among the contributors to the shift in emphasis have been some outstanding economists who left Russia as youngsters after the 1917 revolutions: Simon Kuznets, Wassily Leontief, and Alexander Gerschenkron, whose conceptual innovations in defining and explaining national income growth, formulating and applying input–output analysis, and clarifying regularities in the processes of economic development have served in turn to throw light on Soviet problems. Their influence can be traced in Berliner's essays.

In using contemporary Western economic theory to analyze the Soviet economic system, Berliner found that familiar principles had to be reformulated to explain behavioural responses to unfamiliar pressures. The manager of a Soviet firm, unlike his Western counter-part, finds it easy to sell his output; the major difficulties for him lie in obtaining adequate input. He is under intense pressure to compete, not in turning out high-quality products at low prices, but rather in sacrificing quality and price considerations to ever-increasing demands for sheer quantity. In the seminal essays which follow, the reader will find Berliner spelling out, step by step, the way supply and demand forces interact under these novel con-ditions. This has been genuinely pioneering work.

Trends in Western understanding of the Soviet economy have reflected the emphases noted above. There was initial doubt whether the 'millions of equations problem' could be solved at all, i.e., whether a non-market economy could avert chaos. It has long since become clear that the Soviet economy is viable in the short run and capable of moving forward from year to year, indeed of growing steadily. In the 1930s, 1940s and 1950s, millions of Soviet citizens made heroic and, to some extent, unnecessary sacrifices for the building of a large powerful economy. The capacity to expand output has been clearly demonstrated. As Berliner was the first to show, however, the ability to foster innovation and technological progress, now the decisive test of a modern economy, has proved to be the Soviet economy's weakest feature.

Trends in the focus of Soviet economic policy have been some-what parallel to those in the West, but changes have been notably delayed. Short-run viability was demonstrated in the mid-1920s. Under the pre-war Five Year Plans, starting in 1929, great stress was laid on output expansion making use of large increments of labour and capital, and drawing on large, low-cost supplies of natural resources, to build heavy industry and benefit from a large-scale shift away from agriculture. There was a one-shot infusion of technological progress as advanced plant and equipment from Germany, the UK, and the US were imported, but there was little provision for ongoing incremental innovation. For example the Ford Motor Company contracted with the USSR in 1928 to build a factory at Gorky for making Model A trucks and passenger cars, but in 1932, when Ford offered the V–8 engine as part of the nine-year contract, Moscow declined. Not until the 1950s were V–8 engines produced in the USSR. (See George D. Holliday, *Technology Transfer to the USSR*, Boulder: Westview Press, 1979, pp. 121–2 and 131–2).

The stress on rapid output expansion after 1928 led to drastic, unanticipated declines in the quality of raw materials, finished goods, and construction. Stalin's speeches laid great stress on fostering positive incentives but, after a few years of enthusiastic popular response, the spread of terror and purges fostered fear and cautious conformity instead. Prevailing technology was being mastered, but there was little innovation.

Under Khrushchev and Brezhnev, the importance of positive incentives to stimulate productivity and innovation received more attention, but output expansion after 1953 came primarily, as before, from extensive application of additional labour and capital. Soviet economists and Party leaders groped for within-system changes that would raise efficiency and stimulate technological progress, to little avail. Only with the accession to power of M. S. Gorbachev have the full dimensions of the systemic impasse been confronted. What is wrong, and what corrections are needed?

Here Berliner's pioneering investigations prove to be highly relevant. His perceptive insights suggest the direction in which the answers have to lie. They lie within economics (of course), but not merely within economics as narrowly conceived. One can hold the conviction (as I do) that there are universal economic principles governing the efficient management of scarce resources, yet recognize that the economic principles in practice operate within diverse institutional frameworks. Extension of economic analysis to incorporate key aspects of these frameworks is inescapable if we are to improve our ability to appraise systemic performance and prospects.

Berliner recognized this in the earlier 1960s when he took time off to study anthropology; one result was a critical article, 'The Feet of the Natives Are Large: An Essay on Anthropology by an Economist', which anthropologists were delighted to publish in *Current Anthropology* in February 1962. In 1972 he published an incisive monograph on the production and distribution of social outcomes (*Economy, Society, and Welfare*, New York: Praeger Publishers). One notes that the third and eighth essays in this volume appeared originally in public administration publications. Berliner is thus an exemplary model of the economist whose curiosity and intellectual rigour lead him to incorporate neighbouring areas into his analysis.

Among the economic principles that may be universal is the rule that efficiency requires inefficient producers to be eliminated. Bankruptcy has not so far been a feature of Soviet economic practice, but new regulations now provide for it and it may come into regular use. The firing of inefficient workers is a related precept, also being considered by the Kremlin. If accompanied by retraining of displaced workers and redirection of a firm's resources, application of these rules will clearly improve the economy's technical and social performance. What is not yet clear is how they can be fitted acceptably into the Soviet institutional framework. Berliner reviews the prospects in his concluding essay.

Another issue of principle concerns the decisions governing investment in new capital plant and equipment. Under longstanding Soviet practice, the net income of Soviet state-owned enterprises is to a large extent taxed into the central state budget, whence it can be allocated for investment in directions chosen by the Party. Soviet railroads, for example, generated large amounts of net income in the 1960s and 1970s, but these profits were taken away from the railroads and assigned mainly to pipelines (with only modest amounts going to passenger automobiles and highways).

Under the reforms currently proposed by Gorbachev, however, enterprises will be free to plough back their net income into expansion of their own facilities (though not, probably, to invest elsewhere as they see fit). This change could greatly stimulate innovation and technological progress, but will the Party countenance dispersion of choice over the direction of this progress? What if production of 'boom boxes', VCRs, and other consumer-oriented electronic products proves highly profitable, while development of northern natural gas fields requires subsidies? Will the Party not continue to limit the expansion of 'frivolous' kinds of output?

If some degree of universality attaches to fundamental canons of taxation and government expenditure, it will be interesting to see how they operate within the Soviet institutional framework as price-setting becomes more flexible. Differentiated sales and income taxes are used in mixed economies to cushion the impact of market forces; will they be similarly used in the USSR? Can Soviet budget management contain inflationary forces if administrative controls are loosened? Readers will find Berliner's 1981 essay (Chapter 10) an illuminating analysis of past Soviet difficulties and thus a cogent basis for appraising future possibilities.

Berliner argues in his concluding essay that neither excessively taut planning nor a soft budget constraint can account for Soviet difficulties – that central planning itself is the basic barrier to efficient, innovative economic activity. I wonder, however, whether central planning focusing on *quality*, for products, processes, and services, might not enable the USSR to maintain its preferred institutions while keeping up with its advanced neighbours. Higher quality has been demanded since at least 1976, but only as an addition to strenuous quality targets. If centrally-administered rewards and penalties are decisively linked to the quality of raw materials, construction, manufactured components, and services, then more rapid growth of constantly-improving output will be an indirect result. Can the system make a shift? As the Russian proverb has it, 'We will live, and we will see.'

This foreword is meant to serve as prologue for a most impressive performance, a play in three acts and twelve scenes giving dramatic unity to the most central economic issues arising out of Soviet experience. Berliner thoughtfully sets the stage, presents the players, and chronicles the past. A reflective reader is sure to enjoy his perceptive analysis of the record to date. In addition, these essays offer indispensable guidance for understanding the economic significance of the further acts now unfolded in Moscow.

Haverford, Pennsylvania
September 1987

Part I

The Management of Enterprise

1 Monetary Planning in the USSR*
1950

The first ten articles of the Constitution of the USSR establish the social ownership of the means of production as the political and economic basis of the Soviet state. Article Eleven sets forth the second distinguishing feature of the Soviet economy: 'The economic life of the USSR is determined by the state national economic plan.'

The extent and efficiency of Soviet planning is a subject of absorbing interest to students of the Soviet economy. Interest is heightened by the effusive writings of Soviet economists, which depict the plan as an all-embracing, tightly knit system of relationships and controls which leaves little or no room for errors or misallocation of resources. The plan reaches down to the most minute elements of the economy.

In the Soviet economic system the people's actions are mobilized for the execution of the state plan, and the work of every toiler is in the final analysis subordinated to the common goal[1]

... every worker in the Soviet Union keeps a strict watch over the achievements of the plan on every sector of the economic front.[2]

If errors or dislocations appear, they are quickly detected and corrected, for

The plan foresees all the most important elements of the national economic process ... By means of such (conjunctural) observations, all the changes that take place during the course of carrying out the plan, and the cause of these changes, are explained, and it is made possible to assist in the

*The American Slavic and East European Review (September 1950) vol. IX. pp. 237–54.

fulfillment of the plan and to introduce corrections in the plan during
the course of its fulfillment.[3]

In the writings of the more ardent protagonists, it is difficult
to see room for improvement.

Socialist planned economy raises production to the highest possible point
corresponding to the development of the given productive forces . . . Socialist planned economy excludes any anarchy of production, without – as
we mentioned above – degenerating into bureaucratic centralism.[4]

Such writings have led to a widespread view that the Soviet
Union is free from the various kinds of economic dislocations which
repeatedly convulse free market economies. In consequence of this
view, the announcement of monetary reform in the Soviet Union
in December 1947 was the occasion of considerable surprise in
the Western world, not only because of its severity but because
of its having happened at all.[5] Most of the occupied countries
of Europe instituted monetary reforms between 1945 and 1947,
but these were accepted as a normal form of readjustment of
economic relationships dislocated by the strains of total war. Such
dislocations are perhaps to be expected in free market systems,
but how could they have happened in an economy as completely
planned and nicely balanced as the Soviet?

In fact, the monetary reform was only a dramatic revelation
of one of the many kinds of imbalance that have actually or potentially exercised the Soviet planners since the First Five Year Plan.
These imbalances are mystifying only if one takes the glib view
that planning consists of the organization and coordination of the
economy for the direct transition to a preassigned goal. The fact
is that all along the way the planners are confronted by alternative
paths, each of which bristles with undesired consequences, either
known or unknown. Two assigned aims may prove to be mutually
exclusive and the less urgent may have to be sacrificed to the more
urgent. For example, in the case of monetary reform, monetary
stability during the war had to be sacrificed to the paramount
aim of maximum production for the war effort, and the monetary
reform was the drastic reassertion of the aim of monetary stability
after the emergency had passed. Planning is therefore fundamentally
a problem of choice, usually among means, but often among ends.

The purpose of this chapter is to examine Soviet planning in
the light of the alternatives open to the planners. To reduce the
scope to manageable proportions attention is confined to the
planning of one aspect of the economy – the monetary system.
Part I develops a scheme for the classification of the monetary

system in terms of money flow. Part II discusses the planning of the money flow between the population and the state-controlled economic institutions. The analysis centres about the problem of a high rate of investment, in which the pursuit of monetary stability creates many of the most complex problems of choice for the planners. Part III deals with the money flow among individuals, which, although not directly planned, must be reckoned with by the planners because of its disruptive potential, as exemplified in the monetary reform. Finally, Part IV discusses the limitations of monetary planning in terms of knowledge, obstacles, and rigidities in the economic system.

PART I

For the purpose of classifying the money circulation, the Soviet economy may be divided into two analytically distinct sectors – the socialized sector and the population. The population comprises all persons in their capacity as money income receivers. The socialized sector consists of all corporate economic and administrative agencies whose financial activities form part of the Financial Plan, such as industry, transport, commerce, state-owned agriculture, trade unions, cooperatives and kolkhozy. Three kinds of monetary transactions take place with reference to the two sectors:

1) transactions wholly within the socialized sector, as when a coalmining enterprise receives payment for a sale of coal to a steel mill;
2) transactions wholly within the population, as when a worker buys agricultural goods from a kolkhoznik in the kolkhoz market; and
3) transactions between the socialized sector and the population, as when a worker receives wages for labour performed in an enterprise.

Transactions Within the Socialized Sector
The great bulk of commercial transactions is effected by means of credits and debits on the books of Gosbank, which operates as the centre of a general clearing system.[6] The advantage of this procedure over that of direct commercial payment is in the control[7] exercised by the Bank over the operations of enterprises; not only is the sphere of currency transactions greatly curtailed,[8] but the Bank is authorized to scrutinize all transactions to ensure that they conform to the plan. Thus the effort of an enterprise to purchase

scarce materials in excess of its plan, either for hoarding or for concealing producton inefficiencies, would soon be revealed by an overdrawn account in Gosbank.[9]

Currency payments play a very small part in transactions in this sector. Since purchases involving less than 1,000 roubles are exempt from the clearing system and may be effected in currency, most enterprises carry small sums of petty cash on hand. The communications system (post office, telephone, etc.) and the savings banks are permitted by law to maintain substantial fixed currency balances for daily operations, and these sums are the only large permanent currency holdings in the socialized sector outside of Gosbank.[10]

The chief use of currency in the socialized sector is for transactions with the population, such as payments to the population for wages and pensions, and receipts from the population, such as taxes and proceeds from the sale of goods. Enterprises making payments to the population must withdraw currency from their Gosbank accounts, and enterprises which receive payments from the population deposit their currency with Gosbank, but there may be varied sums of currency in the hands of enterprises in the interim between Gosbank and the population. The funds of all 'budget'[11] organizations are concentrated in Gosbank, but most of the actual transactions with the population are handled by savings banks. Almost all payments made by the socialized sector to the population are therefore preceded by money transfers between Gosbank and a state organization.[12]

Although kolkhozy are not, strictly speaking, state-owned organizations, their financial operations are circumscribed by, and included in, the Financial Plan. For centralized and decentralized deliveries to state procurement agencies, deposit accounts in Gosbank are credited in the same fashion as any enterprise. For the payment of money incomes to kolkhozniki for labour days, kolkhozy withdraw currency from their deposit accounts in Gosbank. In addition, kolkhozy enter the kolkhoz market as sellers, receiving payments in currency. The other agricultural institutions, such as sovkhozy and machine tractor stations, are completely state-owned and pay wages to the workers in the same way as enterprises.

There is a certain amount of purchasing at retail by socialized sector organizations, both in the kolkhoz market and in the state retail network. After 1939 a special fund of retail goods was set aside for sale to urban organizations, partly for cash and partly by non-cash transactions. But all rural organizations and some urban organizations continued to buy retail goods which had been allocated to the population at large.[13] The total volume of retail trade does not therefore represent a flow of money from the population to the socialized sector, but includes some flow within the socialized sector.

Transactions Within the Population
Most of the money payments among individuals take place on the kolkhoz market. Typically the sellers in the market are kolkhozniki, who exchange the produce of their private plots for currency. The buyers are mostly city dwellers, who receive the largest part of their incomes in currency, but rural non-agricultural[14] persons such as doctors and transport workers, as well as kolkhozniki and state farm workers, also enter the market as buyers. The relative proportion of urban to rural buyers depends upon the proximity of the particular market to rail centres or cities.

Agricultural goods play the chief role in transactions among people, but there is a considerable trade in new and secondhand manufactured goods.[15] In the latter case the sellers are non-cooperative artisans of city and village, and persons of all sorts who make or have things to sell. There are indications that there is a certain amount of illegal sale of goods by cooperative artisans, thieves of state and private property, and 'speculators' who purchase goods in state retail stores and resell them at higher prices.

The rendering of services of various sorts results in other money payments between individuals. For example, under the conditions of the housing shortage, it has been made legal for carpenters to build houses for others (providing there is no employment of labour by the carpenter) and to receive payment for the work. Domestic, medical, dental, and local transport services provide money incomes for many individuals. There is also a certain amount of illegal service, among tailors and cobblers, for example, who ostensibly work in cooperatives but in fact carry on a thriving surreptitious private trade.

There are certain money transfers such as gifts and remittances to relatives which are not made in payment of goods and services but nevertheless exercise an influence on certain aspects of the money circulation, especially the geographical aspect. This will be discussed later.

Transactions Between the Population and the Socialized Sector
The sectors have been treated so far as two separate closed systems in which the transactions described can change the distribution of money holdings within each sector but cannot alter the total of either. The type of transaction now to be described provides channels whereby money may flow from one sector to the other

so that the total money holdings of either sector are alterable. The sectors, therefore, can no longer be treated as closed systems, and the direction of money flow now becomes of equal importance with the magnitude.

(a)   Money flow from the socialized sector to the population. Since the state is the most important employer of labour, the bulk of wages and salaries involves a flow of money from the socialized sector to the population. Kolkhozy pay their members according to 'labour days'[16] and cooperative handicraft artels pay dividends, but both are essentially payments for labour services and are analytically the same as wage payments by industry. Socialized organizations also enter the kolkhoz market as purchasers of agricultural and manufactured goods; for example, consumers' cooperative purchase manufactured goods from non-cooperative artisans and others, and public catering organizations purchase some of their supplies from kolkhozniki.

Apart from the purchase of goods and services from the population, the state makes payments to individuals on account of social and cultural expenditures, such as aid to mothers of many children, sickness benefits to workers, old age pensions and stipends to students; and on account of financial operations such as interest on bonds and lottery prizes, claims on state insurance and withdrawals from savings banks.

(b)   Money flow from the population to the socialized sector. The greatest part of this flow arises from the purchase of goods and services[17] by the population from socialized organizations such as retail trade, transportation, entertainment, housing, and public utilities. Obligatory payments by the population to the state include various direct taxes and contributions such as the income tax, communal and housing contribution (*kul't-zhilsbor*), the construction tax, inheritance and gift taxes, local assessments (*samooblazhenie*) and general fees (*poshlina*). 'Voluntary' payments include subscriptions to state loans, trade union dues, purchase of shares in cooperatives and deposits in savings banks.[18]

For the determination of the volume of currency holdings of the population, one must consider both channels of flow between the state sector and the population. If, over a given period of time, the flow of currency to the population exceeds (or is less than) the flow back to the state, there has been an increase (or decrease) in the volume of currency in the hands of the population.

Control of this volume can therefore be effected only by manipulation of these two channels.

PART II

The previous discussion indicates the two sectors in which economic behaviour is within the province of monetary planning. Since the socialized sector is virtually the creature of the state and therefore subject to a much greater degree of control than the population, it is in the latter that the most serious problems of monetary planning are likely to occur.[19] Individuals, it has been shown, receive money payments from two sources – from the state sector and from other individuals. Both types of money flow present their special problems and will be discussed in this and the next part respectively.

The flow of money from the socialized sector to the population raises few problems of planning under the conditions of a zero rate of investment. It is the fact of a high rate of investment such as that maintained by the Soviets since 1928, which introduces the package of troubles known as inflation. Whenever a nation diverts a large part of its resources away from the production of consumer goods[20] to the production of capital goods and armaments, the total value of wages paid out exceeds the value of marketable consumer goods. If this excess is not absorbed, the cumbersome machinery of rationing must be wheeled into action. But although rationing at its best can restore the desired distribution of real income between groups of the population, it cannot absorb the unspendable money holdings of the population. Current money income becomes a progressively smaller proportion of the idle money holdings,[21] and must finally cease to be a measure of purchasing power at all.

The elimination of the excess requires that ways be found either to reduce the flow of money to the population or to increase the flow back to the socialized sector. The former alternative, aside from minor possibilities such as streamlining governmental expenditures and reducing social services, means mostly a reduction of wages.[22] Not only would this have a most deleterious effect on workers' incentives, but it would conflict with the actual tendencies of managers competing for labour in a period of full emploment. The general 'overfulfilment' of wage plans during the four Five-Year Plans is largely due to managers' efforts to procure more labour and achieve a higher output per labourer by means of progressive wage rates, upgrading of workers, and premiums for overfulfilment of norms.

Increasing the flow of money back to the state has been, in fact, the principal means used by the Soviets to cope with the excess. Voluntary and semi-voluntary payments, such as annual state bond drives and encouragement of savings deposits, have been pushed to the full. Direct taxes could, in theory, be made large enough to absorb the whole excess, but the practical difficulties are of the same nature as those involved in a wage reduction.[23] In fact, as the figures in note 17 indicate, direct taxes have played a relatively small role in the solution of the inflationary excess. The major role has been played by price increases.[24]

Raising the prices of consumer goods, however, presents a problem peculiar to planned economies. Keynes' view that workers react more sharply to changes in money wages than changes in real wages (or prices) is based upon the political economy of free enterprise.[25] Wage cuts are initiated by particular employers, and the resentment of the workers affected is focused in the person of the 'boss'. Price level changes, however, have an impersonal origin, and it is difficult to blame them on anything more concrete than the 'system'. Thus, a free market economy which industrializes by a process of 'forced savings' minimizes the degree of social stress. It is different in the case of a planned socialist system, however, for the state has the disadvantage of being directly responsible for price changes. Consequently, while a price rise in a free-market economy results in an amorphous feeling of frustration which directs itself against internal or foreign scapegoats, in the socialist system the frustration is crystallized and directed against the state and its leaders. The socialist state cannot, therefore, enjoy the anonymity of the capitalist promoters of 'forced savings'. Whether it reduces wages or raises prices, it will still receive the full brunt of workers' disaffection.[26]

Hoarding and savings may play a salutary role in the inflationary process, for it is not the gross volume of money in the hands of the population that creates the pressure upon the consumer goods market, but only that part of it which the population is willing to spend. If the desire to save or hoard is sufficiently great, the inflation problem can be met without any price rise at all,[27] for the increase in the quantity of money is balanced by a low velocity of circulation. Since the tendency to hoard is greater in the village than in the city, with a given amount of money in circulation, the larger the proportion of it in the hands of the rural population, the lower the velocity of circulation, and the less the inflationary pressure. Furthermore, with the expansion of consumer goods output and kolkhoz market trade,[28] more money can safely be left in the hands of the population without the danger of a run on the market, for there will be a tendency for people to keep more money on hand for transactions purposes.

If the investment periods extend over an appreciable stretch of time, the dynamic production effect of investment provides an opportunity for easing the inflation. The new producer goods may be used to produce more producer goods, or consumer goods, or a combination of both. Insofar as more consumer goods are produced and prices are not reduced, the value of consumer goods exceeds the total of wages paid out, and the former inflationary excess can gradually be absorbed.

PART III

Apart from the flow of money between the socialized sector and the population, problems of planners' choice may arise from payments that take place among individuals. This type of money flow may result in shifts in purchasing power either between social groups or between geographical regions.

Most of the monetary transactions among individuals take place in the kolkhoz market. It has been estimated that about 10 per cent of the volume of purchases in the kolkhoz market is accounted for by institutional buyers,[29] resulting in a flow of money from the socialized sector into the kolkhoz market. But almost the same proportion of the volume of sales in the kolkhoz market is accounted for by selling activities of kolkhozy, resulting in a flow of money from the kolkhoz market to the socialized sector.[30] On balance, therefore, the kolkhoz market does not cause any net change in the total money holdings of the population, but it does serve to redistribute purchasing power between groups. The steady flow of money from urban to rural classes requires that the state recoup less from the urban classes than was paid out to them, and more from the rural classes. This is done by charging higher prices for state goods sold in the village than in the city, by special agricultural income taxes, and by great efforts to sell state bonds and encourage the use of savings banks in the villages. Part of the difficulty is eased by the greater tendency to hoard in the village, but this may backfire in times of rapid inflation when people try to exchange depreciating money for goods, and the disgorging of accumulated hoards in the village may intensify the pace of the inflation.

During the Second World War, there occurred a notable increase in the money holdings of the population,[31] accompanied by a

greatly reduced supply of state goods. The kolkhoz market responded to this situation by a phenomenal increase in prices.[32] Not
only did the volume of goods bought increase, due to the shortage
of state goods, but the rise in prices caused the value of kolkhoz
market trade to increase more than proportionately. The consequence was a steady drain of purchasing power from the urban
classes to the rural classes from the beginning of the war until
1947.

The shortage of state supplies of consumer goods was met by
rationing the available goods at fixed prices. After the war, when
the supply of consumer goods had reached a level which made
the elimination of rationing possible, the state was confronted with
the problem of large accumulated money holdings of the population. If retail prices were set at a level commensurate with current
money income the goods would have been swept off the shelves
by the large supply of accumulated money holdings. On the other
hand, if prices were set high enough to soak up these money holdings, current money income would have lost its incentive power,
for it would have represented a relatively small command over
consumer goods. The dilemma is analogous to that which arises
under conditions of a high rate of investment.

The solution adopted was simply to reduce the value of the
accumulated money holdings by an exchange of several old roubles
for one of a new type. If the old roubles had been more or less
equally distributed between urban and rural classes, a reduction
of any given magnitude, say by one half, would not have altered
the relative purchasing power of the classes. But the problem was
complicated by the drain of money from the town into the village
through the kolkhoz market, which left the great bulk of the
currency holdings in the hands of the rural classes. Under these
conditions a reduction of one half would have left the urban classes,
as before, with very little reserve purchasing power, but the holdings
of the rural classes would still have been large enough to sweep
all the available consumer goods off the market. In fact, a rather
extreme reduction of nine-tenths was used in the Monetary Reform
of 16 December 1947.[33] For the urban classes, to whom current
income was the chief measure of purchasing power, this extreme
reduction was relatively undamaging, but to the rural classes, whose
purchasing power was measured by the extremely large currency
holdings, the blow was severe. The reform permitted the abolition
of rationing and the return to the free sale of goods at a price
level commensurate with current income, without fear of the power
of one section of the population to purchase all the available goods.

Money transactions between individuals lead not only to disproportions in money holdings of different classes, but also to disproportions between geographical regions. Ordinarily the distribution of consumer goods is planned so that the supplies in a region are proportional to the money income earned in that region. There are many circumstances, however, in which money income earned in one region is spent in another. Along the borders between two geographic regions peasants from one of the regions often sell their produce in a kolkhoz market situated in the other. For example, the peasants of Riazan oblast' sell a large part of their products in the Moscow markets. People from small villages and towns frequently wait to spend their money in the shops of the large cities, because assortments are wider, because some goods are available which are not to be had in small localities, or because of ill-planned distribution. Workers often leave their homes for construction jobs in other places and send or bring their money home to be spent there; this is especially important in the case of temporary or seasonal employment. Finally, resorts, hunting preserves and vacation centres tend regularly to have a greater demand for goods than is indicated by the money income actually earned in those places. These shifts have an effect on the planned distribution of goods and on cash balances of the local branches of Gosbank. Areas into which purchasing power tends to flow must be provided with greater quantities of goods than is indicated in those areas.[34] Where these conditions are of regular occurrence, such as the resort areas of the Crimea and Krasnodar oblast', the volume of excess demand can be statistically determined from past experience, and provision made for it. In the case of one-time shifts, as when big construction jobs are under way and workers must be moved there temporarily, the imbalance must be anticipated and provide for in the plan.

PART IV

The complex problems of monetary planning presented here may well be confusing in the light of the widespread journalistic conception of the Soviet government as a monolithic, totalitarian regime with complete political and economic control of the state. Should not such a power be capable of planning and integrating the totality of economic activity and forestalling by administrative fiat any potential dislocations in the plan? If not, either there are some features of planning which do not respect political power, or the Soviet government has not, in reality, the all-embracing power ascribed to it.

This essay cannot discuss the limitations on planning in their full generality. But certain observations may be made on the basis of the discussion of monetary planning.

As in any conscious organization of efforts, the role of knowledge is critical. There is, however, a considerable range of accuracy with which different things may be known. Actual production is perhaps the most amenable to precise recording. In the sphere of monetary stability, the habits of consumers are rather less readily known. The anticipation of geographical or social shifts of money holdings, for example, must be based upon a wide sample of budget studies. But apart from the difficulty of collecting statistical data from honest informants, there is the problem of inbuilt incentives for managers to distort the truth. Where the reward for success is great, and – more important – where the penalty for failure is severe, one may expect a strong tendency to cover up failure. Thus, there may be a concealment of wages under 'other costs' to avoid prosecution for labour hoarding, or inclusion of substandard output as part of completed production.

A more serious perversion of incentives is that which induces managers to distort not only the truth but the plan itself. Such practices are intimately woven into the framework of the monetary system. In a sense, the very decision to employ money in the Soviet economy was an act of planners' choice. An economy is theoretically conceivable in which all planning is exclusively based on 'material balances', that is, each firm is allotted specific quantities of certain factors and required to produce specific quantities of goods or services. Coordination consists of assuring that planned supplies are, on balance, equal to planned demand for all factors and products. This, in fact, was considered a practical possibility at certain periods of Soviet history. The planners chose, if we may stretch the meaning of the term, to reconstruct the whole balance in monetary terms for the sake of the enormous convenience of reducing all goods and services to a common unit – price.

Controlling plan fulfilment is immensely eased by this, for it is now necessary to examine only two figures, costs and receipts, in order to check on efficiency, instead of accounting for all factors and products in their natural units. This convenience is purchased at a price, however, for managers now also measure their success in money terms. If the material plan requires a manager to produce certain quantities of various products, unless these products are carefully priced so as to equalize their profitability, it is likely that some managers will take advantage of the higher profitability of certain products and increase their production at the expense of the others, contrary to the intent of the plan. Pricing must be correct not only as among the various products, but also as among all managers producing them; since all firms have different production functions in general, each firm would have to be given a different set of product prices, that is, the same product would be priced differently for different firms. In the interests of a homogeneous price system, the aim of equalizing profitability is sacrificed and prices are set according to some rough average. The unintended consequence is the inbuilt incentive to managers to produce according to profitability rather than to plan in cases where the two diverge.

The development of a price inflation creates other potential areas of dislocation in the plan, for rising prices places a premium upon hoarding by managers, an activity which can easily be concealed by reporting profits as normal and investing the excess profits of inflation in scarce raw materials. Labour piracy, over-plan wage payments and so forth are further consequences of the use of a monetary system to implement a real plan.

Consideration of motivations and incentives leads to the concluding and most important observation on the limitations of planning. There is a certain degree of plasticity in people's values; planners can operate on this and mould the shape desired for a given end. Social engineering, for example, can create plant loyalties which may be used to induce workers to exert greater efforts for the sake of their plant's victory in a competition with other plants. There are, however, large elements of rigidity[35] in motivational patterns which planners must take as data and to which they must adapt and conform.[36] The awareness of this is implicit in the motto 'to each according to his work,' which is relevant to the socialist state, whereas the motto 'to each according to his needs' is relegated to the communist society of the indefinite future.

In a sense this kind of rigidity is not a 'limitation' of planning, any more than the heat content of a fuel is a 'limitation' on the production of steel. The engineer determines the heat content, knows the efficiency of the combustion process, and plans his fuel consumption accordingly. Similarly, the economist recognizes that the peasant exerts greater efforts in the cultivation of the collectively owned land if he is permitted at the same time to cultivate a small plot of his own, and out of this recognition emerged the modern Soviet agricultural institution of the household plot and the free market within the framework of the socialized agriculture. But just as the engineer seeks to develop better technological processes for extracting larger proportions of the heat content of the fuel, so the sociologist seeks to devise new ways of inducing peasants to exert greater efforts in the cultivation of the collective crop, by incentive payments and by 'socialist emulation'. These factors are better thought of as data upon which the planner or engineer must operate. The true limitations are the technological processes or social institutions available for extracting the maximum amount of usable heat or peasant effort.

Viewed in this light, planning shows up most clearly as a choice of alternatives. Insofar as planners set goals which are at variance with the motives and behaviour of individuals, caution and compromise must be used in the pursuit of these goals or there will inevitably be disruptions of the plan. There is no doubt, for example, that the Soviet leaders desired to restrain the issue of currency during the Second World War for fear of the inflationary aftermath. Following a passage which describes the dangers of excessive currency circulation, Vosnesensky frankly states that 'it was impossible to avoid currency issue during the war period ... [and] there was more currency in circulation during the war economy than is necessary for peacetime postwar economy'.[37] Clearly this was an occasion when political and economic power were not sufficient to prevent a breach of considerable importance in the monetary aims of the planners, who felt compelled to print money to satisfy the working population despite misgivings over the economic consequences. If the motivational behaviour of workers is viewed as part of the data, the monetary reform was not a breakdown of the planning mechanism, but a case of planning in action under conditions of an uncommonly grim choice.

In short, one should not require of successful planning that it control every unit within the system. In particular, one should not require that the five-year planners transform men, as if they were as plastic as the other factors of production. The measure of successful planning should be the efficiency of the mechanisms and institutions devised for achieving preassigned aims within the limits of the technological and human data.

NOTES

1   N. A. Vosnesensky, *The Economy of the USSR during World War II*, Washington DC, 1948, p. 78.
2   V. V. Obelensky–Ossinsky, 'The Nature and Forms of Social Economic Planning' in International Industrial Relations Institute, *World Social Economic Planning*, The Hague, 1932, p. 340.
3   Ibid, pp. 316, 339.
4   Eugene Varga, *Two Systems*, New York, 1939, p. 141.
5   For a discussion of this reform, see Paul A. Baran, 'Currency Reform in the USSR', *Harvard Business Review*, March 1948.

6   This is reflected in the existence of two kinds of accounts in Gosbank, a current *(tekushchii)* account, and a clearing *(raschetnyi)* account. The latter is held by all *khozraschetnye* organizations, whose operations are primarily within the state sector and whose transactions are part of the clearing system. The former is held by 'budget' (see note 11) organizations engaged mostly in financial operations, and also by kolkhozy, which are permitted a greater degree of freedom in their financial operations than state-owned organizations. Leonard E. Hubbard, *Soviet Money and Finance*, London, 1936, p. 71; also Z. V. Atlas *et al., Denezhnoe obrashchenie i kredit SSSR*, ed. E. Ia. Bregel', Gosfinizdat, 1947, pp. 250–6, 281–2.

7   An illustration of the importance of the control motive in the clearing system is provided by the 'valuta' cheques which were issued in 1931 in order to reduce the congestion in Gosbank after the Monetary Reform of 1930. The cheques were issued in various denominations by Gosbank, could be used in all intra-city and inter-enterprise transactions, and were transferable with endorsement. If not presented for deposit in Gosbank within 20 days they became invalid. These provided the only means whereby enterprises could transact business without going through Gosbank, and hence became very popular with managers. But since they weakened Gosbank's control over transactions, their use was curtailed. Today the clearing *(raschetnyi)* cheque is of the same nature as the old valuta cheque and is also rarely used. Arthur Z. Arnold, *Banks, Credit and Money in Soviet Russia*, New York, 1937; also, Hubbard, op. cit., p. 71.

8   The desire to curtail the use of currency is related to the early revolutionary view that when the state's control was firmly established over the whole economy, 'money' would wither away and the economy would be operated as a book-keeping system in which workers needed only receipts showing that they had performed their work in order to receive their needs from the common store. In the state sector the book-keeping system is virtually achieved, and continued efforts are made to reduce the use of currency by the population. Wide use is made of reductions at the source of income, for example, taxes and subscriptions to bonds. Another device is the 'giro' system of payments in which individuals instruct their savings banks to make recurring payments, such as rent and utilities, directly from their deposit accounts. Although the system is not widely used, a skeleton organization is maintained and one might guess that some time in the future it may be greatly expanded. Arnold, op. cit., pp. 419–21; V. D'iachenko *et al., Finansy i kredit SSSR*, Gosfinizdat, 1940, p. 349.

9   However, under certain conditions, monetary control by Gosbank will not detect dislocations of the material plan. See the discussion on page 12 above.

10 For the purpose of making change and other current operations, enterprises which deal directly with the population are allowed to keep on hand the following percentages of receipts:
Urban retail stores 10%

Rural retail stores 20%
Railroad catering enterprises 50%
Other catering enterprises 25%
Z. V. Atlas, '*O planirovanii resursov Gosbanka i denezhnykh sredstv khozorganov i predpriiatii*', *Planovoe Khoziaistvo*, nos. 9–10, 1937, p. 127.

11 Enterprises are often divided into *khozraschetnyi* and *biudzhetnyi* (budget). The former are those which purchase factors of production and sell goods and services; they are required to follow a system of *khozraschet*, or economic accounting, that is, using factors economically. In most cases this means that receipts must cover costs, although in a very few cases subsidies are still used. Budget organizations are those engaged in money transfer or administrative operations which are part of the state budget, such as social security, financial, medical, and other organizations.

12 Minor exceptions are the payment of wages out of receipts by organizations which sell directly to the public and a few large savings deposits held by wealthy individuals in Gosbank. The latter is the only case in which Gosbank deals directly with the population.

13 U. Cherniavskii, '*Denezhnye dokhody naseleniia i roznichnyi tovarooborot*', *Planovoe Khoziaistvo*, no. 5, 1941, p. 79.

14 In the planning of retail trade distribution, the census categories of urban and rural populations must be further broken down into agricultural and non-agricultural employments. The non-agricultural rural population has a demand pattern more like that of the urban population than that of the rural agricultural population. Rural areas with relatively large non-agricultural elements must, for example, be provided with greater supplies of food products than purely agricultural areas. Ibid, pp. 83–4; also N. C. Margolin, '*Nekotorye voprosy balansa denezhnykh dokhodov i raskhodov naseleniia*', *Planovoe Khoziaistvo*, no. 4, 1949.

15 The kolkhoz market influences the character of the demand for state agricultural goods, because, insofar as it satisfies part of the total demand for agricultural goods, it increases the relative demand for state industrial goods compared with state agricultural goods.

16 The labour day (*trudoden'*) is a fiction designed to express the fact that labour of different kinds has different values. For example, a day's work of a field hand may be rated at 1.5 labour days, while a day's work of a tractor driver may be rated 2 labour days. The total product available for distribution to the members of the kolkhoz is divided in proportion to each person's labour days, not *actual* days.

17 The importance of this element is indicated by the fact that in 1934 and 1938 the outlays on retail goods alone accounted for 77.3% and 79.6% respectively of the total money outlay of the population. In the same years, wages and salaries accounted for 66.6% and 67.6% of the total money incomes of the population. By way of contrast, direct tax payments of the population were only 4.2% and 3.2%

respectively of the total money outlays, and the money earnings of kolkhozniki for *trudodni* were only 2% and 4.4% of the total money incomes. See N. C. Margolin, op. cit., pp. 8, 9. In Margolin's usage, the classification 'total money incomes' includes incomes earned from other individuals, and the classification 'total money outlays' includes payments to individuals. These totals are therefore not precisely identical with the categories used by us, which exclude payments between individuals. Also, Margolin's figures for outlay on goods include public catering but not services such as transportation and entertainment. Nevertheless, the figures give an idea of the order of magnitude involved, and the overwhelming importance of the wage bill and the volume of retail trade.

18 In the early 1930s, as part of the drive to increase private savings, there was strong agitation for paying workers in savings bank deposits. Some trade unions succeeded in making compulsory the payment of part of wages in savings deposits. Arnold, op. cit., pp. 201, 211.

19 This is not to say that monetary disruptions are not possible in the socialized sector. But this leads to the large subject of credit provision and control, which cannot be dealt with here. Since the credit system does influence the money holdings of the population a complete treatment of the problem of a high rate of investment may not neglect it. But the following discussion is not materially changed by the omission.

20 The simplified description of the industrialization process presented here does not include discussion of the possibility of increasing the output of consumer goods simultaneously with a high rate of investment, by a bold programme of economic and technological reorganization. Dobb and others have maintained that, in the industrialization of backward areas, there are numerous opportunities for technological improvements requiring relatively little capital which would raise the productivity of agriculture and release large quantities of agricultural labour at the same time for work in industry.

This argument makes the dubious assumption that there is unemployed capital available in form and quantity sufficient to be used by the newly released labour. It is also likely that if the rate of industrialization is limited by the supply of unemployed labour and resources, it will not be a sufficiently rapid rate to result in the external economies described by Dobb. Dobb, op. cit., pp. 22–3. Also K. Mandelbaum, *The Industrialization of Backward Areas*, Oxford, 1947, and P. Rosenstein–Rodan, 'Problems of Industrialization of Eastern and South Eastern Europe' *Economic Journal*, June–September, 1943.

21 The relation of income to money holdings is the relation of a flow to a stock. Income is measured between two points of time, money holdings at a point of time. In our case money holdings grow continuously whereas income is always the same. The two concepts are used interchangeably by Margolin, the principal Soviet writer on the subject. Margolin, op. cit., p. 64.

22 Insofar as the state has the choice of reducing wages or increasing prices, it is a monopsonist and a monopolist at the same time, with the further complication that its behaviour as a monopsonist influences its behaviour as a monopolist. That is, by exerting its monopsonistic power of setting the wage rate, the state affects the position of the demand curve which it faces as a monopolist. It must be remarked that a monopoly situation defines only a certain relationship between buyers and sellers, and one may be a monopolist and act monopolistically in this sense, without following a profit motive. This definition is in contradistinction to that employed by M. Dobb, *Soviet Economic Development Since 1917*, London, 1948, p. 355, where the author identifies 'acting monopolistically' with restricting output. •

It should also be noted that, with regard to the population as consumers, the government can set price or amount purchased but not both. In the case of the state sector, however, the government can set both the price and the amount consumed. For this reason the monetary problems of a high rate of investment are more serious in the population sector than in the socialized sector.

23 It would be politically difficult for a workers and peasants state to introduce a wage cut or income tax large enough to absorb the excess. A further advantage of price manipulation over these methods is that it reduces the scope of consumer sovereignty, that is, it can be designed to impose any desired *pattern* of consumption on the population, whereas an income tax can only affect directly the *volume* of consumption.

24 The turnover tax is equal to the difference between retail price and the sum of all production and distribution costs. How this tax is accounted for, however, is not relevant to the immediate problem of the inflationary excess. Here the only concern is how the excess is to be siphoned off, not how it is to be disposed once it has been absorbed by the socialized sector.

25 J. M. Keynes, *The General Theory of Employment, Interest and Money*, New York, 1936, pp. 9–13, passim. But see also J. T. Dunlop, 'The Movement of Real and Money Rates', *Economic Journal*, September 1938, which shows that money and real wages have fluctuated in the same direction. This, however, does not disprove the assumption that a wage cut has an instantaneous impact whereas a price rise is gradual and may take some time to be felt. This is the only assumption we need in order to prefer the price rise. Furthermore, the 'money illusion' is not entirely irrational, for a wage cut for any group represents a disadvantage vis-à-vis any group whose wage has not been cut. The less the quantity of information available, the less likely the workers to have a clear idea of how other workers' wages are changing. In fact, most of the steady increase in money wages in the Soviet Union has been unplanned and spontaneous, so that workers never really knew how general the wage rise was. Finally, the qualitative relationship of rising wages to rising prices is much easier to perceive intuitively than the quantitative relationship. The workers

may not know whether wages or prices have risen faster, but at least wages have not stayed the same or fallen.

26 On the other hand, free public discussion in capitalist countries makes workers more sophisticated on the relation of real and money wages, leading to sliding wage scales and cost of living adjustments. In the Soviet Union, limitations on public discussion guard workers against any but the most obvious implications of a price rise. Furthermore, from a practical point of view, prices are more amenable to fixing than wages since workers preserve some degree of bargaining power in any circumstances, if only in their ability to vary the efficiency of their work.

27 In the dynamics of a continuous price rise, however, this advantage may backfire. If expectations are such that people believe prices will continue to rise, and *a fortiori* if they actually continue to rise, there is a positive inducement to dishoard. Large-scale dishoarding of cash seeking conversion into goods will considerably aggravate the inflationary pressure.

28 This may be one reason, although not the most important, for the government's continued tolerance of the expanding role of an institution of dubious political colour. For, since the stabilization of agricultural conditions, the volume of kolkhoz market trade has increased more rapidly than the volume of state and cooperative retail trade. The latter has grown from 80 billion roubles in 1935 to 175 billion roubles in 1940, or 2.2 times. Kolkhoz market trade has grown from 10 billion roubles in 1935 to 31.5 billion roubles in 1940, or 3.2 times. 1940 figures are from *Sovetskaia torgovlia za 30 let*, OGIZ, 1947, p. 14; 1935 retail trade is from TsUNKhU, *Sotsialisticheskoe stroitel'stvo SSSR*, 1936, pp. 606–7; 1935 kolkhoz market trade is from *Planovoe Khoziaistvo*, no. 5, 1936, p. 113.

29 N. C. Margolin, *Voprosy balansa denezhnykh dokhodov i raskhodov naseleniia*, 1939 edn, p. 63.

30 Kolkhozy sold 2,154 million roubles of crops in the kolkhoz market in 1938. The total volume of kolkhoz market trade in that year was 25,500 million roubles. According to these rough figures, 8.4% of the kolkhoz market trade is due to kolkhoz sales.

The kolkhoz sales figure is from Naum Jasny, *The Socialized Agriculture of the USSR*, Stanford, 1949, p. 686. The figure for kolkhoz market trade was obtained by subtracting the volume of state and cooperative trade and public catering, from the total of retail trade; these figures are from TsUNKhU, *Sotsialisticheskoe stroitel'stvo*, 1939.

31 Vosnesensky, op. cit., p. 76, states that over the three years 1942–44 the money in circulation increased 2.4 times.

32 When Soviet writers refer to the stability of prices during the war they mean only state-fixed prices. Whenever prices are fixed in one sector of an economy in time of short supply, the full pressure of the shortage is exerted in those markets where prices are not fixed, in the black market and the kolkhoz market. Ia. A. Kronrod, '*K ekonomicheskoi kharakteristike sovetskoi denezhnoi reformy* 1947

goda', *Izvestiia Akademii Nauk SSSR, Otdelenie ekonomiki i prava*, no. 4, 1948, p. 230; also N. C. Margolin, op. cit., p. 54.

33 The reduction in the value of bank deposits was considerably smaller. Since the savings deposits were held mostly by urban classes, while the currency was held mostly in the village, the monetary reform was more severe to the peasantry. Baran, op. cit., pp. 203–4.

34 Cherniavskii, op. cit., p. 80.

35 Rigidities of this sort are also an advantage to planners, and perhaps indispensable. Imagine trying to plan the activities of a population whose motivations changed with every season. The undesirable rigidities are those which are incompatible with a desired form of action.

36 This is not meant to imply that no efforts are made to change people. Actually, powerful efforts are made in that direction by every means available to the state. Our point is that five-year planners must face the reality of people as they are, and develop economic institutions (and prognostications) on this basis. The success of such institutions should be measured not by how much they have transformed men's incentive patterns, but by how successfully they have harnessed these patterns to a given end.

37 Op. cit., pp. 75–6.

2 The Informal Organization of the Soviet Firm* 1952

INTRODUCTION

The defection of large numbers of former Soviet citizens as a consequence of the last war has provided Western students with a new source of information on the operation of the Soviet industrial enterprise. Formerly the only available sources were Soviet publications which deal, for the most part, with the formal and legal aspects of economic institutions and provide only occasional glimpses of those personal and *informal* relations which are the meat on the bones of a social system. In that literature it is often difficult to tell whether a writer means to describe things as they are or things as they should be according to ideology and law. Part of the literature, however, is a response to the system's need for frank criticism of certain practices, and by an astute reading of published materials Western students have been able to pierce the official façade and sketch out some of the informal features of the system.[1] Nevertheless, the exclusive reliance upon published sources and the absence of personal contact with the people who operate the enterprises have caused the methods of Soviet research to resemble the methods of economic history more than those of contemporary institutional research.

The new emigration from the Soviet Union has afforded an

The Quarterly Journal of Economics (August 1952) LXVI, pp. 342–65. Reprinted by permission of John Wiley and Sons, Inc.

The writer, Joseph S. Berliner, is indebted to the Russian Research Center of Harvard University, which sponsored this interview project under contract to the Human Resources Research Institute of the US Air Force. He wishes to acknowledge his gratitude to Professor Gerschenkron who originally suggested this line of research, and to the many staff members of the Russian Research Center who have contributed the viewpoints of other disciplines to this work.

21

opportunity to talk freely with some of the people who actually managed the enterprises of that imperfectly understood system. Under the sponsorship of the Russian Research Center of Harvard University a group of social scientists travelled to Germany in the autumn of 1950 to interview these people. A large volume of information on many aspects of Soviet life was collected, most of which is still in the process of analysis. The first results of the study of the management of the Soviet industrial enterprise are presented in this paper.

SOURCES AND RELIABILITY

The material on which this paper is based is a group of interviews conducted with twenty-six persons who had occupied positions at various levels in Soviet economic institutions. In view of the small number of people interviewed and of our lack of 'feeling' for the day-to-day experiences and problems of Soviet management, it was decided not to attempt to test hypotheses formulated on the artificial basis of inferences from published sources, but rather to encourage the people interviewed to talk about what they considered important, what kinds of decisions had to be made, what they and their colleagues conceived to be their goals, what techniques were employed in the pursuit of these goals, and so forth. The persons selected were interviewed not as 'average respondents' representing a parent statistical population, but as 'expert informants' capable of stepping outside their occupational roles and reporting objectively on what they had experienced and observed in others.[2] The informants were treated not as data themselves, but as sources of data. There are no calculable criteria for the number of persons to be interviewed in this type of study, but the number should be large enough to cover a wide range of industries and managerial positions.[3] The number of twenty-six is obviously too small for this purpose, but an effort was made to obtain as fair a spread as possible. Table 2.1 gives the breakdown of types of industries and positions represented.

The interviews were based upon a prepared list of topics, covering such matters as planning, procurement, finance, investment and capital maintenance. The length of the interviews varied from two to twelve hours of interviewing time, depending upon the competence of the informant. Questions were posed as broadly as possible in order to encourage the informant to answer in his own terms and to stress those aspects of the question he considered important. Each interview was tailored to fit the experience of the particular

Table 2.1 Positions

Industries	Directors	Chief Engineers	Department Chiefs	Junior Managerial Personnel	Non-managerial Technical Personnel	Inspectors	Technical Planning, Research	Total
Heavy	2	1	4*	2	1	1*	3	14
Light (all-union)		1	2					3
Light (local and cooperative)		1	2*	1				4
Construction	1		2				1	4
Government Planning and Financial Organs					1	1		2
Trade, Law, Procurement	1		1		2		1	5
Total	4	3	11	3	4	2	5	32†

*One informant worked in a commissariat, not in an enterprise.
†Some informants were interviewed on more than one position which they had occupied during the later pre-war years.

informant: those who knew more about the enterprise's financial operations were urged to talk at great length on this subject and those who apparently knew little about them were led to talk on other matters about which they did have knowledge. The informants were interviewed only on positions held between the years 1938 and 1941, a compromise period which combined the advantages of recency and relative stability of industrial organization. This is the period to which this paper refers.[4] The interview protocols constitute a body of documents totalling 670 pages.

Space does not permit a discussion of all the methodological problems which the reader would rightly want to know about in order to evaluate these results. But one problem – that of the anti-Soviet bias of the informants – is so fundamental that something must be said about it. Although there is no doubt as to the anti-Soviet sentiments of the majority of these former Soviet citizens, it would be as idle to reject their testimony categorically as it would be to accept it uncritically. The following are some of the reasons for believing that the informants' discussions of their industrial experience provide valid information:

1 Surprisingly enough, the overwhelming proportion of the non-returners, including those who are strongly anti-Soviet, are convinced socialists. What they point to as negative features of the Soviet economy are such things as excessive bureaucracy, the intensity of the production drive, and certain deficiencies in planning. But in principle they accept economic planning and government ownership of industry (especially the basic industries), and are quick to defend it against the claims of 'capitalism' and 'private property' which are semantically negative concepts to them. Therefore, in this rather technical, non-political interview on their industrial experience and attitudes the informants were inclined to take a much more objective position than, say, in a discussion of the secret police. It is one thing to talk with DPs about the injustices of the Soviet system, but quite another to talk about the socialist economy.

2 Quite apart from anti-Soviet bias, most of the informants were professional engineers, economists, etc., with a natural sense of professional dignity. Most were proud of their technical education, their professional competence and, indeed, of their enterprises too. It was precisely on these subjects that the interviews were focused, not on political matters.

3 The informants were carefully briefed on the nature of this research project, which was objective scholarly research on the Soviet enterprise. It was emphasized that people's judgements

about the Soviet Union would be influenced by our findings, and that it was extremely important neither to underestimate nor to overestimate the efficiency of the economic system. A slight indication of the success of this approach is the fact that several informants asked about the views their compatriots had expressed on certain key issues, wanting to correct any anti-Soviet exaggerations which might have been made.

4   Where conscious or unconscious bias did manifest itself, there is reason to feel that it did not operate in a single direction. Those who desired to magnify the danger of Soviet power would tend to depict it as an economically strong power, and those who desired to disparage the regime would tend to depict it as on the verge of economic collapse. Neither extreme was apparent in the interviews on the industrial enterprise.

5   For a critical appraisal of the interviews, two types of evidence have been employed: the internal checks of consistency among the views of the different informants, and external checks against published sources. Where certain informants held views which were clearly extreme compared with the views of most informants (as on sensitive subjects such as the harshness of punishments for various economic offences), the testimony of these informants was treated more critically. As for the check against published sources, almost all of the interview material can be documented by the literature. The contribution of the interviews is to fill some of the gaps in the existing body of knowledge.

6   Finally, the judgement of the interviewer in the face-to-face interview situation should be given some weight in appraising the integrity of the informants. The writer's opinion, which is shared by his colleagues who interviewed people on other specialized subjects, is that the great majority of informants sought to tell the truth as they saw it, and those who were inclined to exaggerate were rather easy to detect.

The interview material provides some interesting insights into the operation of the Soviet firm, but it cannot be taken to present a balanced picture. The number of informants is too small to provide a basis for any final conclusions. In particular, the quantitative importance of the aspects of management presented here must remain a matter of surmise and judgement. Unfortunately, the limitations of space do not permit a discussion of other aspects of management which undoubtedly exist in the system but for various reasons did not emerge from the interview material. Nor can more than a few illustrations from the interviews and published sources be given. The full documentation of the results presented here will be published in a forthcoming book. The reader should bear in mind that these results do not purport to present all of the incentives or all of the behaviour principles of Soviet plant management, but only those which emerge from the analysis of the interviews.

GOALS OF MANAGERIAL BEHAVIOUR

By reading the interview protocols with an eye for the reasons which the informants gave for doing the things they did, it is possible to make some statements about the goals of management.[5] It should be pointed out that a study of goals and incentives was not anticipated in the research plan and that informants were not asked directly about these matters. Therefore, virtually all the remarks indicative of incentives were uttered spontaneously by the informants in the context of a discussion of some other topic such as planning or procurement.

Premia

Soviet writers frequently point to monetary bonuses, alongside of certain social motivations, as an important incentive for plant management.[6] The great extent to which this incentive has actually penetrated into the decision-making processes of management is testified to by the numerous references to 'premia' in the interviews. In contrast to the basic salary, which is automatically forthcoming in return for a month's *work*, the premium is a bonus paid in return for *performance* equal to or better than planned. The basic salary was practically never mentioned in the interviews,[7] but the frequency of the references to premia indicates that it is the latter which are at the forefront of managerial decision-making. They operate at all levels of management in day-to-day decision-making, not in the analytical sense that a managerial official in an American factory seeks to 'maximize profit', but in the concrete operational sense that the competitive businessman tries to 'make a buck'.

There are three kinds of premia referred to by the informants. The main kind is that paid for successful fulfilment of the output plan. The second is paid in proportion to the overfulfilment of specific tasks, such as cost reduction, economy of fuels, economy of wages, etc. The third is paid for general performance and, unlike the first two, is not based on a fixed schedule of rates.[8]

These categories correspond more or less to the official classification of premia. For example, the rates of premia for overfulfilment of plan have been published for management of large automotive transport enterprises:

	Size of Premia as a Percentage of the Basic Salary[9]	
	For Plan Fulfilment	For Each 1% of Plan Overfulfilment
Senior Management (Director, Chief Engineer)	up to 30%	up to 4%
Intermediate Management (Chiefs of Departments)	up to 25%	up to 3%
Junior Management (Shop Chiefs, etc.)	up to 20%	up to 3%

Since a substantial proportion of management's earnings hinges upon plan fulfilment, there is little wonder that the informants frequently referred spontaneously to premia. It is also important to note that the difference between 99 per cent of plan fulfilment and 100 per cent means a difference of up to 30 per cent in income. This sharp discontinuity places a great strain upon the honesty of plant accounting[10] and also partially explains such phenomena as the safety factor (see below) and the typical breakneck pace of work towards the end of the month [*shturmovshchina*] in order to meet the monthly plan.

Since the striving for premia is uppermost in the minds of management, and since premia are paid according to certain formalized criteria, these criteria become effective determinants of managerial decisions. Soviet management thinks and works, as it were, on a piece-rate basis. In general, the consequence is the exertion of greater effort, which conforms to the interests of the state. However, there are certain conditions in which the premium incentive leads to behaviour contrary to the state's interests. For example, the widespread tendency of management to submit plans which are below actual capacity is based largely on the fact that premia are paid in proportion to the ratio of actual output to planned output; therefore the lower the output plan which the firm succeeds in obtaining, the larger the premium paid for a given volume of actual output. Another example is the fact that the particular way in which premia are calculated may result in an assortment of products different from that planned. As a senior engineer of a production planning department said:

The director of the factory figures that if he puts out 100 machines with the proper quantity of spare parts, he does not get his premium. But if he puts out 102 machines and no spare parts then the chief engineer and all the technical personnel get premia. There is not enough stimulus to producing spare parts.

The tendency of plant managements to submit plans below capacity, and their failure to produce the required product-mix are perennial complaints in the Soviet press.

Profits

Because of the unfortunate use of the word 'profits' in Soviet economic terminology, Western students are wont to think of them as analogous in some sense to profits in a competitive economy. The interviews indicate quite clearly that profits play a rather secondary role as an incentive to Soviet plant management. The firm's plan contains a planned profit target, calculated as the residual between planned value of sales (net of the sales tax)[11] and planned cost of production. Fulfilment of the planned profit target is only one of the several criteria of the firm's success alongside other 'quantitative indices' (e.g., volume of output, total wage bill) and 'qualitative indices' (e.g., reduction of cost of production, increase in labour productivity). But it is primarily for fulfilment of their output plans that managerial personnel earn premia,[12] and it is therefore significant that when the informants were asked why they desired *profits*, they usually reinterpreted the question and answered in terms of the benefits of *output plan* fulfilment, namely, premia. For example, the following discussion with a chief of a production-planning department:

Q. Were you interested in making profits?
A. Yes, if the plan were overfulfilled. Say we had a plan for 3,000 veneers and we produced 3,500. The chief administration[13] would automatically send funds as premia to our leading personnel. They might also send clothing as well as money... The director might get a premium of 5,000 roubles. Also the commercial director and the shop chiefs.

Profits were desirable '*if* the [output] plan was fulfilled', and then the informant proceeded to list not the direct benefits of *profit* plan fulfilment, but the direct benefits of *output* plan fulfilment. In our interpretation, if the firm could fulfil either the profit plan or the output plan but not both,[14] it ordinarily would choose that alternative which provided premia, i.e. fulfilment of the output plan.[15]

It is true that a certain proportion of planned profits and a larger proportion of overplan profits are assigned to the 'director's fund', the benefits of which go to the plant personnel in the form of housing, special bonuses, etc.[16] But, as indicated in note 8, this fund does not have the direct day-to-day incentive quality of the striving for premia. As for that portion of overplan profits which does not go into the director's fund, the informants had no interest in this, because it was thought to be taken away automatically. As a chief engineer of a small rubber products plant said:

If at the end of the year you have made a large supplementary profit, you do not keep it for the next year. The financial plan permits you to keep only a certain amount of working capital... If the profit exceeds the legal amount of working capital, the excess is taken away next year.

Every Soviet firm has a maximum limit placed upon the volume of working capital which it is permitted to possess. Since overplan profits cause this limit to be exceeded, such profits are simply confiscated by the government financial organs. For example, a Soviet handbook for financial officials, after showing the procedure for analyzing the income statement of a chief administration, makes the following recommendation:

Summarizing the foregoing, we come to the conclusion that the enterprises of the chief administration under examination had in their possession an excess of 14,618 thousand roubles in their working capital during this accounting period. This excess was formed as a result of the overfulfilment of the profit plan...

On the basis of the above considerations, we may raise the question of confiscating in the immediate future the surplus of 14,618 thousand roubles from the working capital of the chief administration.[17]

Soviet writers frequently refer to profits as an incentive for capital investment, implying that a large volume of profits strengthens the firm's case in a petition for new investment. For example, one writer showed an annual increase (1945–49) in the proportion of new investment in working capital financed out of profits, as corroboration of his statement that 'the business enterprise is given the right to increase its own working capital out of profits.'[18] Although it is true that planned investment is *financed* out of planned profits, there is no reason to believe that, on the formal level, profits are taken into account in decisions governing new investment. On the informal level, however, a firm which has somehow gained possession of a substantial volume of funds has a good bargaining point in its petition for permission to undertake a small investment programme, for then the chief administration has only to grant permission without having to worry about obtaining funds for the firm. As a chief engineer said:

In order to undertake a small construction job it is necessary only to have the permission of the chief administration... If we have our own funds it is easier to get permission than if you need a loan.

The main source of such funds is indeed profits, but profits which are concealed and not reported. Therefore, except for the small volume of investment financed out of the director's fund, management does not think of its legal profits as an incentive for investment.

The Quiet Life

In combing the interviews for statements of the motivations behind decisions, a concept which cropped up in a number of different interviews is 'to live peacefully [*chtoby zhit' spokoino*] or a variation of this. Actions are explained on the basis of the desire to 'avoid trouble'. But the interesting thing is that in most cases the desire 'to live peacefully' was given as the motivation for an unlawful action. According to a construction materials testing engineer, who travelled widely among construction projects:

In the exchange of materials people are not interested in prices.[19] They are mostly interested in getting materials, and it is all done in a friendly and co-operative way. People realize that they must help each other out so that all can live.

It is not quite clear whether the period referred to was after February 1941, when the exchange of materials was illegal, or before that date when it was at best quasi-legal. In either case, the inference is that, in order that 'all can live', people must do unlawful things. Ordinarily one would expect that people who are motivated to live peacefully would endeavour to stay on the right side of the law. It appears that the conditions of economic success in the Soviet system are such that even cautious people are often compelled to act contrary to certain state injunctions in order to comply with others. As a consequence, law must tend to lose some of its moral force,[20] and enforcement must rely more upon compulsion.

INFORMAL BEHAVIOUR PRINCIPLES OF MANAGEMENT

Given the goals of management, what are the principles of economic behaviour whereby the managers seek to attain these goals? The interviews bring out three modes of behaviour which appear to be sufficiently widespread to warrant consideration as general principles. The development of these principles by management is a response not only to the nature of its goals but also to the specific conditions of the economic milieu within which the goals have to be achieved: namely, perennial commodity shortages, an irrational price system, and complex administrative controls over many detailed aspects of the firm's activity.[21]

The Safety Factor

An expression repeated again and again in the interviews is *strakhovka* (safety; insurance). This concept is related to the practice of measuring managerial performance by means of a series of numerical indices. For example, the index of production performance is the percentage fulfilment of the production plan; the index of efficient use of resources is the percentage fulfilment of the cost reduction plan; the index of labour management is the ratio of the final average wage to the planned average wage. It is an axiom of management that a measure of slack must be preserved, a factor of safety, in order that the planned target can be more easily achieved. The large number of specific techniques discussed in the interviews reflect the striving for a safety factor in every sphere of managerial activity. An example will be given from the area of industrial procurement, which the informants unanimously declare to be the source of more headaches to the Soviet firm than any other aspect of its activity.

The principal method of ensuring a safety factor in the procurement plan is to inflate the statements of material requirements (*zaiavki*)[22] which are approved by the superior organ and become the basis of the procurement plan. As an accountant in a procurement department said:

We always submitted our materials plans 'with a little bit of fat' and the superior organ always returned them 'with the fat cut off'.

In fact, the fat is not always 'cut off', and enterprises frequently succeed in obtaining larger quantities of certain materials than the central planners would have permitted had they known. The device whereby the state seeks to restrain the efforts of plant management to build up a safety factor is the 'norm' (*norma*) of materials utilization. This norm is essentially a coefficient of production which establishes the quantity of a factor which a firm may use for each unit of output. Thus, if the established norm is, say, one pound of cotton per yard of finished cloth, and if the firm's output plan has been confirmed at 10,000 yards of cloth, it may not order more than 10,000 pounds of cotton. Similarly, there are norms of labour productivity, norms of machinery utilization, inventory norms, working capital norms, and so forth, all of which set limits upon the freedom of management to make use of its material and financial resources in its own way. The frequent references to norms in the interviews indicate that much of management's energy goes into influencing and manipulating its norms so that it can build up its safety factor.

One consequence of the safety factor in the procurement programme is the building up of material hoards, a subject of frequent criticism in the Soviet press. Although some of the informants denied that their firms attempted to hoard,[23] most supported the following statement of a chief engineer:

In planning you always try to order more than you need in case something happens. You often receive things you do not need. Every plant has some excessive materials which are not immediately necessary. They often lack things which other plants have in excess, but they do not know about it. They have no legal right to transfer these materials anyhow.[24] They are useless reserves which exist at the same time that other firms have a great need for them. Therefore this is a great loss and a brake on the turnover of goods. Great masses of goods lie in stockrooms and spoil. Sometimes they may lie around for fifteen years. If I order nuts and bolts of a particular size, I am often sent the wrong size, and the things which are sent lie around and rust, maybe for fifteen years. The money involved is insignificant, but you simply can't buy the materials. But in terms of overall waste of materials, millions of roubles are lost in this way.

The other principal manifestation of the safety factor is the striving to have the firm's output plan set at a level well below capacity. Many of the specific forms of the safety factor have long been complained of in the Soviet press, and are well known to Western students.

Simulation

The Russian word, the frequent reiteration of which led the present writer to present it as a principle of managerial behaviour, is *ochkovtiratel'stvo*. Literally it means 'rubbing-in someone's eyeglasses', or in our idiom, 'pulling the wool over someone's eyes'. It refers to the practice of simulating successful performance by a variety of deceptive devices. Four principal techniques of simulation emerge from the interviews.

1 Producing the wrong assortment of products. The firm's output plan consists of a target figure for total value of output and a series of individual sub-targets, expressed in real units, of

the principal products. The firm is supposed to fulfil all of these targets, but in practice the total output target is considered most important, and fulfilment of it is usually enough for the earning of premia.[25] Because the prices at which value of output was computed (the so-called prices of 1926–27) did not reflect the current cost–price ratios of later years, it frequently happened that a given quantity of resources could produce a larger value of output of some products than of others. It was therefore a common practice for a firm to report a large overfulfilment of the value of output target (the main determinant of premia) by shifting factors of production away from the less advantageous planned products into the overfulfilment of the targets for the more advantageous products. Thus the firm simulates plan overfulfilment by producing an unplanned product-mix.

2 Falsified accounting of goods in process. Factories with relatively long periods of production carry over a large volume of goods in process from month to month. In reporting monthly plan fulfilment the net change in value of goods in process is added to or subtracted from the value of finished output in order to calculate gross value of output. The value of goods in process is extremely difficult to estimate, and the firm often exaggerates this figure in months in which its production has lagged. Related forms of simulation are treating incomplete output as if it were complete and ascribing the output of one period to another period.

3 Lowering the quality of output. If the firm cannot meet its plan with the given quantity of resources, it simulates plan fulfilment by reducing the quality of production in ways that make the available resources stretch further. Sometimes this results in truly shoddy production (especially in consumer goods production), but often quality reduction is of a less apparent kind, such as the use of fewer holding screws, or combining two bottle washes into a single operation.

4 Misappropriation of funds. Since financial limits are placed upon various specific aspects of the firm's activity, the firm often simulates conformity to these limits by using funds for a purpose for which they were not earmarked. The most frequent manifestation of this is the payment of wages by means of funds earmarked and entered under repair, overhead costs, administrative expenditures, etc.

The specific techniques of simulation are often the subject of attack in Soviet writings. Although no quantitative statement can be made about the prevalence of these or indeed of any of the phenomena discussed in the interviews, the weight of the evidence supports the belief that they exist everywhere as tendencies, and are widespread as actual behaviour forms. The evidence to date consists of the long-enduring condemnations of these practices in the official literature, the testimony of the informants, and the logical consistency of these behaviour principles with the personal goals of management and the formal criteria of success.

'Blat'[26]

This untranslatable word stands for a widespread practice which seems to be a fundamental element of the informal management of industry. This practice is the use of personal influence, or 'pull', with particular reference to obtaining favours to which the person or firm is not *lawfully* entitled. Unlike the preceding behaviour principles, this has received relatively little publicity in Soviet writings. but a good indication of the deep roots of *blat* in Soviet life is the rise of a number of widely quoted folk-sayings about it, such as '*blat* is higher than Stalin', or 'you have to have *ZIS*'. *ZIS* in this context is a play on words, for it is the brand name of a famous Soviet car, but here it represents the initial letters of the expression 'acquaintanceship and connections' (*znakomstvo i sviazy*).

Like the other behaviour principles, *blat* operates in all aspects of the firm's activity, but is most important in the area of the firm's greatest difficulties, industrial procurement. Most of the major industrial commodities are directly allocated, either by the State Planning Commission (in the pre-war period) or by the commissariat whose firms produce them. The allocating organ issues an allocation order (*nariad*) to the consumer, which the latter must present to the producing firm before the producer has the legal right to sell the stated quantity of materials to the consumer. Much of the firm's energy is centred around the allocation order, as was indicated by the frequency with which this term appeared in the testimonies of the informants. The following are some typical situations in which firms are reported to have met their procurement problems by means of *blat*:

1   If the firm has been unable to procure any allocation order at all through regular channels, it may still be able to obtain the order if it has good *blat* or personal connections with the responsible official in the allocating organ.

2   If the allocation order specifies a quantity less than that asked

by the firm in its statement of requirements, it may be able to repair the deficiency by means of *blat*.

3 If the firm has been unable to obtain an allocation order by any means, it may still be able to obtain part or all of its requirements without the order if it has good *blat* in the producing enterprise or commissariat.

But even possession of an allocation order does not ensure delivery, for the producing enterprise may not have fulfilled its output plan, or may not be able to deliver on time. Hence the firm with the best *blat* will be able to get its order filled first, in the required quantity and quality. On certain occasions *blat* is used to arrange a mutually beneficial exchange of materials which would not have been possible if not for the personal connections between official in the two firms.

Any of the officials of the firm who has a cousin or a good friend or a former colleague in the other firm or organ may effect the *blat* transaction. But the need for this sort of informal procedure is so great that it could not be entrusted to the haphazard personal influence of firm officials. Therefore, there has arisen the interesting penumbral occupation of the *tolkach*, or supply expediter.[27] The word means, literally, 'pusher', which is also the term applied to the booster locomotive added to a long railroad train to increase its power. The supply expediter is sent out by the firm to 'push' for its interests. Sometimes the term is applied to the regular supply officials of the firm when they are particularly skilful in procuring materials by informal means, but the most highly developed form of the supply expediter is a man who specializes in this sort of activity. Often he lives away from the firm, in Moscow or in some other large city where he has the best personal connections. He is usually carried on the books of one enterprise as a 'representative', but he often works on a commission basis for several other firms as well. The informants had some very definite ideas about the prototype of the supply expediter. He is a nervous, energetic man, a master of high-pressure techniques, able to talk his way into enterprises and quickly establish a working friendship with the relevant officials. He is lavish with gifts and entertainment and 'knows how to drink' with all people. His side earnings, based on special commissions and liberal expense accounts, are thought to be extremely large, but a good supply expediter is so important as an asset to the firm that no one begrudges him his income. Furthermore his work is potentially quite dangerous, although he knows how to stay on the right side of the secret police by means of discreetly offered gifts.

Blat plays a role not only in procurement, but in obtaining easier production tasks, in facilitating financial operations, in inducing inspectors to be generous, etc. *Blat* plays an even greater role in the personal enrichment of people and in gaining private unlawful privileges than it does in the operation of the firm. It is an essential thread in the fabric of Soviet society.

EXPECTATIONS FACILITATING INFORMAL METHODS

The prominence of the principles of safety factor, simulation and *blat* testifies to a large degree of looseness and non-monolithic flexibility in the economic system. Management's ability to behave in these ways depends upon certain expectations of other people's behaviour. That is, if large numbers of people engage in *blat*, it must mean that they expect others to be receptive to propositions. The interviews provide some insight into these expectations.

An expression repeated several times is *krugovaia poruka*, which may be feebly rendered as 'mutual support'. As used by the informants it refers to the willingness of officials to neglect their official duties in order to help the firm in its unlawful manipulations or to line their own pockets. The chief accountant has to juggle his books in order to conceal certain heavy expenditures for the supply expediter, or the chief of the quality control department has to accept sub-quality production. Sometimes this support is given willingly, out of an awareness that all benefit from the firm's success. But sometimes an official has to be forced to do something illegal for the sake of the firm, by the director's threat that his premia will be cut off or that life will be made generally miserable for him. When people have worked together in a plant for a number of years, they have usually so compromised themselves that they are too dependent upon each other's confidence to resist further involvement. The following is a vivid description by a senior engineer of a production planning department of the forces making for mutual support:

Sometimes the moulds were badly made, and this resulted in a certain part being too heavy. Therefore, the final product will weigh 14 tons instead of 10 tons. I have to explain this error, but I cannot say that it was due to bad work. I must say that tests show that this added strength is necessary. The director will call in the chief design engineer to confirm this statement. He will have to confirm this or everybody will get into trouble, and he is too small a man to object. If he should refuse to do it, the chief engineer and the director will remember this and he will never get a premium again. If he ever gets into any minor trouble, they will make it very hard for him. The chief design engineer often gets into trouble, because his work is difficult and experimental, and he makes many mistakes. Therefore, he must be on good relations with the director, else they will 'bury him' one day for one of his inevitable mistakes... This mutual relationship is called *krugovaia proruka*. It is very hard to free yourself of it. You can get out of it only if the minister transfers you to another factory.

This involvement in mutual support may extend even to the secretary of the plant Communist Party organization, or to the resident commissariat representative [*kurator*], for the performance of these officials also is measured by their superiors in terms of the success of the firms to which they are attached. Therefore, they are hardly inclined to report the manipulations of a shrewd and successful director or chief accountant. The expectation that numerous officials will countenance the informal manipulations of the firm encourages management to undertake these manipulations.

It is interesting that the commissariat, which is supposed to be the direct arm of state control and pressure upon the firm, was looked upon by many informants as involved in this web of mutual support, and therefore as a source of benevolent aid to the firm.[28] This is partly based on certain long-enduring personal associations between plant and commissariat personnel as well as a certain amount of occupational fluidity between them. The commissariat is expected to be willing to help the firm out of difficulties with extra funds or materials, to ease the firm's plan if it can, to provide it with 'secret funds' for premia,[29] and to overlook deliberately the unlawful operations of the firm. When the commissariat is referred to by the informants as a source of pressure, it is usually with an awareness that this is the reflection of pressure upon 'our commissar' from above, and that basically, firm and commissariat are united by the need to fulfil the plan.

Wherever an official who is supposed to control the firm becomes involved in the web of mutual support, the control system is weakened at that point. It is the officials outside the firm, such as those in the Commissariat of Finance and to some extent the State Bank, who have no motivation to 'look the other way' at the firm's transgressions. These officials are therefore more successful as controlling agents from the state's point of view, although *blat* and the generous gift can operate in these quarters too.[30]

CHARACTERISTICS OF THE ECONOMIC SYSTEM

In considering the behaviour of a specific firm it is necessary to know something about those characteristics of the economic system which form the background for decisions. For the free economy such characteristics are the degree of monopoly in the industry, the nature of the product, the point of the business cycle at which the decision is made, etc. The interviews bring out five such characteristics of the Soviet economy.

First is the relative priority of the firm. This is important not only in the firm's relations with the state, but in its relations with other firms. For the significant thing is that priority awareness is not confined to the highest decision-making organs, but has filtered down into the decision-making process of managerial personnel, and firms discriminate among each other according to relative priorities. Sellers take into account the relative priority of competing buyers in deciding who is to get the goods first. Insofar as allocative decisions have to be made on the firm level as well as the state level, the fact that firms actually operate on the basis of a priority scale more or less similar to that of the state means that these lower level decisions correspond to what the state itself would decide if it were able to make all decisions at all levels. Priority awareness becomes a sort of Lerner 'Rule' for plant management.

In practice this means that there is a tendency for firms to fill the orders of military customers ahead of heavy industry customers, and of the latter ahead of light industry customers. While Western scholars may question the rationality of this 'Rule' of allocation, it probably conforms to the desires of the state. It should be pointed out, however, that in informal inter-firm relations the priority scale used by the firm diverges from the official scale. For example, a textile firm will ordinarily favour an order placed by a military customer over one by another customer. But if the other customer happens to produce ball bearings which the textile firm desperately needs, an informal transaction may be arranged in which the ball bearing producer's order for textiles is quietly placed ahead of that of the military customer. The ball bearing producer, of course, then accepts an unplanned order by the textile firm for the delivery of ball bearings.

The second characteristic is the relatively short tenure of office of plant directors. The informants seemed to think that a director who remains in the same plant more than two or three years is rare indeed. Such fluidity of directors must impair the efficiency of management, and directors must lose a considerable amount of time in getting used to new plants. On the other hand, there are certain beneficial consequences for the state, such as the disruption of a smoothly operating system of 'mutual support' among officials who have worked together a long time in the same plant. But more interesting is the subjective significance of the short tenure of office, for if directors *expect* to be transferred soon, either as a reward or a punishment, their outlook will be more short-run than that of the more constant part of management. It is impossible to tell whether the general tendency for rapid turnover of directors is actually transformed into an expectation for individual directors, but there are indications of a more short-run outlook among directors. For example, several interviews report a struggle between the mechanical engineer, who is responsible for the long-run maintenance of equipment, and the director who would sacrifice maintenance for the immediate demands of plan fulfilment. If the director expected to remain in the plant for many years he would be more sympathetic to the claims of the mechanical engineer. This is an extremely complex question with ramifications into many other aspects of decision-making such as investment, the safety factor, and incentives.

A third consideration is the firm's recent record of performance. A firm with a record of successful operation can count on the continued informal support of controlling agents and on superficial checks by inspectors, which are necessary for the successful informal operation of the firm. But a firm which has begun to fail can no longer count on these things. The chief accountant will fear to break laws if he feels that an investigation of failure is imminent, the party secretary will prefer not to be implicated with an unsuccessful director and will begin to attack him, the Commissariat of Finance will check the firm's reports more closely, etc. The very fact of incipient failure deprives the firm of those expectations and supports which might have helped it to pull itself up, so that it is catapulted at an accelerating rate into failure. Success facilitates success and failure accelerates failure. Therefore in appraising the situation of a firm it is important to know at what point it is located in the spectrum of performance.

Fourth is the peculiar combination of informal and personal relations operating within the framework of a bureaucratic system. Many of the important decisions which affect the firm are made not on the basis of 'arm's length' negotiation involving more or less objective parameters or universally applied criteria but on the basis of personal influence and cloakroom bargaining. The firm's output plan depends to a large extent upon what the plant officials have been able to bargain out of 'Moscow',[31] the supply plan hinges upon how much can be haggled out of the functionary in the State Planning Commission, and the financial plan is based upon currying the favour of a minor official in the Commissariat of Finance. Informants gave illustrations of important investment decisions reflecting the caprice of an important party official. The character of an influential commissar affects the conditions of operation of all firms in the commissariat. The party prestige of the director affects the performance of the firm. Therefore the personal influence which the firm enjoys in various quarters must be taken into account in explaining why, for example, firm A has less trouble procuring certain deficit materials, whereas firm B has less trouble obtaining funds for wages.

Finally, management does not feel that it has full control over all the operations of the firm. Movements may occur spontaneously inside the firm without the foreknowledge of the senior management, and may go a long way before they can be brought under control. The propaganda for *stakhanovism*[32] and 'socialist competition' may set movements afoot in the shops which upset the plant work schedule and endanger some delicate equipment. Party activists and 'climbers' may challenge the firm to accept higher production goals, a challenge which it is difficult for management to ignore. Despite the principle of 'one-man leadership', according to which only the direct superior may give orders to his juniors, functional officials in the party or commissariat bring direct pressure to bear on lower plant management. More important, perhaps, is the fact that organs such as the Party and the secret police have pipelines of information out of the firm which do not pass over the desks of management, so that management may be confronted with data about the plant which it would have preferred not to have known outside the plant, or indeed, which it may not have known about its own plant. This absence of full control over the firm must also play a role in managerial behaviour.

CONCLUSION

The interviews are a window looking into the Soviet firm, but unfortunately the glass has the properties of a colour filter. Only certain wavelengths of light pass through for us to observe. Undoubtedly a different glass would have admitted different kinds of light. It is the task of further research to relate those aspects of management presented here to the larger whole.

There can be little doubt that these results are part of that larger whole. The striking similarity in the independent testimonies of the various informants, and the neat dovetailing of these testimonies with candid hints found in the Soviet sources form too strong a body of evidence to be ignored. The two chief problems ahead are, first, to describe the elements of management which surely exist alongside of those presented here but which failed to emerge from the interviews, and second, to assess the quantitative importance of all of these elements.

For example, among the incentives of management not listed here are pride of work, devotion to the ideal of building for the future, making a successful career, and perhaps the need for recognition, medals, and 'getting one's picture in the papers', as the Russians say. Our interviews do not reckon with directors such as Robert Magidoff's friend Golovenko, who did not care that his 'bones will rot in the mines' as long as he could 'bring to life the entire wealth of the land'.[33] But although his incentives transcended the mere desire for premia, his 'clever and unscrupulously "capitalistic"' handling of the director's fund suggests that his behaviour principles did not diverge much from those described above. It may be that the importance of the economic milieu in shaping behaviour may exceed that of the incentives motivating management, so that managers with quite different motivations from those presented in this paper may nevertheless be forced to follow the behaviour principles which the interviews bring out.

Another director whom our picture of management does not explain is John Scott's Zavenyagin, the director of Magnitostroi. The first quarter that his firm showed a profit, Zavenyagin, 'with a quixotic gesture', declared that he would thenceforth get along without a subsidy.[34] For a director motivated by premia alone, such neglect of a safety factor would constitute quite irrational behaviour. The full picture of Soviet management must account for the Golovenkos and Zavenyagins.

As for the quantitative importance of these results of the interviews, it would undoubtedly enhance our knowledge of the Soviet firm if we could make some statements about what proportion of Soviet managers do the things set forth in this paper and how often they do them. But to require that we measure the strength of the premium incentive or the extensiveness of *blat* is to require that we know more about the Soviet economy than we know about our own. The function of qualitative investigation is twofold; first, to indicate which questions should be asked and which phenomena should be measured when the data and methodology for quantitative research are available; and second, to deal with the kind of knowledge which does not depend upon size or frequency for its relevance but upon patterns and associations.[35] If it is true that the desire for premia is associated with a striving for a safety factor, this is important to know even if we cannot say what proportion of managers are primarily premium-oriented. At the present stage of our knowledge of the Soviet firm we must rely upon such statistical information as we are fortunate to have, and for the rest, continue to gather qualitative evidence in order to arrive at a more balanced judgement.

NOTES

1   G. Bienstock, S. Schwarz, and A. Yugow, *Management in Russian Industry and Agriculture*, New York, 1946; A Gerschenkron, 'A Neglected Source of Economic Information on Soviet Russia', *The American Slavic and East European Review*, vol. IX, February 1950, pp. 1–19; D. Granick, 'Initiative and Independence of Soviet Plant Management', *The American Slavic and East European Review*, vol. X, October 1951.

2   The first approach is sometimes referred to as the 'sociological' method, and is associated with quantitatively oriented studies such as public opinion measurement. The second, the 'anthropological' method, is primarily used for qualitative studies. On the relatively few occasions when interviewing has been used as a method of economic research, the 'sociological' approach has been adopted because the setting of the problem has been an economic system familiar to the experience of the researchers. The objectives have therefore been quantitative, as in Katona's consumer behaviour studies, or the testing of hypotheses, as in the Oxford Research Group studies of entrepreneurial behaviour. Although the Western student of the Soviet economic system is not quite in the position of the anthropologist approaching an entirely unfamiliar society, his 'tactile' appreciation of that system is feeble enough to recommend strongly his use of the anthropologist's method.

Cf. 'Methods of the Survey of Consumer Finance', *Federal Reserve Bulletin*, July 1950; also *Oxford Economic Papers*, no. 1, October 1938, pp. 1–31; no. 2, May 1939, pp. 1–45; no. 3, March 1940, pp. 32–73.

3   The number of interviews was limited in order to reduce the scope of the study in line with the time allocated to the economics portion of the project, and manufacturing industry was made the focus of inquiry. However, qualified informants in related fields were also interviewed.

4   For convenience of presentation, the tense used in this paper is the historical present referring to the period 1938–1941. The names of administrative organs are those used in that period. Although most of the references to Soviet sources are taken from the post-war period, similar illustrations may be found in the pre-war literature.

5   By management we mean all levels from shop chief to director, and by the firm we refer to all manufacturing enterprises which engage in actual physical production. When a statement applies only to one group of management or to one type of firm, this will be specified.

6   E.g., P. Pavlov, *O planovykh khoziaistvennykh rychagakh sotsialisti-*

cheskogo gosudarstva (The Economic Planning Levers of the Socialist State), Leningradskoe gazetno-zhurnalnoe i knizhnoe izd-vo., 1950, p. 139.

7 Sometimes an informant may fail to mention something not because it is unimportant but because it is so important and self-evident that it does not occur to him to single it out. This may be true in the case of the basic salary, which undoubtedly is the main and ultimate monetary incentive. But the salary is fixed and only the premia vary with effort. Therefore in practical decision-making, the effective incentive which calls forth the extra effort is the variable portion of income, the premia.

8 This sort of premium is paid from the so-called 'director's fund'. The director's fund is formed out of the firm's profits, and is used for workers' welfare, for housing, and to a limited extent for paying premia. But this type of premium does not have the same direct incentive effect as the first two because, as one informant expressed it, 'The director's fund was less of an incentive to the technical personnel because the [premia] from the director's fund depended only on the director and you never knew who would get the benefit of it.' The director's fund is therefore a second-rate incentive compared to the direct premia.

9 L. Bronshtein and B. Budrin, *Planirovanie i uchet avtomobil'nogo transporta* (Planning and Accounting in Automotive Transport), Gosplanizdat, 1948, p. 150.

10 The calculation of plan fulfilment, on the basis of which premia are paid, is carried out by the planning department. A chief of a production planning department described how his management encouraged the planning personnel to manipulate their accounts in order to report plan fulfilment: 'In our plant at one time the technical personnel in the planning department did not earn progressive premia. Therefore they were not interested in juggling the figures in order to increase plan fulfilment, so that the other people in the plant could earn progressive premia. Finally, the management itself went to the trust and asked that the planning department be permitted to earn progressive premia also. The trust had no right to do this, but it did.'

11 The sales (or turnover) tax is a commodity tax levied almost exclusively upon consumer goods, and therefore plays a relatively minor role in inter-firm sales.

12 Officially, although premia are to be paid in proportion to output plan overfulfilment, they are not to be paid at all unless other planned indices are met, such as planned cost reduction, correct assortment of products, etc. (Bronshtein, op. cit., p. 149). However, it is clear from the interviews, and corroborated by long standing complaints in the Soviet press that these side conditions are often overlooked. For example, 'The managers of individual plants think that it is enough to fulfil the plan for gross output alone, forgetting about qualitative indices.' ('For Further Development of Socialist Competition', *Current Digest of the Soviet Press*, vol. III, no. 2, p. 36.) Then the article

describes how a plant had won the challenge Red Banner (and therefore presumably had earned large premia) for the highest plan fulfilment, but the Banner had to be taken away from it later because it had failed to produce the correct assortment and to meet its labour productivity target. Whether the premia were also withdrawn is not stated.

13   The department of the ministry responsible for a number of enterprises, to which the enterprises are directly accountable.

14   A situation which apparently sometimes occurred in the pre-war period because output was measured in one set of prices (the so-called 'constant prices of 1926–27') and profits in another set of prices (current prices).

15   The numerous complaints in the Soviet press about 'narrow-minded' directors pursuing profits at the expense of the output plan usually refer to the distortion of the planned assortment and not to underfulfilment of the planned volume of output. They are therefore not contradictory to the above interpretation of managerial preference.

16   A firm may make overplan profits in various ways, such as producing at a lower cost than planned, producing a larger volume of output than planned, etc.

17   S. M. Kutyrev, *Analiz balansa dokhodov i raskhodov khoziaistvennoi organizatsii* (Analysis of the Income Statement of a Business Organization), Gosfinizdat, 1948, p. 110.

18   P. Pavlov, op. cit., p. 105.

19   It is a curious fact that when asked if the firm ever attempted to manipulate the official fixed prices, the informants almost unanimously denied it. Yet with equal unanimity they described widespread practices of giving gifts, favours and concessions of all sorts to the sellers of deficit commodities. Apparently on the formal level all transactions are carried out at the fixed prices, but there are informal ways of granting virtual price increases to sellers. This practice will give little comfort to our index-number colleagues.

20   Cf. Granick, op. cit., pp. 196–7, for a description of the amoral attitude of Soviet managers towards economic laws.

21   The writer is indebted for the observation to Franklyn D. Holzman of the Russian Research Center. Indeed, changes in the economic milieu would cause changes in the behaviour principles even if the goals of management remained the same. For example, if the practice of 'overfull employment planning' were ended, the extent of commodity shortage would be greatly reduced. This would undoubtedly weaken the desire for a 'safety factor', although the goals of plant management might not be appreciably affected. See Franklyn D. Holzman, 'Financing Soviet Economic Development' in Moses Abramovitz (ed.), *Capital Formation and Economic Growth*, Princeton: Princeton University Press, 1955, pp. 229–87.

22   This is one of the key words repeated again and again by the informants which provide an insight into the way Soviet management thinks about the problems of the firm. Other frequently repeated words are the

materials allocation order (*nariad*), the norm (*norma*), the report (*otchet*), the premium (*premiia*), overfulfilment of the plan (*perevypolnenie plana*). It would be interesting to compare a word-count of similar interviews with American and Soviet managers. One might guess that the American equivalents of the words listed above would be 'taxes', 'buyer', 'price', etc.

23 When some informants denied and others affirmed the existence of a certain practice, consideration of the circumstances in each particular case provided a basis for differentiating the conditions in which the practice could take place from those in which it could not.

24 In fact, firms do have a legal obligation to sell these hoarded materials through their superior organizations, as this informant acknowledged later. But much of the hoarded material consists of relatively small quantities of a very large number of items, which makes the handling of it a great nuisance.

25 See note 12.

26 Pronounced 'blaht'.

27 For an official condemnation of the activity of the *tolkach*, see 'Ufa Expediters', *Current Digest of the Soviet Press*, vol. III, no. 5, p. 37.

28 A revealing article in *Izvestiia* describes how a ministry aided its firms in unlawful ways. The quality checkers of the Ministry of Agriculture had rejected some of the output of firms in the Ministry of Agricultural Machine Building. In response to the complaints of the agriculture people, the machine-building ministry took the following actions 'to eradicate sub-quality production': (a) firms were granted permission to sell to other ministries the machines rejected by the Ministry of Agriculture, and (b) the minimum standards of quality were lowered by special order. *'Uluchshat' kachestvo sel'skokhoziaistvennykh mashin'* (Improve the Quality of Agricultural Machinery), *Izvestiia*, 6 January 1951, p. 2.

29 Several informants, including a former director, referred to certain 'secret funds' given to the director by the commissariat or the party, to be used for rewarding plant personnel. The director is accountable to no one for the use of these funds. They are reported to be quite substantial and, if true, must greatly strengthen the hand of the director. It is difficult to assess such statements. Possibly it is an occasional practice which became widely talked about and magnified in importance.

30 The reader will probably think, in this connection, of the scandals in the Bureau of Internal Revenue and the Reconstruction Finance Corporation and other current disclosures of unsavoury practices in American business and government. Although the deification of the 'almightly dollar' has undoubtedly succeeded in corrupting the morals of many Americans, public indignation at these disclosures indicates that there is still a moral resistance to these practices. In the case of the Soviet Union, however, the widespread acceptance of *blat* and favours as a normal means of attaining goals, and the glib way in

which management breaks laws and regulations, makes the following hypothesis worth suggesting: people indicted for using their public office for illegal personal enrichment would be looked upon by the population with sympathy, as unfortunate victims, rather than with moral indignation.

Many of the things reported in this paper ring a familiar note of American practice. That a practice is not peculiar to the Soviet economy alone does not make it less relevant for the understanding of that system. It does draw attention, however, to the important truth that an industrial system has certain imperatives of its own which transcend the particular forms of social and economic organization. The glaring differences between the two economic systems should not blind us to the important similarities.

31 The frequency of the use of the term 'Moscow', standing for generalized authority, reflects the degree of centralization of the system in the thinking of the informants. The trips to Moscow are great and important events in the lives of management, especially senior plant officials. The months of December and January, when the new plans are approved and the annual reports are presented to the superior organs, appear to be a period of great activity and excitement in Moscow. One gets the impression that in these months the trains to and from Moscow are filled with directors, chief accountants, chiefs of planning departments and other officials coming for the annual bargaining over plans, reports, awards, etc. There appears to be a festive air about the occasion, and officials from far-off regions, who come to Moscow less frequently, are filled with the anticipation of renewing old friendships and having a good time on their expense accounts. Commissariats take advantage of the occasion to have business meetings with all their plant officials. A great deal of money is spent in buying special foods and manufactures not available in smaller cities, to be brought home to eager families. The period seems to have much of the spirit of an annual convention of a trade association.

32 A movement to increase productivity by innovations suggested from below.

33 Robert Magidoff, *In Anger and Pity*, New York, 1949, pp. 164–74.

34 John Scott, *Behind the Urals*, Cambridge, Mass., 1942, p. 162.

35 Cf. C. Kluckhohn, 'An Anthropologist Looks at Psychology', *The American Psychologist*, vol. 3, no. 10, October 1948, p. 440.

3   A Problem in Soviet Business
Administration*
1956

Soviet industrial organization has long been plagued by a number of nagging little problems. They have not prevented the state from achieving a considerable success in its prime objective of getting its salaried managers, the men who run the nation's businesses, to turn out impressive quantities of goods and services.

But there remain certain things which the state, with all its power, has not been able to get its managers to do. The intractable is always intriguing, and ones wonders why these persistent thorns have not been eliminated.

Holders of power can rarely expect to achieve a perfect compliance with their wishes, and it is to be expected that Soviet industrial organization would have its share of defects. What is interesting, however, is the particular form they assume. Like the pathology of an organism, an examination of a characteristic defect of a system of organization may be expected to provide an insight into the nature of that system. It is with this end in view that we turn to an inquiry into one such defect in the case of the Soviet industrial enterprise.[1]

Conveniently for us, the leaders of the Soviet state deliver from time to time very candid reports on the state of the nation's industry to the governing bodies of the Communist Party.[2] These reports constitute a set of fairly comparable documents which lend themselves to an analysis of the persistent and the changing features of industrial organization over a period of time.[3] In February 1941, G. M. Malenkov delivered to the Eighteenth Party

*Reprinted from 'A Problem in Soviet Business Administration', by Joseph S. Berliner, published in *Administrative Science Quarterly* vol I:1, June 1956, by permission of *Administrative Science Quarterly*.

Conference a report which, as it turned out, proved to be a summing-up of the state of industry at the end of the pre-war period. Among the many matters which he considered important enough to call to the attention of the assembled party leaders was the following:

Now, Comrades, matters stand thus; in most of our enterprises the output of finished production is carried out unevenly, in spurts, and is concentrated as a rule at the end of the month. Enterprises lack a firm, previously worked-out schedule of production.

Here are some typical examples.

The Kolomensk Machinery Works in Moscow County worked this way in 1940: in the first ten days of every month it produced 5 to 7 per cent of its output, in the second ten days, 10 to 15 per cent, and in the third ten days, 75 to 80 per cent.

The Karl Marx-Leningrad Plant, in December 1940, produced 2 per cent of its monthly output in the first ten days, 8 per cent in the second ten days, and 90 per cent in the third ten days.

In the Moscow Pump and Compressor Plant, in December 1940, 3.4 per cent of the month's output was produced in the first ten days, 27.5 per cent in the second ten days, and 69.1 per cent in the third ten days.

We must put an end to this lack of planning, to this uneven rate of production, to this storming in the work of enterprises. We must achieve a day-by-day fulfilment of the production programme according to a previously worked-out schedule, by every factory, mill, mine, and railroad.

In October 1952, at what proved to be the last Party congress of the Stalin era, Malenkov was again accorded to the honour of delivering the official report. Eleven years of war and reconstruction had elapsed, during which time the preceding generation of industrial managers must have been largely replaced by a new generation. But, again, surveying the broad canvas of Soviet industrial achievements and problems, he lashed out against the same old problem. 'The Party has more than once drawn our industrial executives' attention to this defect,' he said. 'Nevertheless many enterprises continue to work in spurts, producing almost half the month's programme during the final ten days of the month.'

A few months later Stalin died, an uncomfortable collegial form of government emerged, industrial ministries were suddenly combined into a very small number and subsequently decentralized once more, Malenkov fell from the peak of power, and on the next occasion that a major report on the economy was made, it was delivered by Premier N. A. Bulganin. In preparing this first great pronouncement of the new regime on the subject of industrial organization, before a plenary session of the Central Committee of the Party in July 1955, Bulganin chose to call attention to the same matter:

A very serious shortcoming in the work of our industry is the lack of rhythm in production, and the resulting uneven output of industrial production.

Here are three factories... The average fulfilment of the monthly plan at these factories by ten-day periods during the first quarter of 1955 is as follows: first ten days – Russian Diesel, 5 per cent; Spirit of the Revolution, 3 per cent; Kolomna plant, 6 per cent. Second ten days – Russian Diesel, 23 per cent; Spirit of the Revolution, 26.6 per cent; Kolomna plant, 23.3 per cent. Third ten days – Russian Diesel, 72 per cent; Spirit of the Revolution, 70.4 per cent; Kolomna plant, 70.7 per cent. How can one talk of rhythm in the work of these plants when nearly three quarters of the month's work is being carried out in the third ten days?...

Much has already been written and said about the lack of rhythm in work, and decisions have been made. However, it must be admitted that we have been unable to achieve any substantial improvement in this matter.

This practice of 'storming' leads to a number of uneconomic consequences. States of emergency constantly arise; men and equipment are subject to periods of unnecessary idleness; during the days of storming the rate of spoilage increases, overtime pay mounts up, the machines suffer from speed-up, and customers' production schedules are interrupted. It is certainly a practice which the state would wish to eliminate if it could. Yet storming does not occupy a top position on the list of problems facing the state. If it did, perhaps the leaders would have been willing to take the measures necessary to eliminate it. It has not been the subject of a major 'campaign', the technique whereby the state attacks a bothersome problem by mobilizing all its propaganda and police resources and focusing them upon that problem. For this very reason, the practice of storming serves our purpose best by providing a case study of a normal problem in the administration of economic activity.

In examining the reports cited above, one is struck by the absence of an explanation of the causes of storming. Only Bulganin offered a feeble sort of explanation. 'The principal cause', he said, 'is lack of order in the supplying of materials and equipment to industry... Customers usually are sent the major part of their requirements during the second half of the month, and especially during the last ten days.' Now this indeed does explain why the customer has to speed up his rate of production at the end of the month, but it does not explain why the supplier failed in the first place to deliver the required materials in the early part of the month, that is, why the supplier engaged in storming. In effect, storming in one enterprise is caused by storming in another enterprise. This does explain how storming is propagated through the system once it is caused somewhere, but it obviously does not explain why it is caused.

The explanation must be cast in terms of the objectives of enterprise managers and the conditions of the economic milieu within which these objectives must be achieved. The prime obligation of managers is the fulfilment of the monthly output plan. The plan is the document in which the state translates its broad economic objectives into specific production instructions for each of the many thousands of enterprises which make up the industrial system. At the highest level, the National Economic Plan is a listing of the annual production targets for the whole economy, with supplementary targets of investment, increases in labour productivity, reduction of production costs, and so on. On the basis of the National Economic Plan, each of the industrial ministries receives its set of annual targets, subdivided into quarters of the year. The ministries' quarterly targets are then translated into monthly targets for each of their enterprises, which carry out the actual production work.

If the economic objectives of the state are to be achieved, enterprises must meet their production targets in the proper quantities and at the proper times. For this reason, the whole system of incentives which the state has fashioned for the purpose of recruiting high-quality people into managerial positions and motivating them to do their jobs well is geared to fulfilment of the monthly plan, particularly the production target of the plan. First and most immediate is the ample money bonus. Depending upon the importance of the industry and the size of his enterprise, the manager earns a bonus of 30 to 100 per cent of his base salary every month in which he just fulfils his plan.[4] For each percentage overfulfilment of his plan he earns an additional bonus of 2 to 10 per cent of his base salary. The opportunities of adding to an already substantial base salary are thus quite appealing. The director of a coalmine, for example, whose base salary may be about 10,000 roubles a month, would earn a total of 25,000 roubles in any month in which he overfulfilled his plan by 5 per cent.

One need not be a *homo economicus* to be profoundly motivated by such income possibilities. Moreover, the state has seen to it that this money incentive is not in conflict with, but is rather reinforced by, other incentives which may motivate a Soviet manager. Personal advancement, public recognition, and all the prestige which the state can officially confer or channel are available to the manager who regularly fulfils his plans. Demotion is the usual lot of a manager who proves incapable of meeting production targets.

The point is that the state has quite successfully met the problem of eliciting a high level of managerial effort. Soviet managers work hard, not only in terms of their hours of work but in the energy and worry they devote to their jobs. And the focus of their efforts is the fulfilment of the monthly plan.

But fulfilling the monthly plan is no easy matter, and this is the second point to be made. The state has succeeded in organizing a system of establishing plan targets which is calculated to maintain the targets at a high level. Among the various devices developed to achieve this aim is one based on the 'ratchet' principle. According to this principle, when an enterprise overfulfils a plan target, the plan target for the following period must be raised. That is, if an enterprise overfulfils its plan of a million roubles' worth of output in one period, the plan for the following period must be greater than a million.[5] In combination with a powerful motivation for managers to overfulfil their plans, the ratchet principle provides an ever-rising floor beneath which output plans cannot fall. The abundant bonuses induce managers to overfulfil their plans, the ratchet snaps the catch, as it were, beneath the new level of output achieved, and the manager must then exert even greater effort to overfulfil the raised target. This would seem to be a very efficient mechanism for securing the state's objective of an ever-increasing rate of output.

What we have just described is, to be sure, an abstract model of a real process. In fact, managers have been forced to adopt certain methods of defence against the working of this mechanism. Awareness of the action of the ratchet principle causes the prudent manager to beware of overfulfilling his plan by too large an amount, a practice which is contrary to the intentions of the state. Similarly, managers take pains to preserve a 'safety factor' in their production targets, so that they can overfulfil their plans and yet not exhaust their real production potential.[6] But, in general, the effect of the mechanism is to maintain plan targets at a level high enough that the margin of fulfilment is perilously close for most enterprises. This pressure of high targets is perhaps the most salient fact of life for the Soviet manager. Bulganin presented some dramatic evidence of this in his criticism of the high rate of underfulfilment of plans. In 1951, 31 per cent of all enterprises failed to fulfil their annual production plans; in 1952, 39 per cent; in 1953, 40 per cent; and in 1954, 36 per cent. Thus a third of all managers can regularly be expected to underfulfil their plans.

One consequence of this close margin of operation is suggested by another observation made by Bulganin. 'The executives of many enterprises change much too often. In the coal industry, for example, about 40 per cent of the heads and chief engineers of the mines and some 50 per cent of the sector managers change every year.' When a Soviet manager leaves his job, it is not of his own volition.

The picture which emerges is that of a system in which managers work in a rather precarious position. The difference between the successful and the lagging enterprise is not primarily that the former has an easier time of it, but that its managers are more resourceful in overcoming difficulties. Take the Cheliabinsk Tractor Plant, a great and modern establishment which fulfils its plan month after month. Here at least, one might guess, is a smoothly functioning operation. Yet when the Soviet press gives us a glimpse of its day-to-day life, we find another picture. Although the plant fulfilled its plan for the first half of 1955, it had to engage regularly in storming in order to do so. Workers are pressured by management into working on their days off and those who refuse are declared to be 'absentees'. One woman worker was dismissed for refusing to work on Sundays and was reinstated only after the intervention of the trade union. In September, we read, things began to look bad once more towards the end of the month; the director therefore switched the day off from Sunday 25 September to Saturday 1 October. 'It was possible', declares the reporter of the incident, 'with the help of this extra day, to make do, and to make do quite well.'[7] The monthly plan was fulfilled once more and the plant is still numbered among the successful.

With this slim margin of safety, any untoward accident can plunge the enterprise into underfulfilment. The breakdown of a crucial piece of equipment, the rejection of a large lot of production, can throw the enterprise off its production schedule. Even if the manager could meet his target as far as his own efforts are concerned, there is the additional source of trouble referred to by Bulganin, namely that the supplier may fall behind his schedule and thus fail to deliver urgently needed materials on time. Indeed, the unreliability of the system of inter-enterprise supply is perhaps the second most important fact of life in Soviet industry. The economic milieu is therefore such that the manager must often expect to fall behind his production schedule in the course of some month or other.

Given the likelihood of a lag behind the production schedule in some months, what causes the recourse to storming? One might imagine that the lost output would be considered just so much water under the dam: the manager might resume his production schedule when the machine was repaired or the materials arrived, and the month's bonus would be written off as lost. That this does not happen is due to the very special role of the accounting period, the end of the month. Ordinarily, an accounting period is a rather arbitrary date selected for the convenience of planning or for taking stock of performance. Ideally, it should be quite neutral with respect to decision-making; that is, managers should make the same decisions when the accounting date is known as they would make if they did not know on what date the books would be closed. Least of all should the accounting date itself be treated as a datum in the decision-making process. But this is precisely what happens in the Soviet enterprise, and it is this which explains the practice of storming.

This tendency for an arbitrary accounting date to become a factor in decision-making is not unique for Soviet business administration; the effect of tax law on the financial policies of American business leaps to mind. Because of the crucial role of time periods in planning, it is perhaps more serious in the Soviet economy. A vivid illustration of its unfortunate consequences was provided a few years ago by N. S. Khrushchev, in a report on agriculture.[8] For many years it had been the practice to take the livestock census on 1 January. It would seem that 1 January is a rather harmless date; presumably it was selected by an innocent planner with the primary objective of facilitating planning schedules. However, the collective farms have targets of livestock holdings which they are required to meet, as well as targets of meat deliveries to the state. Ordinarily the peasants would bring their stock for slaughter in the early autumn, when they are fattest from the summer grazing. But in order to meet their livestock targets on 1 January, they kept their stock through the cold early winter months so that they could be counted in the census. The consequence was a disastrous loss of weight; and when they finally brought their stock for slaughter after the census date, they had to slaughter many more head of stock than planned in order to fulfil the quota of meat deliveries in kilograms of beef. This had been going on for a number of years before it came to the attention of Khrushchev. The census date has since been moved back to 1 October, and the simple shift of dates has probably solved this curious problem.

Thus an arbitrary accounting date had become a factor in the decision-making process, with the most uneconomic consequences. This is precisely what happens in the case of storming. Because of the crucial importance of the end of the month for the fortunes of the manager, any lag in the production schedule is followed by an acceleration in the rate of production in order that the planned output be attained on that vital date. The greater the lag in the early part of the month, the greater the speed-up towards the end of the month. Given this special role of the accounting period, storming is to be expected as long as lags in production are a normal occurrence.

If storming were confined to the months in which lags occurred, its prevalence would be much more limited than it is. It would be much less troublesome to the Soviets and much less interesting to us. For the remarkable thing is that at the end of the month of storming the manager is not presented with a *tabula rasa*, so that in the following months, if no lag occurred, he might hope to avoid storming. The very act of storming creates conditions which make a lag in the following month inevitable. Of the many reasons why this occurs, we can present only the most important.

A proper schedule of prophylactic maintenance and repair of equipment requires that a certain number of machines be out of operation at all times. But a machine taken down for repair is a machine which is not producing, and thus there is a constant pressure on the maintenance personnel to postpone their work until the pressure is off. 'In the third ten-day period of January', we read in the newspaper of the machinery industry, 'machine "TM–132" was supposed to have been overhauled, but in the shop they decided to wait; "the production programme has to be fulfilled," they said. Soon, however, the machine broke down completely.'[9] And a correspondent of the newspaper of the iron and steel industry observes that 'storming leads to the fact that at the end of the month the equipment is not stopped for maintenance. All stoppages for maintenance are postponed until the beginning of the next month.'[10] The consequence is that the first part of the month following a period of storming is devoted to catching up on the most vital delayed maintenance work and to repairing the damage caused by overwork. Hence the enterprise falls once more behind its current production schedule.

In the discussion of bonuses it was pointed out that the difference between 99 per cent of the plan fulfilment and 100 per cent may be worth as much as double his salary for the plant manager. This sharp discontinuity in earning power is not exactly calculated to bring out the noblest of qualities in a man. When so much hangs upon that one per cent, it is quite understandable that the manager will stretch a point in order to achieve it. The commonest practice is the 'borrowing' of output from the next month and reporting it as having been produced in the current month. The Molotov Weaving and Finishing Mill, for example, was considerably short of its monthly target on 31 August. 'What was most important', states the reporter of the incident, 'there was no chance for a bonus.' The manager called in his accountants, 'giving them strict orders to include the output of the first two days of September in the August plan, and, of course, to draw up appropriate "records" for this purpose.'[11] Since the borrowed output must be 'repaid', the early period of the following month is devoted to producing output which had been reported as completed in the preceding month. Hence the enterprise falls behind its current schedule once more. 'It is like a tight shirt which comes out in front when you pull it down in back,' remarked a former Soviet managerial official interviewed by the writer.

The available descriptions of the storming process indicate that a great deal of energy is expended, while the men work long overtime hours and the managerial officials work 'round the clock'. It is to be expected that when the deadline is over, there will be a letdown – if not in hours, at least in energy expended.[12]

Factors such as these impart a dynamic movement to the output of the Soviet firm, a movement which has all the formal properties of a 'business cycle'. Consider an enterprise which has managed to achieve an even rate of output. Any disturbance to its schedule will now generate a periodic movement in its rate of output, not only in the month in which the disturbance occurs but in a number of successive months. The oscillations will dampen down if the enterprise has succeeded in tucking away a 'safety factor'; that is, if in any month the output plan is small enough that it can be fulfilled with enough time and resources left over to make up for the output deficit of the preceding month. The oscillations will become wider if the initial disturbance is reinforced in succeeding months so that the enterprise falls further and further behind its schedule. This usually ends, as the Russians say, in a great *skandal*. The manager is fired and a new hopeful takes over.

Here, then, is a nice problem for the administrator. Three integral elements of the system of industrial organization are involved; a powerful incentive to produce, a successful technique of maintaining high targets, and a system of planning and accounting. Each in its way is a useful device for what it is designed to accomplish. Yet, in combination, they give rise to this unfortunate and unintended practice of storming. It is interesting to speculate on changes that might succeed in eliminating the practice. Let us at the outset limit the admissible changes to simple measures which would not require far-reaching alterations in the basic features of the system of industrial organization, such as the planning and incentive systems.

In the three Party reports quoted earlier, the only real administrative measure recommended was one put forth by Malenkov in the 1941 report. Certain commissars,[13] he indicated, had introduced a system requiring every director to report daily to the commissar on the quantity of output produced the preceding day. 'These reports oblige the commissar to find the causes of the failure to fulfil the daily targets immediately, and to take immediate measures for correcting the indicated deficiencies.' Where the system had been introduced, stated Malenkov, there had been a significant evening-out of the rate of production.

Whatever hopes Malenkov may have had that this measure would provide the panacea must have been short-lived, for little was heard of it thereafter. At least one reason for the failure began to emerge shortly afterwards. As a measure of self-defence, managers began to resort to the practice of 'prolonging the work day'. In an iron and steel plant, we read, 'by order of Comrade Matevosian, the chief engineer, it was decided to prolong the acceptance of finished products from the rolling mill on March 15 until 1:30 a.m. of March 16. On March 11 Comrade Matevosian authorized the inclusion in the output of the current day, of the output of the quality steel shops which had actually been completed by 6:00 a.m. of the following day.'[14] In other words, the period of the storming cycle was reduced from the month to the day, but the same elements of periodicity continued to prevail. Any measure to eliminate storming must reckon with the boundless ingenuity of Soviet managers.

There were undoubtedly other reasons for the failure of Malenkov's measure. A system of daily reporting must have greatly increased the workload on the normally overlarge number of book-keepers and clerks in the plant administration. The system also required a more formalized set of daily plan targets, a further burden on the planning apparatus in the commissariat and in its hundreds of enterprises. And finally, when the lag in production was due to causes outside the enterprise's own control, such as the failure of materials shipments to arrive on time, the commissariat officials could not be expected to straighten matters out in a single day.

Would it help to lengthen the accounting period, perhaps to a three-month or six-month period instead of a one-month period?[15] This measure comes very close to violating the restriction we have set upon the range of admissible solutions, for it may well require far-reaching changes in the methods of plant administration. The system of bonus payments would have to be shifted to a longer time period. If the bonus for fulfilment of the six-month plan is to be equal to six times the bonus previously available for the monthly plan, the stakes on that last few per cent of plan fulfilment would be so high as to constitute an intolerable strain on the honesty of mortal men. Moreover, the whole system of planning and reporting is geared to a monthly basis, and if the bonus system were not similarly geared there would undoubtedly be an increase in the incidence of underfulfilment of monthly plans. For however harshly storming is indicted, the state is really rather ambivalent about it. Because of the planned interdependence of customers and suppliers, underfulfilment by one enterprise often sends a wave of underfulfilment pulsing through a number of other plants. It is therefore vitally important that each manager exert the greatest effort to fulfil his monthly plan. One suspects that the state would rather have storming-plus-fulfilment than underfulfilment-without-storming. It is true that this problem of the close interdependence of enterprises could be met by an increase in inventories and pipeline stocks, but here too is a measure which would alter the basic principles upon which Soviet industry has functioned in the past.

It is doubtful that an admissible solution could be found by the manipulation of the accounting period. It is true that this approach worked in the case of the livestock census date, but there it was merely a matter of tying the accounting period to a certain natural phenomenon which was not one of the variables of the problem but a datum.

Could a solution be found by focusing on another facet of the problem, the incentive system rather than the accounting period? When really serious problems have arisen, the Soviets have often appealed to what they clearly recognize as a major motivating factor – the bonus. Thus, in recent years, the award of bonuses has been made contingent upon fulfilment of a cost-reduction target and upon the production of the proper quantities of individual items of production (the assortment plan). Judging from the continued complaints about the neglect of costs and product-assortment, this method has not proved outstandingly successful, probably because the state's prime interest in production remains overriding. If the award of bonuses were made to depend on the fulfilment of too many unrealistic side conditions, fewer bonuses would actually be earned, and there is a danger that this potent incentive would be vitiated. If the state introduced and enforced a requirement that no bonus be paid if the plan were fulfiled by storming, most managers would have to write off the bonus as a paper promise.

An alternative solution along these lines would be to offer to the manager who eliminates storming a supplementary bonus which would be independent of the bonus for plan fulfilment. This too is an approach which has been used in the past to motivate managers to put more effort into increasing the production of spare parts and the production of a sideline of consumer goods out of scraps and waste. The trouble is that too many supplementary bonuses tend to deflect managerial attention in the direction of the largest bonus. The Commissar of the Iron and Steel Industry, for example, once introduced a system in which managers could earn a bonus of 50 per cent of the value of fuel saved and 15 per cent of the value of materials saved.[16] The system may well have turned a good deal of effort away from materials to fuel. And when there are possibilities of substitution (perhaps by producing more consumer goods at the expense of spare parts), quite unintended decisions may be made. Thus a supplementary bonus for elimination of storming,which would be large enough to make a difference, might raise new problems in other spheres of managerial activity. It any case, the bonus must not be larger than the bonus for production plan fulfilment, and therefore it would not be likely to eliminate the causes of storming.

We cannot continue here to explore the full range of possible solutions. But enough has been said to demonstrate that storming is so deeply ingrained in the structure of the system that no simple measures can eliminate it. The argument may be concluded by considering that there is no lack of solutions if we are willing to admit fundamental changes in the system of industrial administration. Suppose, for example, that production plans were reduced well below their present high level, perhaps by eliminating the 'ratchet' principle of planning. If there were enough slack in production plans, ordinary lags in production schedules could be easily made up without recourse to storming. Plans would be more often fulfilled, and there would be no need for the postponement of maintenance and the 'borrowing' of output. If plans were more often fulfilled, enterprises would less often be thrown off schedule by the delayed delivery of materials from suppliers. A general reduction of plan targets would thus eliminate two of the three components of the storming mechanism: the high probability of lags behind schedule and the dynamic transmission of storming from one period to the next.

It is doubtful that the Soviets will accept this gratuitous suggestion and, it must be admitted, possibly with good reason. The combination of high targets and high rewards is a most effective mechanism for eliciting a high level of effort from their managers. Lower targets might very well lead to a relaxation of effort and output, which is contrary to the objectives of the state. Storming is a price which the state probably considers well worth paying for the benefits of the present system. For the administrator, it remains an embarrassing defect which his art is powerless to eliminate. 'What we need if we are to solve this,' said Bulganin, 'is not exorcisms but elimination of the causes which breed lack of rhythm.' But it is doubtful that we shall hear anything but exorcisms unless broader changes in the administrative system are admitted.

NOTES

1 The author wishes to thank Dr Richard Axt of the National Science Foundation and Hans Heymann of the RAND Corporation for their valuable comments.
2 The Soviet industrial enterprise may be thought of roughly as a mill or factory under the management of a director and his administrative staff. The director is primarily responsible to a minister or one of his assistants. The minister is part of the executive arm of the state. The broad decisions as to what is to be produced are made by the state and transmitted to the enterprises through the ministries.
3 The three reports referred to may be found in *Izvestiia*, 6 February 1941, pp. 1–3 (the Malenkov 1941 report); Leo Gruliow (ed.), *Current Soviet Policies*, New York, 1953, pp. 106–16 (the Malenkov 1952 report); *Current Digest of the Soviet Press*, no. 7, 24 August 1955, pp. 3–20 (the Bulganin 1955 report).
4 A. Vikent'ev, *Ocherki razvitiia sovetskoi ekonomiki v chetvertoi piatiletke* (Essays on Soviet Economic Development in the Fourth Five Year Plan), Gosplanizdat, 1952, p. 175.
5 The ratchet principle is not an explicit principle of planning but a generally understood rule among managers and planners. In the published sources one catches glimpses of it in the criticism of planners who apply it overzealously (*Stroitel'naia gazeta*, 27 July 1955, p. 2), and in criticisms such as that by Malenkov in his 1941 Report, directed against 'commissariats which not only did not fulfil their 1940 plans but actually reduced their output below 1939'. Usually the ratchet principle operates over yearly periods, occasionally over quarterly periods.
6 Pp. 31–2 above.
7 *Current Digest of the Soviet Press*, no. 7, 9 November 1955, p. 9.
8 *Pravda*, 15 September, 1953, p. 2.
9 *Mashinostroenie*, 9 February 1939, p. 2.
10 *Chernaia Metallurgiia*, 4 March 1941, p. 3.
11 *Current Digest of the Soviet Press*, no. 4, 3 January 1953, p. 16.
12 To this may perhaps be added the survivals of peasant resistance to the harsh and demanding discipline of industrial factory life. There is a very suggestive passage in Marx's *Capital* describing the early capitalists' troubles in disciplining their recently urbanized labour force to the factory regime: 'Work toward the end of the week being generally much increased in duration in consequence of the habit of the men of idling on Monday and occasionally during a part or whole of Tuesday also. . . They lose two or three days, and then work all night to make it up' (Karl Marx, *Capital*, Modern Library, p. 523 n.).
13 In the pre-war period, ministers were known as 'people's commissars'.

14   *Chernaia Metallurgiia*, 22 March 1941, p. 2.
15   The author is indebted to Professor Raymond T. Bye of the Wharton
     School of Finance and Commerce, University of Pennsylvania, for
     this suggestion.
16   *Industriia*, 22 January 1940, p. 3.

4 Managerial Incentives and Decision-Making: A Comparison of the United States and the Soviet Union* 1959

SUMMARY

The rewards in income and prestige in the United States and Soviet economies are such that a larger proportion of the best young people in the USSR turn to careers in heavy industry, science, and higher education, whereas in the United States a larger proportion of the best talent flows into such fields as heavy or light (consumer goods) industry, finance, commerce and trade, law, medicine, etc. Higher education, particularly technical, is more a prerequisite for the attainment of a top business career in the Soviet Union than in the United States.

The principal managerial incentive in Soviet industry is the bonus paid for overfulfilment of plan targets. The incentive system is successful in the sense that it elicits a high level of managerial effort and performance. But it has the unintended consequence of causing managers to engage in a wide variety of practices that are contrary to the interests of the state. Managers systematically conceal their true production capacity from the planners, produce unplanned types of products, and falsify the volume and quality of production. In the procurement of materials and supplies they tend to order larger quantities than they need, hoard scarce materials, and employ unauthorized special agents who use influence and gifts to ease management's procurement problems. The incentive system causes managers to shy away from innovations that upset the smooth working of the firm.

*U.S. Congress, Joint Economic Committee, *Comparisons of the United States and Soviet Economies*, Washington, DC (1959) pp. 349–76.

Since American managers operate in a different economic environment, their problems and therefore their practices differ from those of Soviet managers. But in those aspects of economic life in which the US economy approximates the operating conditions of the Soviet economy, American managers develop forms of behaviour similar to those of Soviet managers. The separation of management and ownership, characteristic of the modern corporation, leads to conflicts of interest between managers and stockholder–owners, and management's pursuit of its own interest leads to activities similar to those of the Soviet manager striving to defend his interests against those of the owner-state. The spread of legislation constricting the freedom of operation of the American firm leads to the evasion of laws and regulations characteristic of the Soviet economy, though on a larger scale there. Finally, under wartime conditions, the burgeoning of government controls and the dominant role of the government as customer alters the operating conditions of the US economy in such ways that it closely approximates some of the normal operating conditions of the Soviet economy. The change is accompanied by black-market operations, hoarding, quality deterioration, and the use of influence, practices which are normal in the peacetime Soviet economy.

1 MANAGERIAL INCENTIVES AND RECRUITMENT

The most important decision a manager has to make is made before he ever becomes a manager; namely, the decision to prepare for a managerial career. The factors influencing this decision are of vital importance for our industrial society. Imagine the consequences if no one aspired to become a manager, or if young people chose management only as a last resort, or if other careers were so attractive that management got only the last pickings of each year's crop of youngsters. It might therefore be appropriate to begin with some reflections on the incentives that the United States and the USSR offer their young people to choose a managerial career rather than some other.

The factors motivating young people to choose one or another occupation are probably not vastly different in the two countries. Family tradition is often decisive; many a youngster chooses a career simply because he wishes to be like his father (or mother). Special talents such as those of the artist, or early conceived deep interests, like the boy who must be a scientist, account for the career choices of some others. But most teenagers have no clear idea of what they would like to be. It is with respect to these youths that it is most interesting to speculate upon the incentive-pulls that the two systems offer for the choice of one career or another.

Education and Career Choice

The role of higher education in career choice is different in the two nations. Higher education is very much more of a prerequisite for the prestigious and high-income occupations in the USSR than in the United States. To be sure, the person with a high school education or less has an increasingly difficult time embarking on the managerial ladder of the large American corporation. But in such fields as trade, commerce, construction and in small business in general, the opportunities are still vast for a financially successful career. College, and education in general, is not of decisive importance. And the brute fact is that a college diploma can always be obtained somewhere in the United States, with very little effort or ability, by just about anyone who can pay the tuition and write a semi-literate paragraph. Those who don't aspire to a managerial position or who fail to make the grade can, as workingmen, nevertheless enjoy a standard of living that is the envy of the world. The point is that the young American who is not inclined toward academic work need not feel that he is out of the competition for our society's best rewards.

This is not true in the USSR. A number of conversations with young Soviet people have convinced me that to be 'worker' is something devoutly to be shunned by most young people who have reached the high school level. There are at least two reasons for this attitude, which seems so anomalous in a 'worker's state'. The first is the enormously high prestige that Russian (and European) culture has always placed upon the 'intelligent', the learned man, the man who works with his mind instead of his hands. The Soviet regime has striven hard to make manual labour respectable, and it undoubtedly has succeeded in endowing the worker with a social position relatively much higher than before the revolution. But the young person who has reached the educational level at which he can choose between being a worker or an 'intelligent' would, other things being equal, choose the latter without question.

Other things are not equal, however. In particular, the income possibilities of a worker are far smaller than those of a college graduate, and this is the second reason for the desperate, and sometimes pathetic, drive for a higher education. Of course, a person must have reached the high school level before he can even begin to think about choosing between the career of a worker or an 'intelligent'. The steady annual expansion in the high school population has had the effect of presenting ever-increasing numbers of young people with the choice, and few of them would freely choose to be workers. If the expansion of the school population had continued, giving more and more young people the opportunity to avoid being workers, it would have raised serious problems for the recruitment of the labour force. The radical reform of the educational system by Khrushchev was undoubtedly motivated, in part, by the wish to avoid that problem.

Thus, the undesirability of a career as a worker has intensified the desire for higher education. Add to this the fact that there is no private enterprise, no small business in which a man could pull himself out of a worker's status and reach a position of prestige and income comparable to the self-made American businessman. I do not wish to state that the door is completely closed. By dint of hard work, ability, and certain other qualities, a Soviet citizen without the college diploma can, from time to time, rise to an important position in some economic hierarchy. But his chances are about as good as those of an equivalent person in a progressive American corporation. And the young person evaluating the importance of higher education understands this.

Finally, the Russian teenager who decides he has to get a college diploma has very few easy ways out. He can't buy his way into college, as the American student can if he has the money. There are no private colleges that can set whatever standards they wish. To be sure there are instances of bribery or influence, but they are certainly the exception. If the Soviet student wants a college diploma very badly, he has to work hard to gain admission and to be graduated. The very intensity of the drive for education, and the competition of many applicants for the limited number of admissions, permits the high schools and colleges to maintain high standards of performance. Moreover the colleges are financially independent of student tuitions: not only are there no tuitions but most of the students earn stipends. The consequence is that the typical Soviet student works harder and has to meet higher standards of performance than the typical American student. The standards are different in the two countries, of course, because of differences in the philosophy of education. But there is no doubt that study is a much more serious business for the young Soviet student than for the American.

One final note on education and incentives. The quality of the managerial (and technical) manpower of a nation depends on the proportion of the population comprising the pool from which the managers are drawn. That is, if half the population were for some reason excluded from the pool, the quality of the managers would be lower than if the whole population comprised the pool. Both nations suffer in this respect from the fact that rural educational facilities are poorer than urban, which reduces the pool of the potential college group. Since the Soviet rural population is larger percentagewise than that of the United States, and since their rural educational facilities are probably relatively worse, they suffer more from this loss. But there are other ways in which the US pool is curtailed more than the Soviet. First is the fact that the private cost of education keeps a substantial portion of talented American young people in the lower income groups out of college. I admit that this fact puzzles me. With the American network of free state universities and with a fairly abundant scholarship programme, I don't fully understand why a competent student who really desired it could not get a college education. It is my impression, however, that systematic studies generally show that the USA is losing an unfortunate number of young people to higher education for financial reasons. If this is so, the USA is worse off than the Soviets in this respect, for their education is absolutely free, and most students of any merit earn stipends besides. Lower-income young Soviet people may nevertheless be unable to go off to college if the family needs their earnings. A young Soviet women told me, in reply to my question, that this was why she never went on to college. She is not a very good illustration of my point, however, for she went on to say that she really wasn't very smart anyhow.

The second group that is largely lost from America's pool of potential managerial manpower is the negro and some other racial minorities. It may well be that the proportion of college graduates among some of the Soviet national minorities is smaller than for the Slavic nationalities; I have seen no data on this. But I would doubt that their loss from racial discrimination is as large.

The third and largest group lost from the American pool comprises exactly half its population – the female half. Sex discrimination certainly exists in the Soviet economy, probably more in management than in science and technology. But undoubtedly the female population enlarges the pool of technical and managerial manpower much more in the USSR than in the United States. The difference in the role of women in the two countries must, I think, enter into the balance I am trying to strike, but it is not a subject on which I would recommend that your committee[1] consider writing corrective legislation.

Let me summarize briefly this discussion of the relationship of education to career choice. Education, and particularly higher education, is more important in the USSR than in the United States as the gateway to a prestigious and highly remunerative career.

Competition is keener for higher education, the cost of education to the individual is less and the standards of admission and performance are higher in the USSR. Both nations lose part of the potential pool of managerial talent, the USSR because of its large rural population, the United States because of financial burdens and racial and sex discrimination.

Competition Among Careers
How does a managerial career compare with the attractiveness of other careers in the two nations? The young American not dedicated to some particular field, but motivated by a roughly equal desire for prestige and money, might select some field such as law, medicine, business, or engineering. He would decidedly not go into education or science. An equivalent young Soviet person would make a somewhat different choice. He would certainly not select law, which has been assigned a most humble role in Soviet society. Nor would he select medicine, for while the prestige is high, the income is low. On the other hand, higher education or science would be an excellent choice. The very title of 'Professor' or 'Scientific worker' would assure him one of the highest places of honour in the society. And an outstanding career in either of those fields would assure him an income ranking in the upper 10 per cent or perhaps even 5 per cent (data are hard to come by) of the population. The difference in the economic and social position of the scientist and teacher in the two countries is of fundamental importance in the matter of career recruitment.

The American who decides to choose a career in the business world has a much wider range of choice than his Soviet counterpart. A great variety of fields offer roughly equivalent rewards in prestige and incomes: advertising, accounting, finance, commerce, trade, sales, light manufacturing, heavy industry. Of all these fields, it is only the latter that would exert a great pull on the young Soviet person. For 40 years the government and party have hammered home the central role of heavy industry, children are instilled with an admiration of technology, and heavy industry has been endowed with an aura of glamour that exceeds even our American fascination with technology. The ideological cards are stacked, in varying degree, against all other branches of the economy. In keeping with the ideology, the prestige and income possibilities in heavy industry are decidedly greater than in the other branches.

Not only will the student be attracted to heavy industry, but he is likely to choose engineering as his path of entry into whatever branch of heavy industry he selects. He would be attracted to engineering for the educational reasons discussed above. Engineering is, moreover, the most direct line of approach to a managerial career.

The Soviet engineering graduate will find his first job opportunities rather different from those of his American counterpart. If he is at the top of his class, the best offers will come from the research institutes, with top starting salaries and opportunities for graduate work. The poorer students will find lower-paying jobs in industry. In the United States the situation is quite the reverse. The most successful students will be snapped up by recruiters from the large corporations, with the best starting salary offers. Some of the top students will, to be sure, spurn the attractive job offers and go on to further graduate work, but I suspect that many of those who go immediately into graduate work are the men who didn't get the good job offers. To be sure, many of the top American students who join the corporations are put immediately into research and development, but as many of them will be working on new passenger car or dishwasher design as will be working on electronic development and automation technique. The Soviet researcher is more likely to be working on the latter than the former.

The young Soviet engineer who goes into industry starts at the bottom of the managerial ladder, as chief of a production shop, or the design or maintenance departments of the enterprise. As new job opportunities develop, he faces the choice of continuing in direct production or taking one of the staff jobs in the enterprise, such as the planning department. If he stays in production proper, his career path may lead to chief engineer of an enterprise or to one of the higher economic agencies. If he moves into staff work, his career may lead to the directorship of an enterprise or of one of the higher organs. Either career leads to the pinnacle of Soviet management.

The paths that are least likely to lead to top management are finance or sales. I would guess the proportion of top management in the United States who started in such fields as finance and sales is much larger than in the USSR. There are no 'colleges of business administration' in the Soviet Union. The ambitious youngster who wants to work for the top of the Soviet business world studies engineering, not personnel and marketing.

Summarizing, industry in the United States has to compete with a wide variety of other branches of economic activity for its share of the best potential managerial talent. In the USSR the values and the rewards are concentrated in relatively fewer fields, and industry is far more attractive than most others. Science and higher education, which scarcely compete with industry in the United States, are a strong competitor of industry in the USSR. Among the various branches of industry, in the United States the light and consumer goods industries compete very effectively for both managerial and engineering talent. In the USSR light and consumer goods industries are much less attractive than heavy industry. And finally the nature of industrial recruitment is such that technical education is much more important as part of the training of a would-be manager in the USSR than in the United States.

My conclusion is that heavy industry, science and higher education attract, by and large, a better and more competent crop of young people in the USSR than in the United States. Moreover, the competition for education is keener in the USSR, so that they get a more rigorously trained (trained in different ways, to be sure) corps of managerial, engineering, scientific and university personnel. On the other hand, such branches of the economy as sales, advertising, finance, trade and commerce, light industry, and law attract a much more competent group of people in the United States than in the USSR. Most of the outstanding people in these fields in the United States would, if they were Soviet citizens, have enjoyed successful careers in heavy industry, science, technology, or higher education. There is, after all, nothing startling in this conclusion. It is but another way of saying that each society gets what it pays for.

2 MANAGERIAL INCENTIVES AND DECISION-MAKING

Material Incentives

The incentives that attract people into management are not necessarily the same incentives that motivate managers to do their jobs and do them well. What are the goals of the manager? What are the considerations that impel him to make one decision rather than the other?

The moving force of our economic system is the pursuit of private gain. The worker chooses the higher-paying job, the businessman accepts the more profitable contract, the investor buys the higher interest security. The usual exceptions must of course be made; the laws must be obeyed, public opinion may sometimes require that one decision be made rather than another, people make wrong decisions, a short-run loss may be accepted for a longer-term gain. But by and large – 'other things being equal', as the economist likes to say – it is private gain that determines economic decision.

The Soviets have at various times experimented with other forms of incentive, for it did not at first seem quite appropriate that a socialist economy should stress private gain. But practicality won out over dogma, and private gain has for the last 25 years been the keystone of the managerial incentive system. To be sure, we still find references to various social incentives such as communist enthusiasm. But we are also reminded that while enthusiasm is well and good, communism, as Lenin used to say, must be built 'not directly on enthusiasm but with the aid of enthusiasm born out of the great revolution; [communism must be built] on private interest, on personal incentive, on businesslike accounting.'[2] Moreover, the incentive of private gain will be with us for a long time. According to the eminent labour economist, E. Manevich, it will not disappear until the day of general overabundance arrives, until the differences between country and city are eliminated, and until the differences between mental and manual labour vanish.[3] We are safe in saying that, for the next several decades at least, private gain will be the central economic incentive in both economic systems.

The form that material incentives take is of some importance. For the American businessman it is clearly profit. If you ask why did he take on this contract rather than that, why did he order this machine rather than that, why did he ship by truck rather than train, the answer would normally be, 'because it's cheaper that way', or what comes to the same thing, 'because he would make more money that way'.

For the private businessman managing his own business, profit is clearly the guide to his actions. But most American business is not managed in this way. The men who actually run the firm are salaried managers, hired by the stockholders' representative body, the board of directors. The profit of the business does not belong to the manager but to the stockholder-owners. The fact is that the private interest of the manager need not necessarily coincide with that of the stockholder. In order to bring the manager's private interest into closer coincidence with that of the owners, most corporations have instituted some kind of bonus system, on the assumption that, if the manager has a direct stake in the profit of the enterprise, his decisions are more likely to be those that will earn more profit.

In fashioning an incentive system for its managers, the Soviet government faced a problem similar to that of the American corporation. For all Soviet enterprises are run by salaried managers. If the Soviet manager's income consisted solely of his salary, it was conceivable that his private interest would not coincide at all points with the interest of the government. Accordingly a considerable variety of supplementary bonuses are available to the managerial staff. The bonuses are designed to motivate managers to make those decisions that the government considers to be in its own interest.

The amount of income earned in the form of bonuses is substantial. In 1947, the last year for which detailed data are available to me, the managerial personnel of the iron and steel industry earned bonuses averaging 51.4 per cent of their basic income. In the food industry at the low end, the percentage was 21 per cent.[4] Since these are averages, many individual managers earned considerably more than this. Bonuses of this magnitude must be a potent incentive indeed.

But incentive for what? This is surely the crucial question. For we can readily imagine an incentive which was extremely successful in motivating action, but action of an undesirable kind. The test of an incentive is therefore not only its motivating power, but the extent to which it leads to the desired kind of decision.

Before proceeding to the relationship of incentives to decision-making, let me clarify the sense in which I use the term 'incentive'. By 'incentive', I mean that consideration which explains why one decision was made rather than another. If a young person decides to find employment in the electrical machinery industry rather than in the furniture industry, the difference in basic salaries in the two industries may well have been the decisive consideration. In this case salary is the effective incentive. But once in the job, the salary does not vary according to whether one operating decision is made rather than another. When the manager decides to put one order into production ahead of another, or to substitute one material for another, it is not his salary he is thinking about. It is usually the size of the month's bonus that will depend on the decision taken. It is in this sense that the bonus is the principal incentive in the operational decisions of the Soviet enterprise.

Production Decisions

Two generations ago people debated the question of whether a socialist economy could possibly work. History removed that question from the agenda. The last generation changed the question to whether the Soviet economy could work at all efficiently. That question has also been answered. These hearings would not otherwise be taking place. My discussion takes for granted that the Soviet economy is reasonably efficient, and that the question at issue is how efficient.

There is little doubt that the system of managerial incentives, broadly viewed, has created a corps of managers dedicated to their work and responsive to the production demands made upon them. Like their American counterparts, they are deeply involved in their work, they worry about production quotas, they demand results from their labour force. As hired managers, they are aware that, if their performance is not satisfactory, there are always other persons spoiling for a chance at their jobs. I have no way of knowing whether the intensity of managerial life is greater in the USSR than in the United States; in both countries there are variations from industry to industry. But there are two reasons why industrial life probably proceeds at a faster tempo in the USSR than here. The first is that the absence of free trade unions makes it difficult for workers to resist pressure for intense operation. The second is that industry is under constant exhortation from government and Party for ever-increasing levels of production.

But the question as indicated above is not whether management is motivated to work hard. It is rather whether the incentive system motives them to do what the state wishes them to do; whether, in other words, they get as much mileage out of their effort as they might get.

One of the most interesting conclusions of the study of Soviet managerial incentives is that the bonus system is directly responsible for motivating management to make a variety of decisions contrary to the intent and the interests of the state. The decisions to be described go far back in the history of the Soviet economy, and have resisted countless efforts by the government to eliminate them. Most of them have survived the great changes in industrial organization of the past several years. They are clearly deeply rooted in the soil of Soviet economic organization.

First, consider the matter of the reporting of information. In a planned economy it is vital that the central planners have as accurate information as possible about the productive capacity of enterprises. The bonus system, however, acts as a prevailing motivation for managers to understate their real production capacity. The reason is that the most important of the bonuses available to managers depends on the extent to which the production target of the enterprise is overfulfilled. If the manager honestly reports his full production capacity, and if for some reason something goes wrong in the course of the month, then he and his staff will lose that month's bonus. It is safer therefore to report a smaller capacity than really exists, in order that the production target will be kept low enough to allow for emergencies. The Russians call this 'insurance' or 'security'. The consequence is that the planners can never be sure that their plans are based on accurate figures. The government is aware of the problem: 'This is fully understandable', writes a Soviet economist, 'because the lower the plan, the greater the opportunity to fulfil and overfulfil it . . .'[5]

Because the higher state agencies cannot trust management's reporting of its productive capacity, various techniques have been fashioned for setting targets high enough to force the firms to operate as close as possible to capacity. One of these techniques is the arbitrary increase of targets over last year's production. As a prominent State Planning Commission economist put it, 'they take as the base magnitude the level of production achieved during the preceding period and raise it by some percentage or other.'[6] Sometimes this technique helps flush out the manager's 'hidden reserves', but in other cases the arbitrary increase in targets leads to impossibly high tasks. Indeed, the spirit of planning is reflected in the systematic use of high targets as a device for keeping managers working at as fast a tempo as possible. In the past targets have been set so high (deliberately, one suspects) that one-third of all enterprises failed to fulfil their annual plans. There is some evidence that, in the last year or two, this policy of deliberate overplanning has been modified, and we are told that in the first half of 1958 only 19 per cent of all enterprises failed to fulfil their plans.[7] This still represents one out of five enterprises, and indicates that the high level of plan targets remains a dominant fact of life for the Soviet manager. The intense pace of plant operation has its distinct advantage from the state's point of view: it elicits from management a high level of effort that might not be forthcoming if the plans were set at a more modest level. But the price paid by the state is the manager's effort to defend his enterprise by concealing his full capacity.

When the target has been set, the manager's bonus depends on the success with which he fulfils it. Most of the firm's production does indeed follow the lines laid down in the plan. But when the end of the month rolls around and, as often happens, production is far short of meeting the month's target, then managers turn to a host of time-tested techniques of meeting – or seeming to meet – the targets. In certain types of production, such as metals, the target is expressed in tons; in such cases the manager might order his shops to curtail the production of relatively lightweight products (special and quality metals) and to throw more men and materials into the production of the heavier products.[8] In textile production we read that the practice of setting targets in 'running metres' (that is, in measures of length, without regard to width) causes managers to overproduce narrow-width cloth and under-produce broad width.[9] In firms with a considerable variety of products, the production targets are expressed in value units –

so many millions of roubles of production. In such cases managers tend to overproduce those products that have high fixed prices (all prices are fixed): they may deliberately use more expensive materials in order to drive up the value of production.[10] These are some of an endless variety of ways in which managers 'violate the planned assortment of production' – to use the official expression of disapproval.

How widespread are these practices? We really don't know. From time to time individual managers are publicly excoriated for such practices, and figures are published to show how widely the planned assortment of production had been departed from. But these may well be extreme cases, and it would be unwise to generalize from them. Occasionally, however, the results of special studies are published, and they give us some idea of the magnitude of the problem. The State Planning Commission recently released the results of a survey of the production practices of 63 enterprises. Of the total production by these enterprises in excess of the plan targets, only 43 per cent consisted of the basic products normally produced by them; 26.5 per cent consisted of 'products not included in the plan when it was originally confirmed', 20 per cent consisted of 'other production', and 7 per cent consisted not of finished products but of an increase in semifabricated parts and goods-in-process.[11] While these data are not precisely in the form in which we would want them, they do provide a good indication of managers' tendency to produce those products that are best from their own enterprises' point of view, rather than those products that the state would most wish to have produced.

Two other consequences of the bonus system (and the pressure of high targets) should be noted. One is simple falsification of reported production. 'Thus, for example', we read in a Soviet article, 'if the plan is fulfilled 99 per cent, the managerial and engineering personnel receive no bonus. But if the enterprise fulfils the plan 100 per cent, they receive bonuses of from 15 to 37 per cent of their salary.'[12] Quite a lot of money hinges on that last percentage of production, and it is no wonder that management may succumb to the temptation to 'fudge' the report a bit in order to earn the bonus. Again, the techniques of covering up for falsely reported production are myriad. To cite only one, production is 'borrowed' from next month. That is, production that is expected to occur next month is reported as having been produced this month. If things go well next month, the 'borrowed' output is 'repaid'; if not, the manager may get into trouble.

More serious than falsification, however, is the deterioration of the quality of production. The poor quality of much of Soviet consumer goods production is well known. In other types of production the danger of detection is greater, and quality standards are less readily violated. But the explanation of management's tendency to shave on quality is the same: the high production targets are so often not attainable, and the manager wants to keep his job. Much of the quality shaving is of a kind that is not easily detected: fewer stitches in the garment, fewer screws in the piece, greener lumber in the building, more impurities in the metal. But if the pressure is keen enough, more extreme forms of quality deterioration will be adopted.

Summarizing, the bonus system is an effective device for eliciting a high level of managerial effort, but in the context of excessively high production targets, it induces management to make certain types of decisions that are contrary to the intent of the state. The production of unplanned products, the concealment of production capacity, the falsification of reports and the deterioration of quality are the unintended consequences of the system of managerial incentives.

Procurement Decisions

The high level of production targets is but half the problem facing the Soviet manager. The other half is the perpetual shortage of materials and supplies. In order to get the greatest possible production from the available stocks of materials and supplies, the state employs a variety of devices to minimize the use of materials in production and inventory. Undoubtedly these devices have served to control wasteful use of resources, and they have also helped channel the flow of resources in the direction most desired by the state. But they have been self-defeating to some extent for they have forced managers to make certain kinds of decision which frustate the intent of the state.

The core of the matter is that managers simply don't trust the planning system to provide them with the supplies and materials they need in the right quantity and quality, and at the right time. The recent decentralization of industrial organization may have improved matters somewhat, but the evidence we have indicates that supply problems are still the most troublesome feature of managerial life. Moreover, the reasons are similar to those we used to read about before decentralization. (This paper was written during Krushchev's years as General Secretary. In that period the national Ministries were abolished and replaced by territorially decentralized Councils of the National Economy. The Ministries were restored after Krushchev's fall from power.) For all important materials the manager must still obtain an allocation order from his home office (usually the Council of the National Economy of his district), which must in turn get the allocation order from the republican or all-union planning commission.

Thus, we still read of the 'existing complicated system of obtaining allocation orders, under which every enterprise must submit detailed requisitions to Moscow a long time before the new planning quarter is to begin'.[13] Because plans are not always finally set at the time the planning period is to begin, enterprises sometimes start with 'advance allocations', that is, temporary allotments of resources designed to keep them operating until the final allocation orders are available.[14] Decentralization of the economy was supposed to have made it easier for neighbouring enterprises to sell to each other without having to go through Moscow. But central purchasing agencies still exist, and agencies anywhere must find something to do. Thus the Chief Purchasing and Marketing Administration located in the republic capitals (Moscow, for example) still insist on being the middle man in purchase and sale contracts between enterprises, even when the latter are located in the same outlying city (such as Sverdlovsk).[15] Perhaps even more serious than the complex supply planning system is the large percentage of enterprises that regularly fails to fulfil its plans, or fulfil them by producing the wrong, or substandard, products. Since the production of these enterprises constitutes the planned supplies of other enterprises, the supplies of the latter are delayed or simply not available. Perhaps enough has been said to explain why 'managers of enterprises did not have confidence in the possibility of getting their materials on time and having them delivered to the factory by the supply depot's trucks'.[16]

What does the manager do to make sure he gets his supplies? Just as he 'secures' his production plan by attempting to conceal the existence of some production capacity, so he 'secures' the flow of supplies in various ways. He overorders, in the hope that if he doesn't get all he ordered, he may at least get as much as he needs. He also orders excessively large amounts of some supplies in order to be able to buy directly from the producer, instead of having to go through the maze of jobbing depots. A survey of 15 Moscow enterprises showed a 10.4 per cent overordering of metals for just this reason.[17] Sometimes management's boldest efforts to obtain supplies are unsuccessful: ' . . . over 300,000 construction workers undergo work stoppages daily because of the absence of materials at the workplace.'[18] In other cases their padded requisitions are accepted and they receive more than they need of some materials. The consequence is the piling up of hoards of supplies of all kinds, one of the most enduring problems of

Soviet industrial organization. The government has waged a long-standing war against hoarding. One of the weapons by which it attempts to hold hoarding within bounds is through the use of quotas of working capital; that is, for its annual production programme the enterprise is allowed to keep on hand at any one time no more than so many tons of coal, so many board feet of lumber, so many roubles worth of inventory. These quotas must be negotiated between enterprise and government, and the enterprise's interest demands that they be set as high as possible. The mutual attempt at outguessing the other leads to a familiar bureaucratic game: '... enterprises try to "justify" and obtain as large quotas of working capital as possible. The financial agencies, aware of this, strive on the other hand to reduce the quotas of working capital.'[19] This kind of planning is hardly calculated to lead to the establishment of the optimal quotas. It is more likely that some quotas will be too large and some too small.

The most interesting of the techniques used by managers to 'secure' their supply of materials is the employment of special supply expediters called tolkachi, or 'pushers'. The table of organization does not provide for this occupation, yet so great is the need that firms manage somehow to employ these people. The chief job of the expediter is to make sure that his enterprise gets the materials it needs and when it needs them. Accordingly he spends most of his time on the road, visiting his enterprise's suppliers, handing out little gifts here and there to assure that his orders are well-handled,[20] picking up supplies of one kind or another that his firm may be able to use or trade for other goods. Much of their activity is associated with the black market, that is, obtaining materals for which no allocation order has been issued. This may be done either by wangling an allocation order out of a reluctant government official by one means or another, or persuading an approachable enterprise official to sell him the things he needs without an allocation order.

Some tolkachi take up permanent residence in the city in which the chief suppliers are located, and only occasionally return to their home firms for consultations. To keep the record clean, they are carried on the books as 'senior buyer', or 'supply agent'. If they are known to be particularly adept at their jobs, they may be asked by other firms to represent them. Nothing is known of their incomes, but there is no doubt that they earn many times their base pay. And they fully earn it, both because of the vital nature of their work, and because the risks they take make them vulnerable to prosecution.

How widespread is the use of these expediters? Again, we catch only occasional hints of their prevalence. The most recent outburst against them reports that the expenses of tolkachi who annually visit the typical large enterprise runs into thousands of roubles. These, however, are only the reported expenses. More often than not their expenses are not reported as such but are concealed under such rubrics as 'exchange of technical information', or 'contract negotiations'. Our latest informant, who is a senior investigator for the State Control Commission of the USSR, is of the opinion that, despite continued official criticisms of the use of expediters, their number has actually been increasing. One of the reasons he adduces is interesting. In 1956, along with a wave of measures designed to give more freedom to plant managers, an order was issued relieving managers of the need to report in detail on all minor expenditures. Travel expenditures were among the items exempted. The measure had the unintended effect of encouraging the increased use of expediters.[21]

The economic effect of the use of expediters is difficult to assess. There is no doubt that they are of vital importance to individual enterprises, but from the national point of view much of their activity involves merely the transfer to one fortunate enterprise of resources that otherwise would have gone to another. Since the higher priority enterprises have less need for expediters, the chances are that the net effect of their activity is to cause more resources to flow to lower priority enterprises at the expense of higher priority ones. On the credit side, however, their wide knowledge of sources of supply, of who has what to sell, is of some importance, and they do arrange for the movement of supplies that otherwise would have lain idle in one plant while another had need for it. In short the expediter possesses a certain kind of knowledge that may be as important to economic organization as the knowledge of the engineer or the machinist. The planning system is able to direct the bulk of the nation's resources with reasonable effectiveness, but substantial quantities of materials and equipment elude the main stream of planning. How to get these resources back into the system is a problem that has exercised Soviet economists for a long time.[22]

In summary, the incentives that motivate managers to strive for the fulfilment of their production targets are the same incentives that motivate them to evade the regulations of the planning system. Because of the tightness of the supply system, which is deliberately engineered by the state, managers are compelled to defend their enterprises' position by overordering supplies, by hoarding materials and equipment, and by employing expediters whose function it is to keep the enterprise supplied with materials at all costs, legal or otherwise. The very planning system that serves to channel most of the nation's resources in directions desired by the state, serves also to misdirect a substantial volume of resources towards uses that are contrary to the wishes to the state.

Investment Decisions

If one were to ask what feature of the Soviet economic system accounts most of all for the rapid rate of growth, the answer would undoubtedly be the high rate of capital formation. The question at issue is whether it is as high as it might be, other things being equal. An examination of the system of managerial incentives will provide part, though by no means all, of the answer to this central question.

Management has a direct interest in obtaining new capital. It adds to productive capacity, and it is good for the record to show steady increases in production. Moreover fixed capital is provided to the enterprise as a free grant by the state, with no interest charge. The problem, therefore, has not been one of inducing management to accept more machines; it has rather been one of dissuading management from ordering too many machines. Far back in Soviet economic history one can find expressions of the problem similar to that recently uttered by Khrushchev in connection with the dissolution of the agricultural machine-tractor stations:

The machine-tractor stations accept any machine whether they need it or not. They don't grow flax, but they take flax-growing equipment. They don't grow cabbage, but they take cabbage-planting machines. Consequently many machines are not used for years and hundreds of millions of roubles worth of state resources are frozen.[23]

The reason enterprises accept any piece of equipment they can get their hands on is similar to that discussed above in connection with materials hoarding. One can never tell when he may need just that kind of machine and not be able to obtain it. If one has a chance to get it now, order it by all means. It may come in handy some day for trading in return for something one might be able to use more readily. And above all, there is no charge for holding the equipment; there is no interest payment, and if the machine is not used there is no depreciation charge either. Hence there is everything to gain and nothing to lose by holding on to as much machinery and equipment as one can obtain.

How to induce managers to take a less cavalier view of capital has been a longstanding concern of economists. They look with some nostalgia at the effectiveness of the profit motive under capitalism in this respect. An eminent Soviet economist put it this way recently:

In order to increase his profit as much as possible, the capitalist strives to use his equipment to the fullest extent possible, and in no case will he buy a machine that he doesn't need at the moment, since every surplus machine slows down the turnover of his capital and reduces his profit. For the same reason he strives to keep his inventories down to the very minimum and to market his finished products as quickly as possible.[24]

Recent economic literature contains a number of suggestions of ways in which Soviet managers might be induced to order only that amount of capital needed for production purposes. One of the more interesting is a proposal advanced by the author quoted above. He suggests that profit be calculated not as a ratio to total production cost (as has always been done), but as a ratio to value of invested capital. In this way the enterprise with too much idle capital will show a lower rate of profit, and profit is one of the principal indicators of overall performance. The suggestion is interesting because it proposes that return on capital be used as a criterion of performance, a rather 'bourgeois' notion. It should not, however, be thought that the proposal envisages reliance on the 'profit motive' as we know it. Profit is an important indicator of the efficiency of plant operation, but the firm does not 'own' its profit, although it shares in the profit in a minor way. As a personal incentive, profit is relatively unimportant in Soviet industry, certainly by comparison with the bonus.

If the incentive system motivates managers to overorder and hoard equipment, the situation is quite the reverse with respect to technological innovation. Concern over managerial resistance to innovation is of long standing, but it has come to the fore in recent years in connection with increased emphasis on automation and modernization of plant and equipment. The reasons for managers' tendency to drag their feet in introducing new products or production techniques are well understood by Soviet economists:

The explanation is, first of all, that the introduction of new technology involves certain risks and requires a considerable expenditure of time; secondly, after new technology has been introduced more difficult plan targets are set and consequently there is less opportunity for fulfilling them and receiving bonuses.[25]

When a manager has a well-running plant, when the workers have learned their jobs and have become experienced in using the

existing equipment, he is reluctant to upset the cart by trying something new. A new production line means trouble. Production bugs
have to be eliminated, workers have to be retrained, time is lost,
and spoilage is high. The chances are that plans will be underfulfilled
and the precious bonuses lost, particularly in view of the tendency
for plan targets to be raised to the rated capacity of the new equipment. It is courting disaster to try new things. If the old machines
are wearing out, it is safer to repair or even rebuild them rather
than introduce the more complicated new models. Outlays on the
rebuilding of old machines often exceed the price of a new modern
machine.[26]

There is another reason why managers shy away from innovation.
Even if the potential gains from new technology are great, it usually
takes a number of years before they are realized. But it is Soviet
policy to shift managers around from plant to plant every few
years. Therefore managers have a strictly short-run point of view.
Why take on all the headaches of introducing a new line when
one is not likely to be around to enjoy whatever benefits may
eventually accrue? Capital investment policy is by its very nature
a matter of long-term planning, and therefore does not commend
itself to the short-run horizon of management.

How does the state combat managerial resistance to innovation?
One technique is direct pressure. Pressure exerted on and by their
own superiors explains much of the innovation that does occur.
Enterprise managers may drag their feet for a long time, but when
the direct order comes down that the new automatic line must
be installed in the next six months, it is eventually acted upon.
Pressure is also exerted through the Communist Party; if the Party
officials in the enterprise are under direct orders from Moscow
that automation must be accelerated, they are in a position to
force the manager to move faster than he otherwise might. Such
pressures are important, although it must be noted in passing that
both the manager's bosses and the local Party people often try
to shield the enterprise from such pressures. They are as dependent
for their careers upon successful plan fulfilment as are the plant
managers themselves.

Direct orders from above are one way of getting management
to innovate. But innovation would proceed more rapidly if
managers could be made to wish to innovate, instead of waiting
until they are forced into it. The literature of the past few years
is full of suggestions on how this can be accomplished. It is
suggested, for example, that attractively high prices be set on new
machines, in order to stimulate the producers of those machines
to put them into production more rapidly.[27] While this measure

might ease the financial strain on the innovating firm, it will not remove the risk that the production plan may be sacrificed. And production is much more vital to the success of the enterprise than finance.

More to the point are the suggestions that the bonus system be employed as an incentive for innovation. Soviet economists seem to have enormous confidence in bonuses as a device for getting management to wish to do what the state wishes them to do. But how to adapt the bonus system to this purpose is more difficult. In the course of years a variety of special bonuses have been introduced for one purpose or another, in addition to the major bonus that comes from fulfilment of the production plan. There are special bonuses available for economizing certain critical materials, for reducing the volume of goods in process, for conserving fuel, for increasing labour productivity, for keeping the plant clean, for reducing the volume of spoilage, for operating the plant without stoppages, for winning socialist competitions, and many others.[28]

This dilution of the bonus system may actually weaken its power as an incentive. If the special bonuses are small, they will not be very effective. If they are large they may detract effort from what is, after all, the main objective of the state: fulfilment of the production plan. For it is interesting to note the evidence that the relative size of the bonus for this or that special purpose often determines the manager's decision to concentrate on this or that objective. There are two types of innovation: relatively small measures such as organizational improvements or inexpensive alterations, and the more dramatic large-scale changes in production techniques. The former are included in the overall enterprise plan each year, under the name of the 'plan for organizational and technical measures' (*Orgtekhplan*). It happens that there are certain bonuses available for the design and introduction of the large-scale innovations, but none for the fulfilment of the *Orgtekhplan*. The consequence is that research and managerial personnel concentrate on the large items, and pay little attention to the small ones, even though the latter could result in great savings with relatively little cost and effort.[29] Thus the very potency of the bonus as an incentive militates against its use for too many special purposes which may compete with each other.

To conclude this discussion, the unreliability of the supply system and the absence of a charge for the use of capital motivates management to order more fixed capital than they need and to hoard machines and equipment. This tendency deflects a certain amount of currently produced capital goods from being put directly into production in their best uses. On the other hand, the incentive system discourages management from taking the risks associated with innovation. Direct orders from above lead to a substantial volume of innovation, and in many cases management may consider certain forms of innovation to be to their interest. The provision of special bonuses for innovation, if they were large enough to compete with the production plan bonus, might help provide an incentive for innovation, and much of the current discussion in the Soviet Union seems to point to this as the next phase.

3 SOME COMPARATIVE OBSERVATIONS

The preceding section has shown that Soviet managers are motivated to make a variety of decisions that are contrary to the interest of the state. Since the state's interest is paramount in the Soviet scheme of things, we may properly conclude that the incentive and decision-making system is 'relatively inefficient', or 'less than perfectly efficient'. Let me caution the reader once more against inferring from this that Soviet managers do not do a good job. They do. There is no doubt that their system works well. If I have chosen to concentrate on the 'pathology' of Soviet management, the purpose was not to create the impression of ineffectiveness, but to illuminate the gap that every economy shows between the actual and the ideal.

A comparison of Soviet and American management will help drive the point home. No one doubts that American management does a good job. But it would be fatuous to allege that it operates with perfect efficiency. An exploration of the inevitable gap between the actual and the ideal in the case of American management will help to place the corresponding gap in the USSR in proper perspective.

A comparison of Soviet and American management is difficult for a curious reason; namely, we don't know enough about the more intimate aspects of American managerial practice. A moment's thought will make the reason clear. The American firm is a private enterprise in the full sense of the word. Its internal affairs are no one's business but its own. No one has the right to pry except with special cause. To be sure, the laws of the land have, over the years, required enterprises to disclose more and more of their private affairs to public and governmental perusal. But large sectors of the enterprise's internal operations are protected from the eyes of curious outsiders.

One of the most striking differences in the conduct of American and Soviet management is precisely in this matter of privacy. The

Soviet enterprise is a public enterprise in the fullest sense of the word. It has no right to conceal its operations from any officially recognized agent of the state. And a great range of such agents have been deliberately endowed by the state with the obligation of keeping close watch on management and disclosing any irregularities or sources of inefficiency that come to their attention. These agents include the 'home office' of the firm (the regional economic council, or formerly the ministry), the state bank, the local governmental body, the central government's State Control Commission, the Finance Department (the tax collector), the local Communist Party boss and his staff, the Party secretary of the enterprise itself, and indeed just about anyone in the enterprise who enjoys the extracurricular activity of attending meetings to discuss the affairs of the enterprise (the *aktiv*).

If we can imagine an American business executive suddenly placed in charge of a Soviet firm, it is this public character of the enterprise which above all would drive him to distraction. It means that any government official can at any time demand to examine any aspect of the firm's operations he wishes to, that at any time he can be hauled on the carpet by the local Party boss to explain a charge made by an irate customer, that any member of his staff (perhaps bucking for his job) can write a letter to *Pravda* exposing him for having made an irregular deal on some supplies, that any scatterbrained worker who wants to 'get his picture in the papers' can rise at a public meeting that the director is obliged to attend, and compel the director to explain why he hasn't yet installed the new assembly line. The point is that the results of this authorized prying often finds its way into the published Soviet economic and political literature, which gives us an insight into the more intimate operations of the Soviet firm that we cannot have in the case of the American firm. But in view of this committee's expressed interest in comparisons of the United States and Soviet economies, I have attempted certain comparisons below which appear to be highly suggestive.

Managers and Owners

The original form of modern business organization was the small firm in which the owner was also the manager. The owner-manager was responsible to no one but himself for his business decisions, and his interest as manager could not conflict with his interest as owner. The development of the modern giant corporation, however, had led to that separation of management and ownership first elaborated in the work of Berle and Means.[30] Under the new conditions the private interests of the hired managers (and the controlling group) need no longer coincide at all points with the interests of the stockholder-owners. This is precisely the relationship between the hired Soviet manager and the owner-state.

Berle and Means concluded from their study that 'the controlling group, even if they own a large block of stock, can serve their own pockets better by profiting at the expense of the company than by making profits for it'.[31] This is precisely what Soviet managers do when they produce unplanned commodities that are advantageous to their firms but not to the state, when they over-order and hoard commodities, and when they resist innovation. Because of the differences between the two economic systems, we should expect that the precise forms that the owner-manager conflict takes would be different in the USSR and the United States. In the United States they are to be found in such decisions as the awarding of subcontracts, the accounting of profit in such a way as to benefit the claims of the controlling group, the awarding of bonuses and other benefits to management, and in dividend payment policy. As in the Soviet enterprise, the accountant is of crucial importance in handling the books of the enterprise in such a way as to make the best possible case for the manager; it is he, for example, who figures out the best way to distract the state's attention from the large expenditures on tolkachi. The accounting techniques are, of course, different in the United States; they involve 'the charging or the failure to deduct depreciation; charging to capital expenses which properly should be charged against income account; including nonrecurrent profits as income though their real place is in surplus; and the creation of "hidden reserves." '[32]

A major difference between the Soviet firm and the American firm is that, in the last analysis, profit remains the criterion of managerial performance in the latter, whereas the Soviet manager is evaluated by a number of criteria that are sometimes mutually exclusive. Both systems have attempted to bring managerial interests into harmony with owner interests by some sort of profit-sharing system. In the Soviet case, it is clear that profit plays a very minor role, compared with bonuses, as a managerial incentive. In the United States the manager shares directly in profit to a very limited extent, and often follows other goals in his decisions. 'The executive not infrequently tends to look upon the stockholders as outsiders whose complaints and demand for dividends are necessary evils...' concluded one American student of management.[33] In like fashion the Soviet manager often begins to feel like the 'boss' and resents the intrusion into 'his' affairs of the state, which after all is the owner. I have described above some of the ways in which the Soviet manager promotes the interest of 'his' enterprise by means contrary to the interests of the owner-state. In the American corporation the forms are somewhat different: '... profits are reinvested in the business for the sake of bigness and to protect the company, and the interests of the stockholders may be given second place to the business leader's conception of what is best for the firm itself.' Executives manifest a 'general unwillingness to liquidate unsuccessful enterprises' and thus put themselves out of jobs, however consistent liquidation might be with the interests of the stockholders.[34] The dramatic growth of corporate self-financing in recent years has strengthened the power of management to expand their own enterprises without having to go through the 'test of the marketplace' for capital.

It was observed earlier that the desire for 'security' and for what the Russians call a 'quiet life' motivates a wide variety of managerial decisions such as concealing production capacity and resisting technological innovation that might rock the boat. Students of American management have also noted the change from the adventurous business tycoons of earlier days to a more professionalized managerial climate in which 'greater emphasis is placed on education, training and a scientific approach, and less on rugged, venturesome, and frequently heedless individualism. The desire for security seems to have increased, and the concomitant of a growing emphasis on security is a diminishing desire for adventure for its own sake.'[35] There is indeed a remarkable parallel to this development in the change in the character of Soviet managers. There would have been a great affinity between the industrial empire-builders of nineteenth century America and the Soviet directors of the first two decades of the Soviet regime.

Those directors were often men of little education who came out of the romantic conflict of revolution, who dreamed great dreams of building an industrial nation and who created an ethos of bold plans and adventurous undertakings. The old Commissar of Heavy Industry, Sergei Ordzhonikidze, would have understood the spirit of the ironmonger, Andrew Carnegie, and the man who built the great ZIL automotive works (now named after him) had the drives and the dreams of the bicycle mechanic Henry Ford.

Time, and Stalin's purges, removed most of those oldtimers and their place has now been taken by Soviet-educated young men born not of revolution but of bureaucracy. Organizations seem to develop 'organization men' types, whether the organization happens to be communist or capitalist. An American reporter visiting a group of communist intellectuals reports that one of them had badgered him with questions about David Reisman's book *The Lonely Crowd*. 'The Communist had read Reisman's book and had been fascinated by it – not, he said, because of its application to life in the United States but because of what he maintained was its extraordinary relevance to the present conditions of life in the Soviet Union.'[36] It is not, on reflection, very surprising that the job of running an industrial bureaucracy should place a common stamp on men of otherwise different backgrounds. The same would probably apply to the running of a large city or a large university.

Managers and the Laws

We have found that the Soviet manager is often compelled to evade regulations or even break laws. Part of the explanation is simply that there are so many laws. If a Chicago manufacturer fails to ship an order to a New York firm, and ships it instead to another Chicago firm, he has nothing to fear but the ire of the New York firm. But if a Kiev manufacturer fails to ship an order to a Moscow firm and ships it instead to another Kiev firm, he has injured a state enterprise and is subject to administrative action, a fine, or even criminal prosecution. If an American firm sells a substandard generator, he may lose money or his business. But if a Soviet firm sells a substandard generator, the director may go to prison. Thus, even if Soviet managers acted exactly as American managers do, we should expect to find more illegal or evasive activity in the Soviet Union than in the United States.

With the growing complexity of our society, more and more legislation is enacted to protect the public from potential abuses. With the growth of such legislation, managers find their activities more and more circumscribed by laws and regulations. The Soviet manager apparently treats such legislation rather lightly when it conflicts with the interests of his firm (and his career and pocketbook). How does American management react when confronted by a spreading web of restrictive legislation?

It is not easy to find out very much about American managerial practice in this respect. Unlike the Soviet press, which throws its pages open to reports of the irregular activities of managers in order to warn others, the American press is likely to shy away from this kind of reporting. Moreover the private nature of American business keeps this sort of activity from coming to light as easily as it might in Soviet industry. Nor is it the sort of thing that businessmen are inclined to talk about very readily. If it is true that a businessman would more readily be interviewed on his private sex life than on his private business activity, then we should require the late Dr Kinsey to help provide the answers to the extent of unlawful or quasi-lawful business activity.

Prof. E. H. Sutherland, the eminent American criminologist and sociologist, made a bold attempt to investigate the phenomenon he refers to as 'white collar crime'. His study is based on the decisions of a limited number of courts and administrative commissions against the 70 largest industrial-type corporations in the country. In the period 1935–44 these 70 corporations were convicted 585 times for such practices as restraint of trade, misrepresentation in advertising, patent and copyright infringements, unfair labour practices, granting of rebates, and a few others.[37] The average was 8.5 convictions per corporation. These data provide some idea of the extensiveness of such practices but they clearly understate the magnitude for a variety of technical reasons. Sutherland's conclusion is that 'a great deal of scattered and unorganized material indicates that white collar crimes are very prevalent'.[38]

The point I wish to make is that when American management finds itself in a position approximating that of Soviet management they tend to react in ways similar to those of their Soviet counterparts. Sutherland's unique study notes many aspects of American managerial practice that are astonishingly similar to those one might find in the literature on Soviet management. 'These crimes are not discreet and inadvertent violations of technical regulations. They are deliberate and have a relatively consistent unity.'[39] It is in precisely this way that the Soviet manager deliberately misappropriates earmarked funds or decides to save on the quality of production. There is evidence that the Soviet manager, aware of the fact that 'everybody does it' and that the investigating agencies have restricted budgets, counts on the law of averages (and his own superior shrewdness) to get away with it. So a member of Federal Trade Commission wrote that 'about the only thing that keeps a businessman off the wrong end of a Federal indictment or administrative agency's complaint is the fact that, under the hit-or-miss methods of prosecution, the law of averages hasn't made him a partner to a suit', and 'Samuel Insull is reported to have remarked during his trial that he had only done what all other businessmen were doing.'[40]

Similarities in managerial practice are paralleled by similarities in attitude to such violations, and towards the administrative agencies enforcing the laws and regulations. The Soviet manager does not think it is 'wrong' to use influence to obtain materials unlawfully, or to fudge his reports to the government. Success is the important thing, and if you are successful you can get away with all sorts of violations. There is evidence that the Soviet manager feels contemptuous of government planners and of Party hacks who try to tell him how to run his business but who themselves had 'never met a payroll'. Sutherland's picture of American management's attitudes contains strains of the same kind.

The businessman who violates the laws which are designed to regulate business does not customarily lose status among his business associates. Although a few members of the industry may think less of him, others admire him ... Businessmen customarily regard government personnel as politicians and bureaucrats, and the persons authorized to investigate business practices as 'snoopers'.[41]

In section 1 of this paper, it was pointed out that a managerial career carries a great deal of prestige in the Soviet Union and attracts a large number of the better students. These youngsters have been raised in Soviet schools and have absorbed the incessant propaganda of the communist regime. Many of them enter industry as green novices fresh from school, filled with high ideals about building the socialist fatherland and working for the common welfare. One wonders about the process by which the naive idealistic young Komsomol member is transformed into the hardheaded manager who knows all the angles for survival in the Soviet business world. Numerous incidents, such as the following, provide a key to the answer. A young Soviet chemist had been assigned to the quality control department of his enterprise. He was quite pleased with himself when his test showed that a sample of production, which had previously been declared acceptable by his laboratory chief, turned out to contain an excess of phosphorus. He reported the 'error' and expected to get a bonus for it. Instead, his boss obtained a new sample, gave it to an outside chemist for analysis, and submitted a report showing that the batch of production was acceptable after all. The young chemist protested, was transferred to another shop, and was finally fired on trumped-up charges.[42]

What happens to such young people? Some never quite get the point and remain ordinary engineers in the plants. Others learn to adapt themselves after a few buffetings and when they decide to play the game according to the real ground-rules, begin to rise in the managerial hierarchy.

It is interesting to note that Sutherland's interviews with American businessmen turned up accounts rather similar to that narrated above. His explanation of the process by which the naive American youngster is initiated into the business of selling used cars, settling insurance claims, covering up irregularities in clients' accounts – indeed, toning down the results of chemical analysis – helps explain the process of transformation of the young Komsomol member:

In many cases he is ordered by the manager to do things which he regards as unethical or illegal, while in other cases he learns from others who have the same rank as his own how they make a success. He learns specific techniques of violating the law, together with definitions of situations in which those techniques may be used. Also he developes a general ideology. This ideology grows in part out of the specific practices and is in the nature of generalization from concrete experiences, but in part it is transmitted as a generalization by phrases such as 'we are not in business for our health,' 'business is business,' and 'no business was ever built on the beatitudes.' These generalizations ... assist the neophyte in business to accept the illegal practices and provide rationalizations for them.[43]

Summarizing, the economic world in which the Soviet manager operates compels him to engage in a variety of illegal or evasive practices. Since the Soviet business world is enmeshed in a much greater web of laws and regulations than the American, the Soviet manager finds his interest in conflict with the laws and regulations more often than his American counterpart. But when American managers' interests conflict with the laws, they too are prepared to take the chance of violating them. Both American and Soviet managers justify their actions by an attitude of contempt for governmental controls and investigating personnel, and by a hardheaded view that 'business is business' and 'everybdy does it'. Young people in both systems who wish to achieve managerial prominence have to learn to play the game according to the rules, or disqualify themselves from the tough competition for the top.

Managers and Overfull Employment

Many of the peculiarities of Soviet management spring from the fact that the economic system works under conditions of perpetual overfull employment. By 'overfull' employment I mean a condition in which there are not merely as many jobs as employables (as under full employment), but the demand for labour far exceeds the available supply. The same applies to other factors of production: materials, equipment, and commodities in general are demanded in far greater volume than the current rates of production. The ability of the Soviet government to maintain, through the planning system, a condition of permanent overfull employment is one of the greatest economic assets of the regime. We err when we interpret evidence of shortages in the Soviet economy as signs of economic weakness; they are rather indications that the economic engine is racing with the throttle wide open.

But just as an engine does not work at its maximum efficiency when it is working at its maximum capacity, so the Soviet economy pays a certain price for the advantages of overfull employment. It is the perpetual shortages of supplies that account in large measure for the losses due to overordering and hoarding. The hunger for goods by both firms and consumers encourages the deterioration of quality. The 'sea of ink' associated with materials allocations, price fixing, priorities, and all the rigamarole of a controlled economy nurtures the spread of the tolkach and the use of influence for personal gain.

The normally functioning American economy does not confront our managers with this kind of problem. Hoarding makes no sense when materials are in adequate supply. Competition and consumer resistance force the quality of production up to standard. The role of influence is narrowly circumscribed when the bureaucratic machinery of government controls is removed. The biggest problem of American managers under normal conditions is marketing, not purchasing. The energy spent by the Soviet firm on obtaining materials is spent by the American firm on selling and advertising.

Thus, the major differences between the practice of American and Soviet management are to be ascribed to the differences in the economic environment. The interesting question is: how do American managers behave when placed in an environment that approximates that of the Soviet manager? The obvious test case is war. During the Second World War, the national emergency forced the United States into a state of overfull employment. Along with this came the total immersion of government into economic life, with a great burgeoning of materials allocation, price fixing, cost-plus contracting, and a prevailing shortage of supplies.

It is interesting to note that the rate of growth of production during the war rose to levels rivalling the current rates of Soviet economic growth. The implication of this fact is important; it means that there is no magic in the Soviet economic system. Our economy could grow as rapidly as the Soviet economy does if our people would consent to being pushed around as totally as the Soviet people are.

But like the Soviet economy, we paid for our high rate of production in various forms of waste. One of the first consequences of the introduction of materials controls was the rise of the black market. The only full-scale study of the black market, to my knowledge, confirmed what many people felt to be the case at the time:

During the war at least a million cases of black market violations were dealt with by the Government. Illegal profits ran into billions of dollars. Business interests and Government vied with one another in estimating the seriousness of the black market; business estimates, curiously, often being higher than those of the Government. Such extensive conniving in the black market in illegal prices and rationed commodities took place among so many businessmen, ordinary criminals, and even the average citizen that serious questions might be raised as to the moral fibre of the American people.[44]

To understand the position of the Soviet manager, we must realize that the American black market flourished at a time when the nation was fighting for its life and public indignation acted as a restraint. But if the economic controls that led to violations could not be justified by a national emergency, they would be thought of as just irritating obstacles, as so many hurdles that the resourceful manager must overcome as part of the risks of the game. There is good evidence that the Soviet manager takes just this amoral attitude towards economic controls, and it is therefore quite understandable that the evasion of controls would be more widespread.

The high quality of American production in normal times is a byword in international markets. But the effect in the economy of shortages was similar to that in the Soviet economy. One of the techniques used by Soviet managers is to represent lower quality merchandise as of higher quality, and to sell it at the higher price. In the United States during the war.

upgrading was one of the most difficult violations to detect, particularly where no professional investigator was available who could appraise the grade or where there were no State or Federal grades stamped on the commodity.[45]

The reports of government investigators read like some of the indignant letters of complaint we read in the Soviet press; men's shorts made of cheesecloth, water-resistant baby's pants which permit a third of a glass of water to leak through after one laundering; 'if you pick up a board by both ends without breaking it in the middle, it's No. 1 Select...' testified an American businessman.[46]

One of the features of Soviet managerial life which helps protect the manager is the feeling of 'mutual support' among various officials whose fortunes depend on the success of the enterprise. The Communist Party secretary doesn't report the manipulations of a successful director because the Party benefits from the success of the enterprise; the people in the 'home office' (the Ministry or the Council of the National Economy) are reluctant to fire a director who violates the laws in order to get the materials his plant needs, for while the next director may be more law-abiding, he may not succeed in fulfilling his plan. This tendency to maintain a solid front against authority is a source of great irritation to the government, which periodically inveighs against it but has not been able to eradicate it. A similar sense of common front prevailed among groups of businessmen.

Nothing better illustrates the degree of organization and consensus among businessmen than their reluctance to testify against each other... Some businessmen felt that the trade would disapprove of behaviour that might undermine the solid front against the Government as well as interfere with supplies.[47]

One of the major differences in the position of management in the two countries is the nature of the penalty for failure. Under ordinary conditions the unsuccessful manager loses his job. But the Soviet manager faces many more situations in which the action necessary to get the job done carries with it the threat of criminal action. Indeed, whenever the Soviet government has found some managerial practice too damaging to its interests and too intractable to the normal sanctions, it has turned to the criminal courts. Immediately after the death of Stalin the punishment for economic transgressions was relaxed, but the new regime has not been able to continue operating without the courts. One of the severest economic problems following the decentralization of industry was the tendency toward 'localism'; that is, each economic region tended to favour the plants in its 'own' region, and would discriminate against plants in other regions. When all exhortation failed, the government had to turn to the law. Today, a manager who fails to honour the orders of plants outside his own region is subject to 'administrative action, fines, or even criminal punishment'.[48]

Financial penalties, such as fines, have rarely proved successful as restraints on Soviet managerial behaviour. American managers seem to have reacted the same way to the fines imposed for black-market violations. 'The don't hurt anybody.' 'It just comes out of profits, like a tax.' 'They make so much money on the black market they can afford to pay steep fines.' But imprisonment was another matter. 'Jail is the only way; nobody wants to go to jail.' 'A jail sentence is dishonorable; it jeopardizes the reputation.'[49] This would not be quite the same in the case of the Soviet manager. At least during Stalin's lifetime some of the best people served their time in jail, and it definitely did not destroy their reputation among their neighbours; although the neighbours might be wary of associating with them. One has the impression that large numbers of Soviet managers feel the chances are fair that some day they will do their stretch, hopefully for a minor transgression.

The wartime economy of shortages injects the government into business life not only as an agency of control but also as the largest customer of many firms. In the Soviet case we have noted the importance of the tolkach, the expediter, the peddler of influence. We might note in passing that the economic system of Nazi Germany, in which government had also assumed a dominant role, also gave rise to this chap. The Germans called him the 'contact man'. As described by an American student of the German economy:

To influence the powerful agencies of control, however, he [the German businessman] has good use for what might suitably be called a private relations department. Under the Nazi system of control of business by an absolute government, the contact man, or graft, or both, take the place of the public relations executive.

The contact man is primarily a political figure. His job is to pull wires. He knows the influential members of the all-pervading Nazi Party in a position to bring pressure successfully to bear upon the men in charge of controlling agencies... Two types of contact man are known to be used: one is an independent agent whom the businessman hires, or attempts to hire, whenever necessary; the other is carried on the payroll of the business in a more or less permanent capacity.[50]

The words might well have been written about the Soviet economy. In that sector of the US economy in which government plays a dominant role as customer, the symbols of the mink coat or Dixon-Yates, depending upon one's political persuasion, come to mind. 'Washington', wrote Senator Paul Douglas, 'is indeed full of lawyers and "representatives" whose primary commodity is "influence".'[51] The techniques of the American influence-peddler differ little from those of his colleagues in the Soviet or Nazi economy. Gifts and quid pro quo favours are standard among Soviet tolkachi. Another way in which Soviet enterprises manage to exert influence is to have one of 'their' men placed in other organizations that can be of use, rather like the unusually high employability in industry of retired military personnel. During the war the problem was particularly acute because of the American government's desperate need for skilled managerial personnel, many of whom were on loan from corporations with which the government placed contracts. But the use of influence is not confined to government–business relations, as Senator Douglas pointed out in his critical defence of the ethics of government personnel:

As a matter of fact, the abuses which have been exposed and properly denounced in the field of Government are quite widespread practices in private business. Thus the 'padding' of expense accounts is so common that they are often referred to as 'swindle sheets.' Purchasing agents and buyers frequently exact toll from those who seek to sell to them, and their Christmas presents and other perquisites appreciably increase their income. Business managers and directors think nothing of awarding contracts, insurance, and underwriting privileges on the basis of friendship and relationship rather than the quality and prices of the goods and services supplied. All this is taken as a matter of course in private business, although it obviously increases costs and intercepts gains which should go to stockholders and consumers.[52]

While gifts, pay-offs, and bribery play their role in the Soviet scheme of things, the subtler and much more pervasive technique of influence is known as *'blat'*. To have good *blat* with someone means that one has an 'in'; one can always count on him for a favour because of friendship or family ties or some other relationship of confidence. *Blat* may be used to obtain everything from a new apartment to a carload of coal. The prominent British observer, Edward Crankshaw, has called *blat* the most significant word in contemporary Russia.[53] The way in which the American equivalent of *blat* is cultivated is described in one final quotation from Senator Douglas:

Today the corruption of public officials by private interests takes a more subtle form. The enticer does not generally pay money directly to the public representative. He tries instead by a series of favors to put the public official under such feeling of personal obligation that the latter gradually loses his sense of mission to the public and comes to feel that his first loyalties are to his private benefactors and patrons. What happens is a gradual shifting of a man's loyalties from the community to those who have been doing him favors. His final decisions are, therefore, made in response to private friendships and loyalties rather than to the public good.[54]

Summarizing, many of the differences between Soviet and United States managerial behaviour spring from differences in the economic climate in which they operate. The stress on quality and appearance, the drive for innovation and technological development, and the interest in cost reduction reflect the force of competition and the buyer's market. Such similarities as have been observed in managerial behaviour, spring from features of the economic environment that are common to the two systems, such as large-scale organization and the intrusion of government into the economy. Under wartime conditions the American economy takes on more of the features of normal Soviet economic life, and the consequence is that American managers adopt more of the normal practices of Soviet management.

NOTES

1 Subcommittee on Economic Statistics, Joint Economic Committee, Congress of the United States.
2 *Voprosy ekonomiki*, no. 6, 1958, p. 74.
3 *Voprosy ekonomiki*, no. 1, 1959, p. 35.
4 Documentation and further discussion of this section's argument may be found in the author's 'Factory and Manager in the USSR', Harvard University Press, 1957.
5 *Voprosy ekonomiki*, no. 3, 1959, pp. 61, 67.
6 *Voprosy ekonomiki*, no. 4, 1957, p. 70.
7 *Planovoe khoziaistvo*, no. 10, 1958, p. 5.
8 *Voprosy ekonomiki*, no. 7, 1958, p. 51.
9 *Voprosy ekonomiki*, no. 6, 1959, p. 19.
10 *Voprosy ekonomiki*, no. 6, 1958, p. 129.
11 *Planovoe khoziaistvo*, no. 10, 1958, pp. 5–6. The study deals only with that portion of the firm's production in excess of their planned targets.
12 *Voprosy ekonomiki*, no. 3, 1959, p. 67.
13 *Planovoe khoziaistvo*, no. 4, 1959, p. 58.
14 Ibid., p. 65.
15 *Voprosy ekonomiki*, no. 5, 1959, p. 75.
16 *Planovoe khoziaistvo*, no. 5, 1959, p. 85.
17 *Planovoe khoziaistvo*, no. 5, 1959, p. 84.
18 *Voprosy ekonomiki*, no. 8, 1957, p. 50.
19 *Voprosy ekonomiki*, no. 7, 1958, p. 120.
20 The gifts are not always very little. An expediter sent out recently to get tires for his trucking firm, was given 62,000 roubles in cash for the trip. He spent 42,000 roubles for gifts. He is now in prison. *Izvestiia*, 4 April 1959, p. 2.
21 *Izvestiia*, 4 April 1959, p.2.
22 Recently there have been numerous suggestions that enterprises and economic regions publish catalogues of the commodities they produce and the surplus materials and equipment they would like to sell. The expediters are rather like walking catalogues. *Planovoe khoziaistvo*, no. 4, 1959, pp. 64, 96.
23 *Planovoe khoziaistvo*, no. 7, 1958, p. 121.
24 Ibid., p. 122.
25 *Voprosy ekonomiki*, no. 1, 1959, pp. 44, 45.
26 *Voprosy ekonomiki*, no. 4, 1957, p. 69.
27 *Voprosy ekonomiki*, no. 6, 1959, p. 16.
28 *Voprosy ekonomiki*, no. 3, 1959, p. 66. Not all these types of bonus are available to the director himself, but they are available to different groups of managerial personnel.

29 *Voprosy ekonomiki*, no. 2, 1958, p. 136.
30 Adolph A. Berle, Jr., and Gardiner, C. Means, 'The Modern Corporation and Private Property', Macmillan, New York, 1945.
31 Ibid., p. 122.
32 Ibid., pp. 202–3, 335.
33 Robert A. Gordon, 'Business Leadership in the Large Corporation', Brookings, Washington, 1945, p. 309.
34 Ibid., p. 309.
35 Ibid., p. 311.
36 *The New Yorker*, 6 April 1955, p. 52.
37 Edwin H. Sutherland, *White Collar Crime*, Dryden, New York, 1949, p. 26.
38 Ibid., p. 10.
39 Ibid., p. 217.
40 Ibid., p. 218.
41 Ibid., p. 220.
42 *Mashinostroenie*, 17 February 1939, p. 3.
43 Ibid., p. 240.
44 Marshall B. Clinard, *The Black Market*, Rinehart, New York, 1952, p. vii.
45 Ibid., p. 224.
46 Ibid., p. 45.
47 Ibid., pp. 306–7.
48 *Planovoe khoziaistvo*, no. 7, 1958, p. 14.
49 Clinard, p. 244.
50 L. Hamburger, 'How Nazi Germany Has Controlled Business', Brookings, Washington, 1943, pp. 94–5
51 Paul H. Douglas, 'Ethics in Government', Harvard Press, Cambridge, 1952, p. 56.
52 Ibid., p. 25.
53 *New York Times Magazine*, 3 June 1951, p. 35.
54 Douglas, op. cit., p. 44.

5 Planning and Management*
1983

INTRODUCTION

In July 1979 the Party and government of the USSR issued a decree announcing a variety of changes in what is now called the economic mechanism. The decree evoked a flurry of interest at the time but, in short order, public attention turned to other things. There are two lessons in that incident. First, the process of modifying the system of planning and management has become routinized. The public has become used to the periodic announcement, usually in advance of the next five-year planning period, of a series of changes that had been agreed upon since the last such decree. Second, for the most part the changes are technical rather than fundamental, involving such matters as new success indicators or revised planning procedures.

The capacity of the system to review its methods of operation periodically and to seek ways of improving them must be regarded as one of its strengths. There is a view abroad, however, that the range of alternatives considered, in the public discussion at least, is too narrow to score a significant advance. If Mr Brezhnev were immortal, that restriction might continue indefinitely. But as the USSR enters the last decades of the century, there is a strong possibility that the range of discussable alternatives may widen, not only because of human morality, but also because of the growing strains to which the economy will be subject.

The objective of this paper is to explore that wider range of alternative systems of planning and management that may be considered as the next two decades unfold. It is well to begin, however, with a review of the recent history of economic reforms.

*Abram Bergson and Herbert E. Levine (eds) *The Soviet Economy Toward the Year 2000*, Allen and Unwin, London (1983) pp. 350–90.

SOME REFLECTIONS ON RECENT HISTORY

Five cases of changes in the economic mechanism will serve as the specimens in this dissection of the past. The details are familiar to this audience and have been so well studied elsewhere (Schroeder, 1979) that they need not be recounted here. The purpose is rather to review those cases for the light they can shed on the views held by the governors of the economic system about that system. Two questions will be asked about each of the cases. First, what were the governors seeking to accomplish by that particular change? Second, what does that change reveal about their conception of how their system works? The first question is designed to identify the objectives of the leadership, and the second to understand their implicit model of their own economy. That sort of knowledge about past efforts to change the economy should provide some insight into the future course of such efforts.

The selection of the five cases examined below is somewhat arbitrary. Two of them, the Territorial Reorganization of 1957 and the Economic Reform of 1965, would appear on everybody's list of the most important efforts at system change. The others have been chosen not necessarily because of their prominence but because they deal with different facets of the planning or management system. Other analysts would select other cases, covering areas I have omitted, like agriculture. The five that have been chosen nevertheless represent, I believe, a reasonable selection of changes from which to seek some instructive generalizations.

The Territorial Reorganization of 1957
The problem to which the reform was addressed was the diversion of resources into uses different from those provided for in the plan. To some extent the issue was the deliberate violation of the plan; for example, when ministries instructed their enterprises to alter their shipping plans in favour of customers within their own ministries. In other cases the issue was not violations of the plans but restrictions on the flow of resources in ways that were contrary to the intent of the plan. A typical instance was the enterprise that possessed excess stocks of some scarce commodity while a neighbouring enterprise's production plan foundered for lack of that commodity; but the redirection of that commodity from the first enterprise to the second was inhibited because they belonged to different ministries.

The source of the problem, as seen by the reformers, was captured in the slogan, *vedomstvennost'* or 'departmentalism'. That may be interpreted to mean that ministries tended to maximize the indicators of their own performance, which in system terms is equivalent to sub-optimization by the component units at the expense of the performance of the system as a whole. The solution was thought to be a restructuring of those components by repartitioning them in such fashion that the identity of the sub-optimizing units – the ministries – was obliterated. If there were no ministries there could be no sub-optimization by ministries.

It is difficult to imagine, in retrospect, that the reformers did not anticipate what the consequence would be; that only the specific form of the objectionable behaviour would be changed, but not that behaviour in general. There had been ample evidence in the past of *mestnichestvo* (localism) in decision-making by regional government and Party organizations. The outcome was indeed so predictable that a compelling case can and has been made that the whole purpose of the exercise had nothing to do with economics at all but with politics; namely, that the reform was Khrushchev's gambit for crushing the power base of the Moscow bureaucracy by transferring their power to his supporters in the provincial centres. If that was indeed the history, then we are misled in trying to draw too many lessons out of the economics of the reform. But one can recognize the political element in the reform without having to hold that there was no serious economic purpose behind it. If the reformers failed to anticipate the turn that the economy actually took after the reform, it may be because they expected either that (a) *mestnichestvo* could and would be more easily contained than the old *vedomstvennost'*, if only because none of the 110–odd provincial economic leaders could wield the power of a major industrial minister, or (b), even if that were not so, the cost of *mestnichestvo* would be less than that of *vedomstvennost'*. We know in retrospect that both of those propositions were wrong, but they could have been honestly held by reasonable men at the time.

The episode offers several insights into the thoughts of the system's governors about their system. It is clear that there was no question of the principle of central planning as the basis of the economic mechanism. They recognized that planning was not perfect, but that was not the issue to which this reform was addressed. The problem was that even perfect plans are not self-executing, but require persons and organizations to carry them out. The task of government was to create a management structure in which managers would make those decisions that are in closest conformity to the plan. In seeking out the villain, of the several levels of management at which the problem could have been attacked they chose the level of central management – the ministries. Presumably they saw enterprise-level management as less at fault, or perhaps as more compliant. The effective power of choice lay with the central management, and if the central management could be made to behave correctly, enterprise management could be expected to comply. In any event, even if they were not quite that starry-eyed about enterprise management, it was their judgement that the greater damage was being done where the greater overall decision-making power lay – with the central management.

Finally, the problem was seen not simply as one of incentives but of structure. If it were merely incentives, they might have sought to design new incentives – perhaps new success indicators – to induce ministers to alter their decisions. The fact that they did not take that tack indicates that they did not see that as the source of the problem. They must have felt that it was the branch structure of the management system that induced the unfortunate behaviour, and no amount of fiddling with success indicators would eliminate the pressures towards maximizing the performance of the branch.

The Territorial Reorganization was introduced in 1957. It is well to recall that that was a period in which the Soviet economy was still growing very rapidly. The reform was the first major effort to eliminate some of the grosser sources of inefficiency in the rigid system of planning and management inherited from Stalin. The evidence of waste was abundant, but the system was thought to be performing quite satisfactorily at the time. The objective of the reform was to enable it to do even better. The beginnings of the decline in the growth rate date from the late 1950s. By the mid-1960s it was increasingly evident that the decline was not a short-term aberration but was perhaps something systemic. The next major reform was introduced under new conditions; the economy had seen better days and its governors wished to find a way of bringing those days back.

The 1965 Economic Reform

The problem that motivated this reform was similar to that involved in the Territorial Reorganization: enterprises were making a broad range of decisions that were contrary to the intentions of the plan. And as in the earlier reform, the source of the problem was again held to be the organs of central management; that was the meaning of the slogan, 'petty tutelage'. But one new source was identified this time. That was the use of poorly designed success indicators that directed enterprises into making incorrect decisions.

The petty-tutelage problem was an issue in organizational theory; the question was, what were the optimal levels at which various types of decisions should be made. One can detect in the solution the primacy of informational concerns. That is, the decision to devolve a wide range of choices from the level of central mangement to that of enterprise management reflected the view that those were areas in which enterprises had more precise and timely information at their disposal than the central ministries.

The success-indicator problem, in contrast, was an issue in economic theory; it was indeed the first reform in which economists rather than politicians and planners had a hand. By identifying the source of the problem as the notorious *val* (gross value of output), the reformers implicitly acknowledged that they were dealing with a process of maximization under constraints, and that in such a process it is important to get the objectives function right. That way of thinking about the economic mechanism was a giant step forward from the reasoning of the past, which held that the problem was simply to get managers to 'fulfil the plan'. It led eventually to the formulation that is currently in wide use; 'what is best for the economy should be best for the enterprise.'

The choice of sales revenue and profit as the new success indicators was a reasonable first step in the direction of designing an optimal objectives function for enterprise management. Though not usually put into the same category, the introduction of a capital charge may also be regarded as a contribution to the improvement of the success indicators. For when profit is promoted to the level of a major argument in an objectives function, it becomes more important to be sure that the relative costs of factors of production are properly accounted for.

The change in the success indicators required a corresponding change in the incentive structure, which had formerly been linked primarily to *val*. The new system of incentive payments involved nothing new in principle, however. All the elements were there before, in the form of the Enterprise Fund, although the magnitude of the contributions to the various incentive funds was changed.

In the course of a few years several features of the original 1965 reform were modified. Among the major modifications was the gradual increase in the number of indicators for which the enterprise had to account to the ministry. The reason for the retreat is instructive because it bears on a problem that arises in all efforts to reform the system of planning and management. The central allocative instrument is still the national plan. Gosplan must be held responsible for the consistency and optimality of the plan, and someone else must be held responsible for assuring that that plan is executed. As long as the executors are the ministries, they must be given authority equivalent to their responsibility. The Economic

Reform was an attempt to permit enterprises, on informational grounds, to make a wide range of decisions that affected plan fulfilment, but to hold the ministries responsible for the results. In effect, the ministries were put in the position of being held responsible for decisions that they were forbidden to control. The impossibility of that organizational arrangement led eventually to the reassertion by the ministries of control over those kinds of enterprise decisions for which they had to account to the Party and the Council of Ministers.

In that piece of history there is an important lesson regarding the limits of decentralized decision-making under central planning. A governing unit (for example, a capitalist corporation) can delegate decision-making authority to lower units on grounds of informational efficiency if it determines its own objectives function; it can decentralize purchasing while retaining control over pricing, for example. The test of that organizational arrangement is its own evaluation of whether the results are better in the light of its own profit and other objectives. But if a governing unit (like a Soviet ministry) is not an autonomous organization but is responsible to a higher organization for a very detailed plan of operations, then it cannot be limited in the kinds of controls it may exert over its operating units. Specifically, if the material balances in the national plan are carried out in physical or gross-value units, then the ministerial executors of that plan must be held accountable for the production by their operating units of the specified physical quantities or gross values. They simply cannot be denied the power to telephone their enterprises towards the end of the month to inquire how close they are to fulfilling their gross-output targets. And once the telephone calls are made, the message is fully absorbed.

To be sure, a ministry itself may delegate certain decision-making authority to its enterprises on grounds of informational efficiency. But the range of such decentralized authority is likely to be very limited, and to deal with secondary choices for which the ministry itself is not directly accountable. Thus the lesson of the Economic Reform is that genuine decentralization of authority to enterprises is strictly limited by the directive nature of a detailed national economic plan.

With respect to success indicators, the prospects are brighter. What is involved is the choices that must be made that are not dictated by the terms of the plan. The usual instances are choices among qualities not specified in the plan, or choices of output-mixes in excess of the minimal assortment-plan targets (i.e. plan overfulfilment.) Since the goal is to induce those decisions that are most consistent with the objectives of the plan, the shadow prices implicit in the plan could serve that purpose, with profits as the maximand in the objectives function. Nevertheless, if the ministry is still held to account for quantities or for gross value of output, it is those magnitudes that will prevail in enterprise decisions.

The Price Reform of 1967

The primary goal of the Price Reform may be judged from the kind of evidence that was presented as justification of the need for such a reform. What was thought to be the most persuasive evidence was the widely published data on the vast spread of profit rates among products and branches, ranging from highly subsidized branches like coal to highly profitable branches like machinery production. Among the reasons that such diversity of profit rates was regarded as bad, the following predominated:

1 subsidies are bad in general, because they encourage inefficiency and neglect of cost by producers who anticipate that the government will subsidize the loss;
2 high profits are generally unearned, and represent rental elements in income; they are inequitable, and they also weaken cost discipline;
3 large profit differentials between commodities bias product-mix choices by producers and input-mix choices by purchasers.

The goal, therefore, was to reestablish a price structure in which most enterprises earned the normal profit rate and a few of the best and worst earned a bit more or less in proportion as their work diverged from that of the 'normally operating enterprise'.

What does this concern about profit differentials reveal about the leadership's analysis of the economic system? For one thing, it reveals a certain normative notion of what prices should be. The ideal presumably was one in which most enterprises earned the normal rate of profit and a few earned somewhat more or less, the excess or shortfall of profit serving both as a success indicator and as an incentive. However, the basis of pricing was to remain average branch cost plus normal profit. The objective was that prices play not an active but a neutral role in decision-making. The trouble with large profit differentials is that they convert price into an active element in decision-making, in the sense that managers depart from rational or socially desirable decisions because of the profit-related consequences of wide price variability. In other words, the ideal was not that price should serve as an allocative device; the plan was still the primary allocative instrument. The objective was rather a price structure in which a profit could serve as a success indicator (which requires *some* degree of variability) without at the same time serving as an allocative device by influencing production choices.

Thus the Price Reform was a reaffirmation of central planning as the allocative mechanism. Managerial decisions were to be made on the basis of plan assignments whenever those assignments were clear, and not on the basis of price and profit. The Price Reform recognized, however, that for a broad range of decisions that had to be made by management there was no clear indication of which alternative contributed most to the fulfilment of the national plan. The Economic Reform of 1965 had designated profit, along with sales, as a major criterion of performance and therefore implicitly as a proper basis of choice. By eliminating the large profit differentials of the past, the Price Reform was designed to assure that the choices made would be in closer conformity with the objectives of the plan.

There were two exceptions that are noteworthy. One was the pricing of new products. In a separate decree issued in 1965, before the Price Reform, the pricing of new products was reorganized on lines entirely separate from those of established products (Berliner, 1976, chs. 10–12). That decree introduced certain highly active functions for prices in the case of new technology. Profit rates were deliberately differentiated in order to induce management to choose the higher-profit alternatives. It is significant that this concession was made in order to promote technological innovation. Central planning is at its best with well known technologies, and at its worst with technologies not yet fully developed or even yet unknown. In assigning an active function to prices and profit in this case the system's governors demonstrated a new awareness that in this major area of economic activity central planning suffers from certain limitations and that more decentralized decision-making can be helpful.

The second exception was the introduction of rent-like fixed charges on commodities like petroleum and timber. The use of such charges was a victory for the marginalists and quasi-marginalists who had finally persuaded the leadership that, at least in those cases in which the difference between marginal and average cost is very large, price should be used actively to discourage consumption. In this case it is not only managerial decision-making that is to be influenced but also the plan itself. In deciding whether to use oil or coal in a new power plant, for example, it is the marginal cost of the two fuels that planners must take into account.

Hence the purpose of this new provision is to improve the quality of central planning as well as that of managerial decision-making.

Production Associations

This reform consists of the merger of groups of enterprises into new super-enterprises under a single management. In one class of mergers the key feature is that a formerly independent R & D institute is a part of the new association, and sometimes the dominant member. These are the science–production associations. The other production associations follow the familiar pattern of the vertical integration of enterprises, although there are some cases of horizontal integration.

The problem that motivated the founding of the science–production associations is clear enough. It was the unsatisfactory rate of technological progress. This in fact is the first of the reforms under review in which the problem of technological progress lay at the heart of the reform, although it played a role in the others. But if technological progress were the only objective of this reform, one could not explain why the merger movement was extended to encompass virtually all of the non-agricultural economy; for most of the mergers do not involve R & D institutes. One must therefore postulate a second objective, which appears to be yet another stab at the problem of enterprise-level decision-making. The specific facet of the problem in this case was that enterprises produced outputs that did not take sufficiently into account the requirements of their industrial customers. The second objective is related to the first in that it was not merely the quantities of output but also their qualities that were at issue. That is, the concern was not simply that enterprises produced types of products that did not correspond to the needs of users, but also that the quality of outputs did not correspond to the needs of users.

The selection of the production association as the device for getting at these two problems suggests a change in the analysis of the source of the problems by the system's governors. In earlier reforms it was assumed that enterprise managers were motivated to make correct choices. The problem was that they were misdirected, by the ministries in the case of the Territorial Reorganization, and by the success indicators and also the ministries in the case of the Economic Reform. In turning to production associations, it appears that the leadership has given up the view that by creating the appropriate environment (better success indicators, better prices, less misdirection by central management) enterprise management could be counted on to get things right. The pro-

duction associations have virtually eliminated enterprise management, as it had operated for forty years, as a significant level of
economic decision-making. The former enterprise manager now
occupies a position that is rather like a glorified version of what
in the past was the position of shop chief. The new approach is
to take responsibility out of the hands of the enterprise managers
and to relocate it at a level that is very much like the central
management of the past. The production associations may be
regarded as micro-ministries, in the sense that they enjoy powers
over the former enterprises similar to those formerly enjoyed by
ministries over enterprises. They have also acquired some powers
that formerly were lodged with the ministries.

With respect to the ministries, the reform is a measure of decentralization (Gorlin, 1976, pp. 180–2). It is also a vote of confidence
in the superiority of 'administrative levers' over 'economic levers'.
Before this reform, the strategy was to find ways of inducing enterprise managers to behave by creating the proper conditions for
them to behave. Now they are to behave because they have a new
superior authority that tells them what to do; an authority not
as remote as the ministry and with a span of control not as wide
as a ministry, so that it is in a much stronger position to be informed
and to impose compliance.

This interpretation of the analysis that underlay the reform
applies both to the general problem of enterprise decision-making
and to the specific problem of technological progress. With respect
to the former, producer enterprise A will produce and deliver
precisely the outputs required by user enterprise B because they
both have the same boss whose career is on the line and who
knows the capacity and needs of both enterprises. With respect
to technological progress, producer enterprise A will quickly put
into production a new product developed by the R & D Institute
because, again, they have the same boss, who may in fact have
been the former director of the Institute when it was an independent
ministry organization. Nor will the Institute lose interest in the
practical success of the product innovation once it has gone into
production, as in the past, because the general director of the
association is responsible for both units.

Thus the production–association reform is a break with the past.
It reflects the continued concern with the problem that had been
the major concern in the past – enterprise-level decision-making.
But it adds a major new concern – the promotion of technological
progress. Moreover the solution chosen reflects a change in the
strategy that guided past reforms. Instead of seeking ways of
improving the quality of decentralized decision-making, it has with-

drawn decision-making authority from enterprise management and relocated it at a more central level.

The Comprehensive Planning Decree of 1979
The reforms in the management system discussed above were widely heralded and have been deemed important enough to have acquired names of their own. It is interesting to note that while other changes in the planning system have proceeded through the post-Stalin period, history has judged none of them significant enough to have merited a name of its own. It is possible that the planning decree of 1979 (*Ekonomicheskaia gazeta*, no. 32, 1979) will pass on in anonymity like the others. I have given it a name not because I judge it to be of name-deserving proportions but because a review of the past would be incomplete without some notice of the changes in the planning system, and the most recent one is the appropriate candidate.

The decree may be regarded as a continuation and extension of a series of changes in the planning system that have been proceeding for some time, rather than as a break with the past or as the opening of a new direction. I suggest the term 'comprehensive' because it roughly captures the sense of those changes. First, the planning process now comprehends a longer spread of time; the five-year plan rather than the annual plan is now officially designated as the fundamental plan, and it is to be based on a twenty-year programme of scientific–technical development and on a ten-year plan that sets forth the main directions of economic and social development. Second, the planning process now comprehends both branch and regional planning; all USSR ministry plans are to be submitted to review by the republic councils of ministers, and the latter are to present to Gosplan their plans for all their enterprises. Third, the decree mandates a more comprehensive set of balances than in the past; balances are to be employed in the ten-year main-directions plan and in the five-year plan; interbranch balances are to be used for major products; and regional balances are to be used for the production and distribution of major products.[1]

Two problems can be identified as those with which the system's governors sought to deal in the planning decree. One is the promotion of technological progress. The incorporation of ten-year and twenty-year plans into the current planning process is intended to build into current planning a basis of consistency with the long lead times of technological advance; that is, to avoid current decisions that lock the economy into directions that may be inconsistent with the probable direction of future technological advance. The technique adopted is to require that current plan decisions be checked for consistency with longer-run structural choices that have already been made, and with the forecasts of future technological developments.

The second problem is, once more, enterprise-level decision-making. The reforms in the management system discussed above were all directed at the problems that arise when managers have to make decisions. The necessity for managers to make decisions arises out of imperfections in the planning process; that is, with perfect planning there would be virtually no need at all for decisions to be made by enterprise managers. The system's governors must assume, however, that there will always be considerable scope for managerial discretion, either because the central plan cannot realistically provide for all possible detail, or because of errors in plans, or because of changes in plans. Accepting the inevitability of managerial discretion, the purpose of the management reforms was to improve the quality of those decisions. But the second string to that bow is the improvement of the planning system. The more comprehensive and detailed the plan, the smaller the volume of planning errors, and the less frequent the changes in the plan, the less the need to rely on managerial decision-making.

The implication of this view of the relationship between planning reform and management reform is that planning is thought to be good and management bad. The less the discretion that needs to be given to management, the better. In this interpretation, the move toward increasing comprehensiveness of planning reflects the hope that eventually everything can be balanced in advance so that management can be reduced solely to carrying out preplanned instructions. On the face of it, there can be no quarrel with the notion that in a planned economy plans should be as specific as possible. But that doesn't necessarily mean that they must be comprehensive. The alternative view is that there may be some optimal level of comprehensiveness beyond which the marginal benefit of more detailed planning diminishes and that of decentralized managerial solutions increase. It is true that as planning techniques improve the optimal level may involve greater detail. The extension of comprehensiveness does not therefore necessarily mean that the leadership is shifting the balance deliberately. But it appears to me that the push is in that direction. Better planning continues to be thought of as a way of decreasing the inefficiency associated with an obdurate management.

Some Lessons of History

I make no claim that mine is the only story that a brief review of recent economic reforms can tell. Had a different list of reforms been selected for examination, or had another analyst considered the same reforms with a different eye, the story might be different. I trust, however, that this account is a plausible one and serves as a useful prelude to an inquiry into the possible shapes of the future.

The first conclusion is that the reforms give no evidence of a disposition to doubt the efficacy of the system of central planning as the basis of the economic mechanism. On the contrary, the 1979 Planning Decree affirms the intention to strengthen the planning system by improving the quality of the national plans. In this respect the efforts of the last several decades have probably been successful. The technical equipment now available to planners, including electronic data-processing equipment and mathematical-modelling techniques for checking the consistency of plans, have no doubt been helpful. We may expect that the plan-making process will continue to improve in the future, although the growing complexity of the economy increases the size of the task from plan to plan. We may also expect that each five-year plan of the future will, like the most recent, be preceded by a decree incorporating in the forthcoming plan a series of newer techniques that have been in the process of experimentation and are ready for adoption.

The second conclusion is that the problem of management has been less tractable than that of planning, and that there have not been significant advances in improving its quality. In principle, planning and management should be expected to complement each other; planners draw up the plans and managers see to their execution. In fact, the relation appears to be viewed by the system's governors as one of tension. Planning is the friend while management is the enemy. Evidence of inefficiency is most often explained as the consequence of bungling or mismanagement. Brezhnev expressed what is probably the general view of politicians when he laid the blame for a series of excesses at the feet of people who 'no matter how much you talk to them, no matter how much you appeal to their conscience and their sense of duty and responsibility, nothing helps'.[2]

To see the problem as one of poorly trained or venal people is to close one's eyes to possible defects of the system itself. It obscures the fundamental problem: that central planning, which must inevitably be imperfect, makes extremely difficult demands upon management. The central managers – the ministries – are responsible for the execution of a detailed set of targets, all of which cannot be fulfilled in the normal course of events. There is no 'bottom line', although gross output comes close to serving as the ultimate criterion. Their own record of performance depends on that of hundreds of enterprise (or production–association) managers, who must also constantly make a variety of decisions for which there is no clear guide in the plans. Hence alongside the tension between planners and managers, the system's governors have also to contend with the tension between ministries and enterprises. Most of the reforms have attempted to come to grips with the latter problem. In the Territorial Reorganization, it was decided to solve the problem by abolishing the ministries. In the Production–Association reform it was decided to abolish the enterprises instead. It is difficult to foresee any clear basis for a more effective distribution of authority between the two levels in the context of central planning.

Finally, the history of the recent reforms reflects the growing appreciation of the importance of technological progress. The reforms of the 1950s and 1960s concentrated on the coordination of management and planning and on the increase in static efficiency. But in the more recent reforms technological progress has been at the forefront of the objectives. The change in emphasis coincides with the gradual acceptance of the view that the decline in the growth rate reflects a fundamental change in economic conditions, which is reflected in the formulation of a change from 'extensive' to 'intensive' growth. How to adapt the system of planning and management to the new goal of promoting technological progress is likely to be the central concern of those who bear the responsibility for the economic reforms of the future.

THE CONSERVATIVE MODEL

The status quo rarely has passionate supporters. The passions are normally on the side of change. Support for the status quo is usually based on a lack of conviction that the untried alternatives will produce a better future than the present. That is likely to be the case if the Conservative Model is chosen as the basis of the future system of planning and management in the USSR. It is doubtful that many people, even among the system's governors, regard the present structure as having great merit in its own right. That was not the case two decades ago. At that time Soviet economists certainly, and political leaders probably, looked over the world of economic systems and pronounced their own as exceptionally good. Today the system may still command strong support, but very likely in the Churchillian vein, as a rather bad system, 'except for all the others'.

The Conservative Model retains all the basic structural features of the present system, but it should not be thought of as unchanging in form. Judging from the recent history of reforms, we should expect repeated efforts in the future to try new ways of dealing with old problems. Certainly the planning system will be continually changed by the incorporation of new techniques of central planning. What will remain unchanged is the commitment to central planning as the basis of the economic mechanism. Beyond that, each analyst is free to forecast efforts to change whatever is his own favourite source of inefficiency in the economy. My own guess is that many of the production associations will be dismantled after a period of time, in favour of a system containing a broader mix of large and small enterprises. The reason for this guess is that the size structure of enterprises in the USSR, even before the production associations, was strongly skewed towards large enterprises, compared to the size structure in the technologically advanced capitalist countries (Kvasha, 1967). With respect to efficiency and certainly to innovation there must be some range of activities in which there are diseconomies of scale. There are also likely to be further changes in such perennials as the success indicators of enterprise management. The indicator newly introduced in the July 1979 planning decree – normative net output – may well prove to be exceedingly costly to administer and is likely to bias decisions excessively in favour of labour-intensive choices in a period of tight labour supply. There may be some renewed flirtation with profit as a more general success indicator, but the pathological antagonism to the appropriation by enterprises of unearned economic rents will stand in the way; large profits in particular seem to constitute *prima facie* evidence that they were unearned, probably as a consequence of favourable price changes. New experiments in the use of contractual relations may be tried, and also new Shchekino-type efforts to reallocate labour among enterprises by various incentive devices. The recent sharp increase in the price of gasoline suggests that price policy may be called upon more often to ration scarce commodities. Price revisions every few years will continue to keep relative prices from diverging excessively from average branch costs, and there may be some further incorporation of scarcity pricing into the price structure. Extrapolating from the past, planning may become more detailed, and with the growth of electronic data-processing capacity, the number of balances is likely to increase; however, there may be a reaction at some point because of the mounting complexity of the plan-making process, and a return to more aggregated planning.

Certainly there will be new measures designed to promote technological progress and the quality of production. Some would attempt to make use of 'economic levers' through new forms of incentive payments. But most will consist of 'administrative measures'; changing the structure of authority, holding more people responsible for the completion of assigned tasks, penalties for not fulfilling quality assignments.

To accept the Conservative Model is to give up the goal of attaining the technological level of the leading industrial countries. For I take it as fairly well established that whatever the merits of the Soviet economic mechanism, the promotion of technological advance is not one of them. But that is an outcome with which the Soviet leadership ought to be able to live. There is no reason why the USSR cannot maintain a position that lags permanently behind that of the technological leaders in world industry by, say, an average of about five years. There would be some loss in productivity because of delayed innovation, but that loss would be offset to some degree by savings in research and development expenditures as well as in the costs of learning-by-doing that the country pioneering in any new development must bear. It would be a reasonable strategy for the Soviets to wait until each new major breakthrough is announced elsewhere, and then to proceed to develop their own version on the basis of whatever information can be perused, purchased or purloined. For it is an axiom in the R & D community that the most valuable piece of information in technological advance is the information that a certain result has been successfully accomplished by somebody. The strategy of waiting until the results have been accomplished elsewhere is not only cost-saving but is also appealing to R & D people operating in a risk-averse bureaucratic structure. Moreover, the Soviets have shown that technological excellence can be maintained in a few priority areas where these are deemed crucial for defence or other national purposes.

Taking the foregoing as the essence of the Conservative Model, the question here is what are the outcomes that can be expected from the adoption of that model. Since the model involves no significant changes from the past, the past can serve as a guide to the economic outcomes to be expected in the future. There is little reason to expect any discontinuous increase either in static efficiency or in the rate of growth. None of the major reforms of the past has succeeded in doing what their initiators must have devoutly hoped for – attaining a quantum leap in efficiency. Indeed the term 'reform' has disappeared from the public discussion and has been replaced by the expression 'improving the operation of the economic mechanism'.

The evaporation of the spirit of reform may reflect the view that the system of central planning and management has now reached the practical limit of its perfectability. An economic system is like a technological innovation. When first invented, a steam engine or an internal combustion machine represents a major advance over its predecessor, but it is a very inefficient mechanism in terms of its own potential. In the course of time its efficiency increases, very rapidly at first and more slowly thereafter, with successive waves of 'reforms' or 'improvements'. Eventually it attains a degree of efficiency that can be regarded as the effective maximum that is realistically attainable within the limits of its basic conception; there is only so much one can expect to get out of a machine the basic conception of which is a piston in a cylinder. It is rather like a Kuhnian paradigm in the development of scientific theory; not much more can be expected to happen until someone breaks out of the paradigm with a very different conception of how power may be generated.

That vision may be applied to the invention of central economic planning as an economic mechanism by the Soviet leadership of the thirties. In the course of time it became a more efficient mechanism than it was when first introduced. But like all inventions, the possibilities of improvement within the basic paradigm may have been largely exhausted by the 1960s. It should be noted that the economic mechanism was designed in a period in which the strategy of economic progress consisted of what was later described as 'extensive growth'. It is perhaps still a reasonably successful model for that purpose. The problem is that the conditions within which the economy operates today are not such as to generate high rates of extensive growth. Three per cent per year more or less may be the most that can be expected of an economy designed according to that model. It is in that sense that the economy may be doing as well as can be expected under that economic mechanism.

It is entirely possible, of course, that this judgement may be too pessimistic. To assert that there are few opportunities for further improvement is to imply, paradoxically, that the economy is highly efficient, in the sense of operating close to its production-possibilities frontier as defined by the existing economic structure. A future government may yet find ways of extending that frontier. Some such ways have been proposed at this conference: the creation of enterprises specializing in production for export, correcting those relative prices that create perverse incentives in agriculture, providing greater autonomy for small-scale production units within the collective farm. Without abandoning the Conservative Model, its limits may be extended by adopting some of the features of the other models discussed below. While a bold package of such measures may prove that the Conservative Model contains greater potential than its recent record reveals, the history of the reforms sketched out above does not offer great encouragement. Individual changes in prices and organizational structures that make good sense in themselves have not produced the desired results because they clashed with the imperatives imposed by the dominating structures of central planning and management.

Suppose then that the Conservative Model does not in fact produce better results than those forecast on the basis of the experience of the recent past. The question is whether the leadership can continue to be satisfied with it; that is, to turn to no alternative model but simply to muddle through with only small variations on old themes. I think they can, on one condition – that the decline in the growth rate decelerate and eventually stabilize. A constant rate of growth, even if very low, would constitute a chronic condition that does not ordinarily lead to disruption. It is the acute problems, such as those encountered with continuous decline, that must ultimately lead to disruption. With a chronically low but stable growth rate, the century could end with a whimper. Otherwise it might end with a bang.

We cannot judge what the minimally sustainable growth rate is – three, or two, or one per cent per capita. However, it is safe to say that it is likely to depend primarily on the consumption level. A threshold level of consumption may be defined, in political terms, as the level below which dissatisfaction would result in outbursts of disorder that would strain the authorities' instruments of political control. It would be an error for the leadership to believe, however, that there is no danger as long as consumption levels exceeded that political threshold. For there is another threshold at which the economy would begin to suffer from the erosion of incentives. If that incentives threshold, which must be higher than the political threshold, were not maintained, then it would prove to be impossible to maintain even that low level of stable growth. Output and consumption would decline reciprocally until the political threshold were reached, and then the whimper will turn into a bang. Hence, the key to the question of whether slow growth will turn from chronic to acute will depend on whether the rate of growth can be stabilized at a level sufficiently high to maintain consumption above the incentive threshold.

The Soviet leadership may possibly have some rough notion of the range within which the incentive threshold lies, but outside analysts can do little more than guess. My own guess is that a steady increase in per capita consumption of 1–2 per cent per year would 'provide consumers with a sense of forward motion' (Gertrude Schroeder, 1983). Under the baseline projection of

SOVMOD, GNP would grow at 3.2 per cent and consumption per capita at 2 per cent (Bond and Levine, 1983, Table 1.1, p. 13). With a bit of luck that outcome should keep the economy above the incentives threshold. Under the low-productivity scenario, however (ibid. Table 1.3, p. 18) GNP grows at 2.3 per cent and consumption per capita at only 0.7 per cent. At that rate it is conceivable that the erosion of incentives would preclude the stabilization of the growth rate, and consumption may decline to the perilous level of the political threshold.

There is a fair chance that the economy can stabilize at the levels of the baseline projection of Bond and Levine. The long period of declining growth may presage continued decline in the future, but it need not. It may signify instead that the economy has been readjusting from the high growth rates of the past to low but stable growth rates in the future. In that case poor performance in static efficiency or in technological progress need not compel the abandonment of the Conservative Model as long as consumption does not fall below the incentive threshold.

THE REACTIONARY MODEL

The political characteristics of a neo-Stalinist reaction are not difficult to portray. One thinks first of a restoration of the power of the secret police, perhaps not quite to the level of the Stalinist terror but well beyond the present level. Contacts with capitalist countries would be greatly reduced, the iron curtain reimposed, a zenophobic nationalism reinstituted, and ideological, political and social discipline generally tightened.

If one asks, however, what changes would have to be made to return to a Stalin-like economic system, the answer is not self-evident. The exercise is a reminder that, however great the changes in Soviet political life since Stalin, the essentials of the economic system have not been that greatly changed. The inclination of the leadership under the Reactionary Model is towards the restoration of discipline and order, and they will view their mission as the reassertion of strong central control. But they will find that the clock has moved so little in the system of planning and management that it hardly needs to be turned back very much.

In the organization of central planning, while the political leaders under the Reactionary Model may harbour a Stalinist contempt for theoretical economics, the practical value of 'optimal planning' would overcome the aversion and it would elicit strong support.

For it promises a possibility of centralization of decision-making and control far beyond anything dreamed of in Stalin's time. It is, in the words of a close student of the subject, an ideal instrument for an 'autocratic political mechanism' (Katsenelenboigen, 1978, p. 41). However, the possibility of introducing that form of plan making is still too remote to be of use in the near future. Short of that, it is difficult to imagine that the leaders of the Reactionary economy could contrive ways of extending the scope of central planning that are not already contained or implicit in the 1979 planning decree.

With respect to the management system, because the 1965 Economic Reform has been so greatly modified, there are few changes that will be seen as essential for the restoration of central control. No great purpose would be served by eliminating the capital charge or restoring *val* as the dominant success indicator. Those small ways in which the present-day enterprise manager is less accountable to the centre than in the past are not likely to be eliminated. What might be changed is the spread of *khozraschet* (financing an organization's expenditures out of its own revenues) to the agencies of central management – ministries and chief administrations. To the extent that centralization is the desideratum, the degree of independence that *khozraschet* would provide for these units would probably be regarded as unacceptable. The inclination would more likely be to proceed with the creation of the superministries that have been discussed from time to time. Similarly, to the extent that contract-financed production has replaced planned production, for example in the financing of R & D organizations, that practice may well be ended.

Another of the post-Stalin moves toward decentralization was the establishment of the wholesale trade programme. That measure started out as the bold idea of offering an alternative to the 'material–technical supply' system. The programme for a large network of well stocked stores where enterprises could purchase small quantities of whatever was needed never did materialize. What evolved instead was a system of warehouse supply, differing from the Stalinist system only in that it is managed by the hierarchy of *Gossnab* rather than by the ministries' own supply organizations. It is difficult to imagine that a neo-Stalinist leadership would find it a matter of some importance to abolish *Gossnab* and turn its functions back to the ministries. *Gossnab* may in fact be regarded as the more centralized supply system, even though its operating units are territorially based.

The production associations would very likely find favour with the Reactionary leadership, resembling as they do the vast scale of enterprise that was characteristic of Stalin's time. One of the virtues of that organizational form is that it reduces the task of central planning by 'internalizing' within the superenterprise a certain number of transactions that were formerly inter-enterprise transactions and therefore the responsibility of the central planners. The more self-contained the producing unit, the simpler the job of the planners. There has been a growing trend toward self-containment in recent years that merits more attention than it has received. Many enterprises, for example, have begun to develop their own subsidiary farms to provide produce for their own workers (Rumer, 1980). That development is an extension of a very old practice by management of seeking independence of the uncertain supply system by the practice of 'universalism', or the in-house production of as much of their inputs as they can manage. That practice has been criticized in the past, and the present Conservative leadership has taken a dim view of it. In the aforementioned speech Brezhnev was sharply critical of what he described as 'a recent widespread practice for local agencies to recruit people from enterprises to do various kinds of work – help with the harvest, work in procurement organizations, on construction jobs, on beautification projects and so forth'. A Reactionary leadership, however, may be less concerned with the contraction in the division of labour and the loss of the economies of specialization that this 'new feudalism' entails. It may be inclined to support large universalist enterprises that encompass a variety of activities and that relieve the burden on the central planners.

Thus planning and management will be somewhat more centralized under the Reactionary Model than under the Conservative but the difference in that respect cannot be very large. The major differences between the two models will be found not in organizational forms but in policies. High on the list would be a policy of tightening labour discipline. One might envision a return to the severe laws of the late 1930s, making it illegal to leave one's job without authorization and providing criminal penalties for such violations as lateness to work, unauthorized absence from the job, and drunkenness. There might also be a disposition to return to the high-investment growth strategy that was associated with the rapid-growth years of the post-war period, although that would require a disavowal of the intensive-growth views that have prevailed subsequently. The corollary of a high-investment strategy would be a return to a policy of slow growth of consumption, or even possibly a decline. That would very likely be a subject of dispute even among supporters of a Reactionary Model, on a variety of grounds. First, the popular hostility it would arouse would challenge even the greatly tightened political controls. Second, there would be serious doubts about the efficacy of that strategy at this time in history. Third, since agriculture is no longer the predominant sector of origin of national income, the growth-rate gains from the suppression of the consumption of the agricultural population would no longer be as great as they were thought to be in the past. However, the recent trend towards the virtual transformation of the collective farms into state farms might be accelerated rather than reversed, on the assumption that the collective farm had been an enforced compromise and the state farm is more consistent with a neo-Stalinist structure.

Since a neo-Stalinist model implies the existence of a neo-Stalin, the leadership must be presumed to possess the power to carry through the changes that it finds necessary. One is a strong drive against 'speculators' and the second economy. Another is a purge of the managerial élite, both at the central and at the enterprise level. The Stalin period was characterized by rapid upward mobility of managers which, while purchased at some cost, nevertheless conveyed certain clear benefits: in weeding out dead wood, in cementing the loyalty of the new managers, in lowering their average age, and in generating an unusual level of effort (though perhaps at a cost in the form of increased risk aversion). One might guess that the long tenure enjoyed by the present managerial corps has contributed to a decline in its quality. It is interesting to note, in this context, that in present-day China the virtual lifetime tenure of the Party and management élite has come under increasing criticism, and Vice Premier Deng and his supporters seem determined to end that practice. A new and secure Soviet leadership might very likely see things the same way, though perhaps not with respect to themselves.

Finally, we are likely under this model to see a return to a policy of relative autarky, in an effort to reduce the volume of contacts with the West. Some level of import of advanced foreign technology would be maintained, but the new regime is likely to place a greater weight on the ideological costs of involvement with the West and to assign less value to its economic benefits than the Khrushchev-Brezhnev governments.

In evaluating the prospective economic performance of the USSR under the Reactionary Model, one tends to regard it as a mere romantic nostalgia for a simpler and in some ways better age that never really was and that could not be successfully restored under present-day conditions. But it would be an error to dismiss it entirely, for it might well bring some benefits of a purely economic kind.

For one thing, it might offer some short-run gains in the form of freeing up of the 'hidden reserves' that are so often the object of special campaigns. A few well publicized trials and convictions might lead to the disgorging of excess inventories and a scaling-down of the diversion of resources from public to private uses. The tempo of production is likely to be sped up and labour discipline tightened generally. It would not be surprising if the change were followed for a time by a significant rise in productivity and output.

If the economy is indeed characterized by a large degree of under-employment, in the form of excess numbers of workers whose marginal productivity is very low, as many Soviet economists claim to be the case, the tightening of political controls in a time of labour shortage may make it possible to launch an effective drive to reallocate labour to more productive use. One can imagine a campaign in which every enterprise would be obliged to deliver a quota of young workers to be relocated to the labour-short areas in the East, much as the collective farms once delivered their quotas for the staffing of new industrial enterprises. Whatever form it finally takes, the neo-Stalinist regime would very likely regard the reallocation of labour as one of its prime objectives, and that may be expected to have a favourable impact on economic performance.

In the longer run, it is possible that the recentralization of economic activity may also produce some economic gains. The view is sometimes expressed that the present-day Soviet economy is the worst of possible worlds. Change has not proceeded far enough to yield the benefits of genuine decentralized markets, yet the central planning and management system has given up control of a variety of functions in the interest of decentralization. The system, according to this view, is neither flesh nor fowl and enjoys neither the advantages of true markets nor of full central planning. Either alternative would be better than the particular mixed economy that has evolved out of the Khrushchev–Brezhnev regimes (Zielinski, 1973, pp. 312–21).

In evaluating this point of view, one may question, as we have, whether the reforms of the post-Stalin years constitute a significant degree of decentralization. Nevertheless there may be merit in the argument that many of the forms of decentralization have brought little genuine benefit. An instructive case is the conversion of the R & D institutes from budget financing to contract financing, a change that was introduced for the purpose of increasing the client's interest in and power over the work produced by the institutes. The instrument of a contract is crucial to the operation of a market economy, and it may seem that the replacement of administrative orders by contracts in the Soviet economy is a measure of market-like decentralization. However, the contexts are so different that it is an error to associate the word 'contract' with any of the real functions played by that instrument in a decentralized economy. For one thing, the client regards the payment for the services as made with 'the government's money'; if it is in the enterprise plan, financing is provided for it in the plan. Secondly, the contractor's income is limited by the conditions of the incentive structure. Regardless of how profitable the innovation is, the size of the reward is stipulated in the statutory incentive schedule, and the balance of profit is simply appropriated by the Ministry of Finance as a 'free remainder'. It would be an exaggeration to say that there is no difference at all between a management system in which the R & D institute operates under a plan and reports to an official in the Ministry, and one in which it operates on the basis of contracts entered into with enterprises. But the nature of the dependence of a market-economy firm on its contracts, and that of a Soviet firm on its contracts, are of different orders of magnitude. In that sense this act of formal decentralization, like so many others, is more a matter of detail than of critical importance in the decision-making process.

Plan-making should proceed under the Reactionary Model in much the same manner as under the Conservative Model. Nor is there any reason why, with intelligent administration, innovation should not proceed as well under a Reactionary Model as it does at present. The same material-incentive system would be employed as at present, and the prestige of science would be undiminished. Presumably the tightening of political and ideological controls would not extend to the extremes of Stalinist terror, nor to Lysenko-like constraints on science. The major loss perhaps would be that which would result from the decreased level of scientific contact with the more advanced countries, including very likely some decrease in the import of advanced technology. But if the leadership should accept realistically the policy of a permanent technological lag, the loss would not be regarded as very large. Only as long as the objective is to overtake and surpass the West in technological attainment would the decrease in scientific contact be of major significance.

The prospects for agricultural performance are probably much poorer under this model. The continued transformation of the collectives into state farms will satisfy some aspirations for ideological purity, but it is not likely to reverse what comes through the literature as the widespread demoralization of the agricultural labour force. Restrictions on private subsidiary agriculture are likely to be tightened, with a further loss in agricultural output. Agriculture may well be the sector in which the Reactionary Model will encounter its major failures.

I conclude that, with the exception of agriculture, the economy may exhibit some sharp short-run gains relative to the recent past. It is also entirely possible that in the longer run it could outperform the Conservative Model, particularly if it is successful in tightening labour discipline and in massively reallocating labour among jobs. However, a major condition is that it avoid the excesses of Stalin, for Stalin was the worst part of Stalinism. An intelligent Reactionary leadership may well squeeze more out of the economy than the cautious and compromising leadership of the recent decades.

THE RADICAL MODEL

If the Reactionary extreme is the recentralization of planning and management, the Radical extreme must entail the decentralization of planning and management. The characteristics of the model may be taken from the Hungarian experience. One may think of it simply as central planning without directive targets to enterprises. But that innocent-sounding formulation involves more than a simple modification of the centrally planned economy. For without the power to assign directive targets to enterprises, much of the fabric of central planning unravels. If enterprises cannot be required to produce according to directives, they cannot be held responsible for the delivery of specified intermediate materials and supplies, and the time-honoured system of material–technical supply must be largely abandoned. In the absence of directive targets, the criteria for evaluating enterprise performance must be modified, and it is then difficult to imagine any criterion other than some suitably modified form of profit. But if profit is to serve as the dominant criterion of performance, it will become the effective objective function for management, and it is then necessary to assure that the prices and costs in terms of which decisions are made are reasonably reflective of marginal social benefits and costs. That must entail the abandonment of forty years of centralized administration of average-cost-plus-normal-profit pricing. Similar changes would have to be introduced in the management of the labour market, the financial system, and in other parts of the economy.

Party and government control of the economy would very likely continue to be maintained in several areas. First, most investment, particularly investment in social overheads and in new plant and equipment, would continue to be a central function, and it would become the most powerful instrument for determining both the rate of investment and the direction of growth. Investment would be financed by taxation, on profits and personal income, and also on the basis of a capital charge and depreciation allowance. That is, the state would continue to own all productive assets, and would require a return on them from the collectives that hold them in trust. Incentives would be derived from some profit-sharing plan.

Secondly, the state would continue to maintain an interest in prices, primarily in order to prevent excessive use of market power to maintain monopoly prices. To the extent that the objective of state policy would be to trade some efficiency for equity or for some other social goal, the option of price regulation would be maintained for that purpose as well. The legitimacy of selective state price control would be based not only on state power in general but on the state ownership of the assets of enterprises. That is, the state continues not only to own the enterprise but to exercise national sovereignty.

Third, it is safe to say that the Soviet leadership will have very little interest in supporting self-management or other forms of worker control. The more delicate problem is the policy to be taken towards the possible increase in involuntary unemployment.

Fourth, income taxation (or perhaps consumption taxation, which would make more sense in an investment-conscious economy) would be relied upon to regulate income distribution. Commodity taxation could be employed for financing public expenditures, but it could not be used to regulate the powerful new entrepreneurial forces that (one would hope) would arise and would tend to widen the income distribution. For if the Radical Model succeeds in generating vigorous entrepreneurship, there will be large incomes to be earned in eliminating disequilibria in the centrally planned economy. The function of eliminating disequilibria has been one of the main economic responsibilities of the Party in the past (Grossman, 1983). The income distribution problems will be particularly pressing during the transition period because of the large disequilibria inherited from the period of central planning that have not yet been diminished by market forces.

Turning to the question of how the Soviet economy might fare under the Radical Model, one must begin with such hard evidence as we have on that type of system operating in another country. The form of radical decentralization that the Soviets are most likely to draw upon is the New Economic Mechanism introduced in Hungary in 1968. One conclusion is clear; Hungary has produced no Economic Miracle. When the East European countries are ranked by order of their long-term growth rates, Hungary comes at about the centre of the group, behind such less developed countries as Romania and Bulgaria, as one would expect (Marer, 1977). Nor has that relative position changed, for while Hungary's growth rate increased in the years following the 1968 reform, so did that of most of the other countries that retained their central planning systems (Portes, 1977). Per capita consumption increased during 1970–75, but that was also the case in Romania during the same period. It is true, however, that Hungary was particularly hard hit by adverse changes in its markets abroad, and suffered from a number of costly policy errors while learning to control the new economic mechanism. Under the circumstances, Portes concludes, Hungary probably did better than it would have done under the old central-planning system.

One suspects that the statistical record may have missed something important. Most knowledgeable observers, including Hungarian economists who tend to be among the most severe critics of their own economy, report that without question there has been a considerable improvement in the quality of goods and services generally. The usual formulation is that the growth-rate performance has not been distinctive *but* the quality of goods and services has increased greatly. An alternative formulation might be that the quality of goods and services has increased greatly *but* the growth-rate performance has not been distinctive. If a significant quality change can be attributed to the system change, that is no mean claim. Perhaps the judicious conclusion is that the Hungarian economy performs generally better under the new mechanism but not by an order of magnitude. Certainly one hears no Hungarian pining for the good old days.

Hungary is no Japan. But then again the USSR is no Hungary, and one must entertain the possibility that the new economic mechanism in the USSR might perform better or worse than in Hungary. In one major respect the USSR is like Hungary. The Hungarian reform has been limited by a set of political considerations, which include a commitment to extensive job security and to strict limitations on income differentiation (Granick, 1973; Portes, 1977). Those same considerations are likely to prevail in the USSR and to limit the effectiveness of the reform in the same ways. The USSR has one potential advantage in the size of the domestic market, which could yield some of the benefits of inter-enterprise competition, but job security and income differentiation concerns could spill the wind out of the sails of competition. There is no cogent reason for expecting the USSR to perform better under this type of decentralization than Hungary.

There is one reason, however, why the USSR might be expected to perform worse. Western analysts have been struck by the vigour with which the patterns of the former centrally planned system reasserted themselves under the new Hungarian decentralized system. Hungary, however, had lived under central planning for only two decades. The managers, politicians and economists who engineered the reform of 1968 had lived the first thirty-odd years of their lives in a market economy. They found no mystery in a system in which no one tells the enterprise what it should produce and from whom it is to obtain its supplies. Many, we may also suppose, had conceived a certain fondness for aspects of that kind of economic arrangement, socialists though they are. In the USSR, by contrast, hardly a soul is now alive who remembers such a system. The notion that somehow the 'right' amount of coal can be produced even though no one tells the coalmines how much to produce is not an idea that is easily grasped if one has not lived it. I can cite two pieces of evidence for this view. One is a recent study by the International Communications Agency (ICA) on Soviet perceptions of the US, based on interviews with Americans who have had close associations with Soviet officials at high levels of authority. The study reports that 'Soviets who study the US have long assumed that hidden somewhere in the economic system is the key to American success, and that there must be a planning mechanism for the American private sector'. Even Soviet experts on American management and industry 'seem puzzled that the private sector has no apparent planning center. They know that the system works, but they are puzzled how' (Guroff, 1980). The second piece of evidence is the observation by a prominent émigré authority that most Soviet economists sincerely believe the price mechanism to be only a temporary necessity (Katsenelenboigen, 1978, p. 15). While there is a sophisticated minority who have learned to comprehend the nature of general-equilibrium decentralized systems, they are not the ones who will be managing the government and economy. The 'legacies' of the centrally planned period that Neuberger once identified in the case of Yugoslavia have been found to operate in the Hungarian economy as well (Hewett, 1981; Neuberger, 1968). The legacies of a half-century of central planning must be expected to be particularly restrictive. Kenneth Boulding once remarked that the bus from capitalism to socialism runs only during the early stage of capitalism. If a nation misses the bus, capitalism is there to stay. The same may be said of the bus from central planning to socialist markets. The Hungarians caught it in time, but central planning has endured so long in the USSR that the Soviets may have missed the bus.

There are two aspects to the legacies that one structure bequeaths to another. The first may be described as the human-capital aspect. In moving from one technology to another, while new capital is being built up in the form of knowledge and experience in the operation of the new technology, old capital is being lost as knowledge and experience of the old technology disappears. That process applies to social as well as physical technology. There is a vast stock of human capital that supports the operation of a decentralized economy that is lost after a few generations of not having been learned and used.

The second feature of the legacy is the large number of points in the old system that are in disequilibrium with respect to the requirements of the new system. I refer to the structure of productive capacity relative to the structure of the demand for output under the new system, and similarly with the structure of wages and prices. Because of supply inelasticities, many of those disequilibria are likely to be large, and to endure for relatively long periods of time, making for potentially large rental incomes. It is doubtful that the market processes under the new system could readily close those disequilibria without the emergence of very large inequities. After a half-century of central planning, those disequilibria in the USSR are likely to be of massive dimensions, and therefore a source of a great deal of social tension and economic strain.

For these reasons the Radical Model established in the USSR may not secure even that modest improvement in economic performance that it secured in Hungary. And yet there could hardly fail to be some gains in the quality of goods and services, similar to that reported in Hungary. The requirement that a producing unit be obliged to decide what to produce by consulting potential purchasers rather than by instructions from the ministry – which is the heart of the model – cannot fail to discipline management to respond actively to demand, providing that demand is not in excess. To the extent that it is politically difficult in socialist countries (and increasingly in capitalist) to permit the market to determine the penalties for failure, the tightness of that discipline is attenuated, but it is likely to prevail to a greater extent than under the central planning of output. Similarly the enterprise as purchaser – now both obliged to and permitted to seek out its own sources of supply – is likely to assign a higher place to cost considerations in its calculations. These observations apply also to the quality of innovation. If the decision to introduce a new process or product is genuinely that of the enterprise, it cannot fail to be more resistant than in the past to pressures to adopt inferior work produced by the R & D centres, and more inclined to seek out and introduce genuinely superior innovations. Again, to the extent that the politics of distributional equity cuts into the rewards for risk taking, the beneficial effect of the Radical Model on innovation will be attenuated.

Perhaps that is as far as speculation should be permitted to range. My judgement is that the USSR under the Radical Model would experience some benefit in the quality of its goods and services and in the rate and quality of technological innovation, but to a degree not quite equal to the modest gain experienced by Hungary.

THE LIBERAL MODEL

I call the Radical Model by that name because it involves the total abandonment of directive target planning. From the present Soviet perspective it is difficult to get more radical than that without being downright revolutionary. This last model is properly called Liberal because it conserves the traditional planning methods for most of the economy while liberalizing the present restrictions on private initiative.

It might also be called a neo–NEP model. Like that first great reform, it would come as a response to mounting economic difficulties. In the present case those difficulties are not nearly as critical as they were at that time, but then neither is the scope of this reform as extensive as the earlier one. The heart of this reform, however, is the same as that of the other: the withdrawal of the socialized central-planning sector to the 'commanding heights' of the economy. This time, however, the 'commanding heights' comprise the overwhelming portion of the whole economy. Its boundaries may be demarcated by whatever limits the leadership finds politically and economically optimal. Within those boundaries the economy operates as in the past, with enterprise directive targets, material–technical supply, centralized price administration and the rest.

Outside of those boundaries, however, individuals or small groups would be encouraged to engage in any economic activity for private profit. They would be permitted to employ the labour of other people; wage rates would presumably not fall below the levels in the state sector, which remains an employer of last resort. The size of the private enterprises would be limited by law; initially the limit would be fairly small, but if the reform were successful the limit might be raised in the course of time. Enterprises would be permitted to own capital and to rent land from state agencies. They would be required to file periodic reports with the Central

Statistical Agency and with the Ministry of Finance, on the basis of which taxes would be levied.

Neo–NEP enterprise would flourish in those activities in which smallness of scale has a comparative advantage. First is the consumer-service sector; food services, home-care services (clothing repair, washing and cleaning, plumbing, carpentry) and appliance repairs. Second is handicrafts and the manufacture of consumer goods in short supply (warm winter clothing) or of higher quality than is produced by state industry. Third is all manner of retailing services; small shops that purchase both state-produced and private-produced goods and compete with the retail services provided by government shops. Fourth is construction work by small *artels* for both private persons, cooperatives, and private and state enterprises. Fifth is special-order and job-lot production work for industry. Sixth is the supply of specialized services to industry, like R & D and technical consulting. The supply of goods and services to industry is particularly important because it would provide the flexibility that state planning is unable to offer. It may serve the function that small-scale enterprise serves in the modern oligopolistic capitalist economy. In Japan, for example, small-scale enterprises take up the slack of the business cycle and serve as valuable supplementary sources of supply for the large corporations. In the US the small enterprise is often the vehicle for innovations that, if successful, are subsequently bought up by larger firms. It is very likely, as Dr Kvasha (1967) argued, that the absence of the small enterprise is a significant gap in Soviet organizational structure for the promotion of innovation and for industrial efficiency generally, a gap that must have widened since the Production Association reform.

Several critical decisions would have to be made on how the neo–NEP sector would transact with the state sector. The first is the conditions under which private enterprise may purchase materials and equipment from state enterprises. One possible arrangement is that the physical-output targets of state enterprises be divided into two parts, the quantity to be delivered to other state enterprises, and the quantity to be sold to private enterprise. The state deliveries would be handled by the planning agencies by use of the standard method of material balances, while the deliveries to private industry would be handled on the basis of market demand analysis. The deliveries to private industry may thus serve as a useful balancing instrument for the central planners. Suppose for example, that in the first trial balance of wood nails, the planners find that the state industry's demand for nails exceeds the supply proposed in the draft of the enterprise production plans.

Balance could then be attained simply by reducing the quantities that the planners had originally allocated to private enterprises and increasing the quantities allocated to state enterprises. The consequence could be that in that year private industry would have to scramble for nails, develop substitutes, or reduce its output; or resort to bribery, to which we will return presently.

Second, a decision would have to be made on the prices of transactions between state and private enterprises (transactions between private enterprises and consumers need not be regulated). One approach would be to employ a purchase tax on sales by state to private enterprises. The former would receive the same price for its product regardless of whether it was sold to state enterprises or to a private enterprise, but the private purchaser would have to pay the state tax. The purpose of the tax is partly to recapture any subsidies in the enterprise wholesale price, and partly for the political purpose of strengthening the competitive position of state industry against private enterprise. That is to say, private enterprise would have to contribute more than a marginal gain to the economy in order to justify the ideological cost of tolerating it.

Third, the private retail network would provide a higher quality and larger range of many consumer goods and services than are available in the state stores. The higher prices may kindle popular hostility if it is felt that the private stores are 'crowding out' the distribution of state-supplied goods. It is therefore important that the state continue to supply the traditional array of consumer goods and services at conventional prices. They would continue to be rationed by queuing, while those whose incomes or preferences are different could purchase at the private stores.[3] Similarly, the state sector must continue to act as employer of last resort, as it in fact does now. Workers would not therefore be at the mercy of their employers as in a capitalist system, for if they are dissatisfied with the pay or working conditions in the private sector, their alternative is not unemployment.

For evidence on how the economy would perform under this model, one might go back to the experience of the original NEP. But the more relevant evidence is that of the present-day second economy. The lesson that is usually drawn from that peculiar institution is that the centrally planned economy tends to spawn corruption. The story may be told differently, however. The lesson of the second economy is that within a socialist system there is a vast store of initiative that cannot be tapped through the normal institutions of central planning. To benefit from that great productive potential, the economy must provide some institutional arrangement in which it can flourish in a socially responsible way. The introduction of a controlled domain of limited private enterprise would be such an arrangement.

Every participant in this conference can supply his own anecdotes on the kinds of initiative that burst forth even under the present inhibiting conditions. I shall mention only two that I have found particularly instructive. One is the case of the Fakel' firm. It was formed by a small group of engineers and scientists in Novosibirsk for the purpose of providing research, development and innovation services to industry on a spare-time basis. Operating out of a few dormitory rooms, they solicited contracts from enterprises, drawing upon consultants' services as needed from specialists in the area. In about four years they received 3.5 million roubles from 263 contracts, which they claim to have saved 35 million roubles for the economy, for which they received fees for themselves and their consultants. Their activities sparked an intense controversy, and they were finally forced to close down because of the objections of the State Bank and the Ministry of Finance (Löwenhardt, 1974). The second is the case of the agronomist I. Khudenko, who was given a free hand in farming a tract of unused state farm land. Operating under the form of an 'extended link', Khudenko and a few colleagues ran the operation virtually as a private farm with phenomenal success. The controversy was more bitter in this case and Khudenko was found guilty on criminal charges and died in prison in 1974 (Katsenelenboigen, 1978, p. 66). The vast store of tales like these testifies to the existence of a powerful innovative and productive potential in the nation that would flourish under the Liberal Model.

Like the Radical Model, the Liberal Model is that of a 'mixed' economy'. There is a critical difference between the two, however. The Radical Model is a mix of central planning and markets, but all enterprises are state enterprises. What is radical about it is the abandonment of directive target-planning of enterprises, which is the heart of Soviet-type central planning. The Liberal Model retains the traditional form of central planning for most of the economy. It is a mix of state enterprises and private enterprises. I would not quarrel with the view that a mix of that kind might be regarded as more radical than the abandonment of directive planning. The main point is that the two models reflect different judgements about the pathology of the Soviet socialist economy. The Radical Model reflects the view of the major body of Western economic theory of socialism deriving from Lange and Lerner. That theory is pre-occupied with issues of Pareto efficiency and looks upon markets as a way of increasing the efficiency of socialist economies. The

Liberal Model directs attention not to allocative efficiency but to something like Leibenstein's X-efficiency. It says, in effect, that the problem of centrally planned socialism is not in the central planning but in the socialism, or at least in the monopoly of socialist organizations. Concern with that issue, incidentally, can also be found in Lange (1938) in his remarks about the danger of the 'bureaucratization' of economic life even in his market model of socialism.[4]

If the evidence on the Radical Model is the experience of Hungary, the relevant evidence on the Liberal Model, I have found to my surprise, is the experience of the GDR. That stern government permitted private craftsmen to operate throughout its history, and while there was some retrenchment in 1972 by the nationalization of the larger private firms, small-scale production continued to be given the 'fullest support of the Socialist Unity Party and the state' (Scott, 1974, p. 196). In their judicious comparison of the performance of the two Germanys, Gregory and Leptin (1977) credit the toleration of private enterprise in handicraft, retail trade and agriculture in the GDR as one of the reasons for the success of the incentives policy of the country. The dismal state of Polish agriculture might be regarded as evidence of the failure of private enterprise in a socialist context, but the stronger argument is that the fault in that case was the gross mismanagement of agriculture policy by the national leadership. For the USSR under the Liberal Model, the prospect for agriculture is not full-scale private farming after the Polish example, but perhaps a full commitment to the 'link' as the basic unit of socialized agriculture. Like the 'team' in the People's Republic of China, the link can be made sufficiently small to restore one of the central elements of X-efficiency, namely, the direct association of one's income with one's effort. Along with the elevation of the link, the spirit of the Liberal Model requires that the state give full support to private subsidiary agriculture. The link and the private plot would constitute the kind of 'wager on the strong' with which an earlier Russian reformer – Peter Stolypin – had sought to release the peasant's initiative from the restraints of the commune.

Two issues that would have to be faced are corruption and income distribution. The first issue is not whether the Liberal Model will produce corruption. It certainly will. The question is rather whether corruption will be larger in scope and more detrimental than that which is presently generated under central planning. The answer is not at all self-evident. The large expansion in lawful opportunities for earning private incomes will increase the gains from the illegal diversion of state property to the private market. On the other hand to the extent that the private sector succeeds in closing the disequilibrium gaps, the volume of bribes currently demanded by custodians of state-owned goods in short supply will be reduced. Moreover the Liberal Model would convert into acceptable 'red markets' some of the variously coloured markets that Katsenelen-boigen (1978) has detailed, thus reducing the volume of corruption by defining as legal that which was formerly illegal. The principal objective of this model, however, is not simply to distribute already produced goods more efficiently but to stimulate the production of new goods and services that would not otherwise have been produced. Corruption in that kind of activity would have less undesirable social consequences than that which merely redistributes real income in favour of those who have access to goods and services in short supply. Hence it is quite possible that corruption will be less of a problem under the Liberal Model than under the present system.

More than any of the other models this one will test the limits of income inequality that the society is willing to tolerate. The period immediately following its adoption will generate the largest individual incomes because of the large disequilibria inherited from the present system. In the course of time, however, as the backlog of unrepaired TV sets is worked off and the supply of hand-knitted wool gloves expands, the initial transient windfall incomes will moderate in size. The eventual steady-state income differentiation may still be larger than the political system can tolerate. In that case it would be perfectly reasonable for the leadership to take measures to rein in the scope of the private sector. A society has the right to decide what combination of income and inequality it prefers. An informed social choice, however, requires that the price of greater equality be known. The experiment with the Liberal Model will provide both the leadership and the population with a clear measure of the price currently being paid, if there is such a price, for the prevailing degree of equality; and of the price that would have to be paid if the Liberal Model is eventually abandoned.

Finally, the Liberal Model has the virtue of administrative and political flexibility. The Radical Model would be difficult to implement in parts: to operate certain sectors without target planning while in other sectors traditional central planning prevails. As in Hungary, it is an all-or-nothing proposition. The Liberal Model, however, is infinitely divisible. Certain types of private production can be declared lawful while others remain unlawful as at present. If either the level of corruption or the degree of income differentiation should exceed the politically acceptable, the boundaries of the private sector can be constricted. The income distribution problem can be separately controlled by tax policies that can make whatever discriminations are thought to be desirable.

The longer any model endures, the greater are the interests that become vested and the greater the resistance to reversal of policy. But that risk is slight under the conditions of present-day Soviet society. One need only to think back to the original NEP to be convinced of the difference. At that time NEP was a risk of major proportions because the state-run commanding heights didn't command a very large part of the economy. The political fears of the Left were entirely justified; the strengthening of private enterprise in trade and small-scale industry, and particularly in an agriculture that engaged some 80 per cent of the population, could very well have eventually generated a political force to challenge the usurped power of the relatively small Communist party. The Liberal Model poses no such threat in Soviet society today. The ideological awkwardness would be small compared to the economic gain from what may be the most effective model for the Soviet economy of the future.

POLITICAL ISSUES

When the choice is finally made, the economic prospects under the various models will no doubt enter into consideration. But it is politics and not economics that will dictate the choice in the end. In reviewing the array of political forces I shall first discuss the political disposition of the major social groups, and then consider the political viability of each of the four models.

For the urban working class, there are two primary concerns; job security, and the level of consumption. The evidence for the latter comes primarily from the Polish experience, and we may err in transferring the lesson directly to the Russian working class, which may be much more compliant. There is no direct evidence that Soviet workers are prepared to go to the barricades over the price of meat, but the Soviet leadership acts as if they thought that might occur. What is more certain is that a decline in real income would at some point lead to an attenuation in incentives, with possibly worse consequences for productivity and growth.

The centrality of job tenure to the workers is evident in the longstanding inability of the Soviet leadership to find a politically acceptable way of redistributing workers among jobs. The Shchekino experiment, in which part of the wages of dismissed redundant workers was added to the wage fund of the remaining workers, was the boldest move to date in that direction, but it has not had a major impact. Evidently the prospect of dividing up the wages of their dismissed comrades did not prove to be an incentive sufficient to crack labour's solidarity on this issue. Soviet analysts of innovation regard the difficulty of dismissing technologically redundant workers as a major obstacle to innovation (Berliner, 1976, ch. 5). Nearer at hand is the evidence of the Hungarian reform, much of the potential of which had to be forgone out of a concern to avoid a clash with labour on this issue. The Yugoslav experience, on the other hand, testifies to the capability of at least one socialist government to survive extensive unemployment. But the Soviet leadership is probably correct in its own assessment that it is not an issue on which it would want to be tested.

The key to peasant sentiment is the private plot. That is the institution that is the focus of his potential political involvement, and alterations in the official status of that institution have a major impact on his material and psychic life. By contrast, the steady conversion of collective farms into state farms seems not to have aroused a ripple, suggesting that the difference between those two organizational forms has long since ceased to be salient to the peasants. One has the impression that farm life continues to be highly unattractive to young people who must be restrained from fleeing from it by social and legal pressures. The attachment to the private plot suggests that the peasants would be attracted by the possibility of greater individual autonomy over a larger piece of land. But they have had no experience with the fluctuations of farm prices and incomes that accompany that autonomy in uncontrolled markets, and it is not at all certain that they would gladly pay that price for a larger say over their own land.

The intelligentsia are likely to be the least resistant to change in the economic mechanism since the basis of their social position is least system-specific; there will be jobs for journalists and engineers under any likely economic arrangement, though the stars of some would rise while others fall. The liberal intelligentsia are likely to be disposed towards more decentralized systems that allow greater freedom for individual action. But the technical intelligentsia may well be disposed towards more conservative systems. Sharing with enterprise management the responsibility for trying to keep the trains running on time, and with no practical experience in the operation of decentralized systems, they are likely to see the solution in better planning, organization and management. Perhaps only among economists has there developed an understanding of decentralized systems and some attraction to them, but close observers regard their number to be rather small. For most economists Soviet means central planning (Katsenelenboigen, 1978).

Enterprise managers are second to none in their grumbling about the inefficiencies of the centrally planned economy within which they operate. The general view, however, is that their grumbling is of a highly conservative kind. They want the supply system to work better and the ministry to be less bureaucratic in attending to the needs of their enterprises. All the vibrations suggest that they are quite content in principle with a system in which they are told by someone else what to produce and where someone else has the responsibility for providing them with the inputs they require. It is doubtful that they would see much virtue in a system that required them to take the risks of guessing what unspecified customers would be willing to buy from them and that permitted other enterprises to steal away their customers. Doubtless they believe they merit higher incomes than they earn, but they are aware that the combination of their pay, perks, and prestige places them in the upper echelons of society. They have achieved as a class a form of job security they never attained under Stalin, when the rapid turnover of managers was a characteristic feature of their lives. Most have held their jobs for very long periods, a state of affairs that disposes them to both managerial and political conservatism. The question of the political power that management can muster in defence of its interests has been the subject of controversy (Azrael, 1966). The most recent test of that power was the introduction of Production Associations, which threatened a substantial number of enterprise directors with the loss of their authority to the general directors of the Associations. The evidence is mixed. Many Associations were indeed formed, and although initially a controversy broke out over the status of the directors of the merged enterprises, that status was eventually largely submerged (Berliner, 1976, pp. 136–43). On the other hand, the Production Association reform appears to be proceeding very slowly, and one of the reasons is thought to be the intense opposition of managers, as well as of some ministry personnel (Gorlin, 1976). The evidence is not conclusive because this reform divided the interests of managers; those who expected to be promoted to the general directorate of the Production Associations had a great deal to gain. Hence it cannot be thought of as an issue on which management would have a unified interest. Nevertheless the rearguard action mounted by what must have been a substantial number of managerial officials was evidently successful in retarding the pace of the reform and constricting its scope, perhaps permanently.

With respect to labour relations, the demise of the Shchekino experiment suggests that management has little stomach for the job of taking on labour in a campaign to cut costs by dismissing redundant labour. Nor would they gladly share their power with worker representatives under some form of genuine self-management or democratization of the workplace. The system of central planning and management thus makes for a very comfortable position for enterprise management; protecting them from workers' demands for participation that might arise under greater decentralization and relieving them of the responsibility to economize on labour in ways that would threaten workers' job security.

About the interests of the central management – the ministerial bureaucracy – there can be no doubt. They are to central planning as capitalists are to capitalism. Close to the pinnacle of power and prestige, they are as 'establishment' as one can get, save perhaps the Party. The more centralized the system of planning and management, the larger the power they wield. To be sure, under most conceivable models of socialism there will still be national economic ministries, for the state will always be obliged to implement national policies and to monitor the activities of enterprises; and for that purpose national bureaucracies are necessary. But to be a ministerial official under decentralized conditions is to be a much less substantial person.

This group is likely to be the strongest defender of the system of central planning and management against efforts at substantial change. Yet their power would be limited in a conflict with a strongly supported Party policy. The classic test was Khrushchev's Territorial Reorganization, which was directed against precisely this stratum of officialdom and virtually dismembered it, with large numbers of ministry officials being sent out to the provinces to staff the new territorial economic councils. Their return to office with the restoration of the ministries after Khrushchev's departure is evidence not of their power *per se* but of the growing awareness that that reorganization had been a failure and needed to be reversed. More recently their power has been tested again in what is reported to be extensive ministerial opposition to the Production Associations. That reform has created a class of new association managers presiding over much larger domains than the old enterprise managers and therefore much more substantial people who are less easily intimidated by ministerial power. Here too, however, the opposition was a rearguard action and the reform has been pushed through, although the slowing of its pace may be attributed to continued ministerial as well as managerial resistance (Gorlin, 1976).

I take it as self-evident that the Party and policy *apparat* must be regarded as conservative in economic matters. The same is probably true of the military officer corps, although it ought not to be surprising if the nature of their responsibilities lay them more open to alternatives. The responsibilities I have in mind are the maintenance of a fighting force equipped with the armaments required to defeat a coalition of countries all of whom are more technically advanced. No other group in Soviet society confronts foreign competition in so stark a form. I know of no evidence on the subject but it should not be surprising to learn that the military, in the vital quest for technological advance, and of necessity knowledgeable about the technological processes and products of its potential antagonists, might prove to be a force for greater autonomy at lower levels of the production system.

About the Politburo itself, three things may be said. First, in the short or medium term the composition of that body will change greatly. Precisely what the political–economic orientation of the new leadership will be is impossible to know, but it is a good bet that it will feel freer to entertain a wider range of alternatives than can be expected of the present leadership. Second, a younger leadership is likely to take a longer-run planning horizon and may therefore be more impelled to take action, drastic if it need be, to arrest the decline in growth and to 'get the economy moving again'. Third, any drastic action must be threatening to some substantial interests in the country. The new leadership will therefore have to establish a power base upon whom it can rely for support, as Khrushchev sought to rely on the provincial Party *apparat*. For these several reasons, of all the groups we have discussed in this review, the top Party leadership may be the most likely agent of change in the economic mechanism, carrying it out as a 'revolution from above'.

Among the national minorities, nationalist sentiments may conflict with class interests. Russified or Sovietized Party officials and managers are likely to see their interests in the same way that their Great Russian colleagues do. But where nationalist feelings run deep, centralization means Moscow which means Russian domination. A significant portion of the Party and managerial groups among the minorites are therefore likely to support decentralizing measures primarily because they will reduce the power of Moscow over their lives. The Yugoslav experience may appear to suggest the contrary; there the smaller Southern republics have promoted centralization while the larger Northern ones have pushed hard for a weakening of central government. One of the major factors in the Yugoslav case, however, is the division of the country among the less developed republics and the more developed. It is the poorer republics like Montenegro that have fought for centralization because the more powerful the central government the greater the redistribution of income and investment in their favour. For the same reason, the richer republics like Slovenia have supported increased republic power, as a means of slowing down what they regard as the draining of their resources for the support of the less productive republics to the South. The Soviet case is notably different, for at least two reasons. First, republic differences in per capita income and consumption are probably much smaller in the USSR than in Yugoslavia, although I know of no evidence on this question. Second, a number of the national minorities enjoy higher living standards than the Great Russians; particularly the Baltic nations and perhaps Georgia and Armenia as well. Nor are Central Asians notably far behind the Great Russians, if at all. Hence the special feature that operates in the Yugoslav case is not salient in the Soviet. The nationalist-minded members of the national minorities will see the issue not primarily in income distribution terms as in Yugoslavia but in political terms. From that perspective any reform that will reduce the power of Moscow will command support.

If this review of the interests of the relevant groups conforms even roughly with political reality, it implies that the Conservative Model is most likely to prevail unless one of two conditions obtains. One condition is that the rate of growth under that model fails to stabilize at a level above what was described earlier as the incentive threshold. If it falls below that level, the erosion of work incentives would trigger off new forces that would make for continued decline. Even if the economy did not yet fall to the political threshold, but certainly if it did, a change to another model would be inevitable. The second condition is that in the succession politics after Brezhnev a new and younger leader either (a) develops a power base strong enough to force a change over the opposition of major vested interests, or (b) wins the support of a major social group, Mao–like, by forcing a change that is strongly supported by that group.

We are not charged, in this conference, to foretell the future; to forecast, in this case, whether either of these conditions will in fact obtain. The probability is large enough, however, to pursue the question of which of the other models might be adopted if the Conservative Model is abandoned.

The strongest political support, it seems to me, can be marshalled in favour of the Reactionary Model. It is the alternative that does the least violence to the interests of the groups that are most closely tied to the regime – central and enterprise management, the Party *apparat*, the military and so forth. There would be some loss to these groups from the restrictions that are likely to be placed on the second economy. But the organized system of special shops would presumably be continued. The experience of the 1980 Polish workers' strike may lead to a reconsideration of the special shops, the abolition of which was one of the workers' demands. But political wisdom may dictate the retention of those privileges nonetheless, because it is precisely those social groups that would be most counted on to forestall such workers' action.

The Reactionary Model would also command strong ideological support from a variety of sources. There are first those Party loyalists for whom strong Party leadership and control of the economy are matters of deep conviction and are believed to be the only proper way to run a Marxist-Leninist society. Most observers hold that few people in Soviet society are motivated by Marxist-Leninist ideology today, and I do not dispute it. But the ideology I have in mind is not the grand socialist idealism associated with those revered names, but simply the set of ideas on the right way to manage the Soviet state and society that emerged from the Second World War. In any case, certainly much larger is that portion of the society that would support the Reactionary Model because it promises a return to a more orderly, less contentious, and perhaps simpler way of life. Though the words ring strange in Western ears, internal observers report a widespread nostalgia for the 'blessed' Stalinist times, when 'there was rigid discipline in the country, when there were no difficulties, for example with labor power' (Katsenelenboigen, 1978, p. 57). That this sentiment is also widely held among the élite was corroborated by the ICA survey, which found that while Soviet professionals are attracted to many features of American society, like access to information and freedom of travel, they 'believe that similar access by the Soviet *narod* (people) would unbalance the society' and that 'widespread freedoms would lead to chaos in society and perhaps undermine their own positions' (Guroff, 1980, p. 16).

How the *narod* would respond is harder to guess. It is likely that a strong law-and-order policy coupled with the usual combination of xenophobia, nationalism, anti-semitism and anti-intellectualism will command extensive populist support. The tightening of police controls will affect mostly intellectuals and 'speculators', and while there will be some loss in consumption levels from the curtailment of the second economy, it is the producers for those markets and not the consumers who will be dispatched to the camps. If, as I have argued above, the economy will perform somewhat better under the Reactionary Model, the extent of that loss may be small.

A critical question is the response to the tightening of labour discipline, which is a major condition for the economic success of the Reactionary Model. Certainly the programme would have to be presented as part of a great new national campaign, perhaps even packaged as a programme to raise the consumption level of the people. Something of the sort would be necessary to sustain the compulsion that would be required to pull workers away from the 'collective' in which they have worked all their lives and assign them to work in other enterprises and in other regions. In the short run there is a fair possibility that an imaginative political leadership can pull it off. In the longer run, however, it is more problematical.

The Radical Model runs counter to the interests of all the main groups that support the traditional regime. Most of the officials of the central planning and central management bureaucracy would be out of jobs. Enterprises would still require directors, but they are not likely to be the same persons who directed the factories in the past. As in Hungary, an effort is likely to be made to mollify the directors by assuring them of their job security under the new system (Granick, 1973). But the managers whose skills and outlook were cradled in a system of *mat-tekh-snabzhenie* (centralized supply of enterprise inputs) are not likely to survive in a genuinely decentralized system; particularly if, unlike the Hungarians, they have never lived in one. They are likely to resist this model as strongly as the central managers.

The workers are likely to perceive a decentralized system, correctly, as a threat to their job security. And as in Hungary, the regime would have to give such strong assurance on that score that one of the major potential benefits of decentralization would be lost. Similar assurances had to be given in Hungary (Granick, 1973), but because of its older legacies, the cost would be greater in the USSR.

In fact, in surveying the various interest groups, the only ones that are likely to support the Radical Model are the national minorities, a small group of economists and perhaps a smattering of liberal intelligentsia who would support any weakening of the central bureaucracy as a step towards more personal freedom. Perhaps if the model included some extensive decentralization of agriculture as well, it might also command the support of the peasantry.

If this judgement about the very weak support for the Radical Model is correct, it raises the interesting question of why the USSR is different from Hungary and Czechoslovakia. In the latter case decentralization had vast support in the country, including eventually large sections of the Party. In Hungary the support was perhaps not as extensive but one has the impression that decentralization nevertheless commanded fairly broad support. The difference, I suspect, is that in Eastern Europe the system of central planning is identified with rigid Party orthodoxy and, ultimately, with Russian domination of their countries. To smash central planning is to strike a blow at a Soviet-like Communist Party, and symbolically at the USSR. From this perspective, hostility to the USSR was an important political factor in enabling the leadership to marshall support in favour of decentralization. But if the USSR is vital in promoting the Radical Model elsewhere, who will be the USSR's USSR? Perhaps China.

If the Radical Model is to be adopted in the USSR, it will come about only because the small band of liberal economists have somehow got the ear of the new leader and persuaded him that it is the best course for both himself and for the country. But that, as we have argued above, would be a hard case to make, for the Hungarian performance has not (yet) been so successful that its effectiveness is beyond dispute, particularly for the USSR. If the leader nevertheless did decide that the Radical Model was the best course for the USSR, he must then face the prospect of engineering a revolution from above, for he will have no support from the conventionally loyal groups. Nor is he likely to turn, like Mao, to an unconventional group like the students in order to create a new power base. The military might conceivably be neutral on the technical issue of whether the decentralized model will outperform the centralized, but it will hardly rally around a leader who contemplates a new revolution in favour of decentralization. A revolution from above of this magnitude would require that the new leader first concentrate in his hands the personal power of a Stalin. On the other hand, Stalins don't decentralize.

It should now be evident why the Liberal Model would command much greater support than the Radical. No one loses his job, for the centrally planned sector operates largely as it did before. The Party leader who introduces that model will, moreover, have a new basis of support in both the producers in the new private sector and the consumers who will have access to a significantly improved range of goods and services. For if the assessment presented above should prove to be correct, the population will experience a sharp improvement in the quality of life, sharp enough to leave no doubt about the success of the policy and the person who gets the credit for it.

Among the political obstacles, one thinks first of the ideological. But an imaginative leadership should have little difficulty presenting the model in a favourable light, providing that Mr Suslov has passed from the scene. It is, after all, modelled on the NEP, and what Soviet leader would not wish to be the one to pick up the baton of Lenin? Moreover the NEP is associated in the public mind with a period of hope and prosperity; I have heard even young people refer to it as the 'golden age' of Soviet history. The Liberal Model could also supply the missing part of an ideological puzzle that has been created by the adoption of the notion that the USSR has entered the new historical stage of 'mature socialism'. It is clear that central planning was the appropriate economic model during the stage of the building of socialism, but now that socialism has entered the stage of maturity the historical process should be expected to produce a new set of production relations. The dialectician should expect a negation of the negation, producing a social formation similar to the older one but on a new and higher plane. Viewed from that perspective, central planning was the negation of private enterprise. The negation of central planning can reasonably be thought to be a new form of private enterprise, but on a higher plane in the sense that it is now socially responsible because it is embedded in a mature socialist society. Moreover since the transition to mature socialism is accompanied by the scientific-technical revolution, the historically progressive economic system is one that enables the society to reap the fullest benefits of that revolution. Central planning was an appropriate economic model in a period in which the task of socialism was to adopt the advanced technology of the time that was already known and in operation in the capitalist world. That historical task having been completed, a new economic model is required that not simply adopts known technology but also produces yet unknown technological knowledge in the age of the scientific–technical revolution. Central planning is the historically correct form for applying known technology, but planning the yet unknown is a qualitatively different task. Hence the rise of a new synthesis in which the private initiative of socialist men and women serves to promote technological innovation in the matrix of a centrally planned socialist economy.

I conclude that the prospects for change in the system of planning and management depends on the performance of the economy under the Conservative Model. If the growth rate should stabilize at a level that may be low but that nevertheless exceeds the incentive threshold, that model will be retained and the century will limp quietly to its end. Chronic cases do not normally evoke extreme measures. Only acute attacks, like depressions or rebellions, galvanize a society into such measures. If the Conservative Model cannot stabilize the growth rate even at that low level, the accumulation of social and political pressures will propel the leadership into either the Reactionary or the Liberal Model. Both are likely to improve the performance of the economy, but the greater potential lies with the latter. If the counsels of political prudence prevail, however, the lot will fall to the former.

NOTES

1 The decree deals not only with the planning system but with the management system as well. The major new departure with respect to management is the introduction of a new success indicator – normative net value of output. The intent of the new indicator is to eliminate the benefit that enterprises derive from their assortment plans in favour of products with a large proportion of purchased inputs.

2 *Pravda*, 28 November 1979, Transl. in *Current Digest of the Soviet Press*, vol. 31, no. 48:8, 26 December 1979.

3 It may not be possible to mollify populist egalitarian hostility to the two types of stores. One of the demands of the Polish workers in the 1980 strike was the abolition of the 'special shops' open only to the élite. The private enterprise shops would be open to all purchasers, but they may kindle resentment nonetheless.

4 There is a third position, which may be taken as the Yugoslav interpretation. This interpretation shares the Radical view that markets are superior to central planning, and it shares the Liberal view that enterprises should not be state-owned. It parts company with the Liberal view, however, in holding that the best alternative to state-owned enterprise is not private enterprise but self-managed enterprise. The notion of worker self-management is so far out of the bounds of the thinkable in the USSR that I have not explored that model here.

REFERENCES

Azrael, Jeremy R. (1966), *Managerial Power and Soviet Politics*, Cambridge, Mass: Harvard Univ. Press.

Berliner, Joseph S. (1976), *The Innovation Decision in Soviet Industry*, Cambridge, Mass: MIT Press.

Bond, Daniel L. and Levine, Herbert S. (1983), 'An Overview' in Abram Bergson and Herbert S. Levine (eds), *The Soviet Economy Toward the year 2000*, London: Allen and Unwin.

East European Economies Post-Helsinki (1977), Papers, Joint Econ. Comm., US Congress. Washington DC: Govt. Printing Office.

Gorlin, Alice C. (1976), 'Industrial Reorganization: The Associations' in *Soviet Economy in a New Perspective*, Papers, pp. 162–88, Joint Econ. Comm., US Congress. Washington DC: Govt Printing Office.

Granick, David (1973), 'The Hungarian Economic Reform', *World Politics*, vol. 25, no. 4, pp. 414–29.

Gregory, Paul, and Leptin, Gert (1977), 'Similar Societies under Differing

Economic Systems: The Case of the Two Germanys', *Soviet Studies*, vol. 29, October, pp. 519–42.

Grossman, Gregory (1983), 'The Party as Manager and Entrepreneur' in Gregory Guroff and Fred V. Carstensen (eds.), *Entrepreneurship in Russia and the Soviet Union*, Princeton: Princeton University Press.

Guroff, Gregory (1980), 'Soviet Perceptions of the US: Results of a Surrogate Interview Project', Washington, DC: Internat. Communications Agency, 27 June.

Hewett, Edward A. (1981), 'The Hungarian Economy: Lessons of the 1970s and Prospects for the 1980s' in *East European Economic Assessment*, Papers, Joint Econ. Comm., US Congress, Washington, DC: Govt. Printing Office.

Katsenelenboigen, Aron (1978), *Studies in Soviet Economic Planning*, White Plains: M.E. Sharpe.

Kvasha, Ia. (1967), 'Kontsentratsiia proizvodstva i mel'kaia promyshlennost', *Voprosy ekonomiki*, no. 5.

Lange, Oskar (1938), 'On the Economic Theory of Socialism' in B. Lippincott (ed.) *On the Economic Theory of Socialism*. Minneapolis: Univ. of Minnesota Press.

Löwenhardt, John (1974), 'The Tale of the Torch – Scientists–Engineers in the Soviet Union', *Survey*, vol. 20, no. 4 (93), Autumn, pp. 113–21.

Marer, Paul (1977), 'Economic Performance, Strategy and Prospects in Eastern Europe' in *East European Economies . . .*, pp. 523–66

Neuberger, Egon (1968), 'Central Planning and Its Legacies: Implications for Foreign Trade' in Alan A. Brown and E. Neuberger (eds), *International Trade and Central Planning*. Berkeley: Univ. of California Press.

Portes, Richard (1977), 'Hungary: Economic Performance, Policy and Prospects' in *East European Economies . . .*, pp. 766–815.

Rumer, Boris (1980), 'The "Second" Agriculture in the USSR', Mimeo, Russian Research Center, Harvard University.

Schroeder, Gertrude E. (1979), 'The Soviet Economy on a Treadmill of "Reforms" ' in *Soviet Economy in a Time of Change*, Papers, Joint Econ. Comm., US Congress, Washington, DC: Govt Printing Office, pp. 312–40.

Schroeder, Gertrude E. (1983), 'Consumption' in Abram Bergson and Herbert S. Levine (eds), *The Soviet Economy Toward the Year 2000*, London: Allen and Unwin.

Scott, Hilda (1974), *Does Socialism Liberate Women: Experiences from Eastern Europe*, Boston: Beacon Press.

Zielinski, Janusz G. (1973), *Economic Reforms in Polish Industry*, London: Oxford Univ. Press.

Part II

Technological Progress

6   The Static Efficiency of the Soviet Economy*
1964

In the discussion of economic efficiency, all roads lead back to Pareto. The optimality criterion directs us to seek for evidence that permits us to judge whether the bundle of goods produced is such that no other attainable bundle could contain more of some goods and no less of any other goods. Two types of evidence can be marshalled. The first is theoretical in character and is based on the conditions that must be satisfied if an optimal bundle is to be obtained. With no empirical data at all, for example, if we knew that the methods of price formation were such that prices could not be expected to correspond to marginal rates of transformation, we could conclude that insofar as prices governed resource allocation, that allocation could not be optimal. The second method is based on empirical data. If we found evidence that the system tended to leave productive resources unused, or used in less productive employments, or that output was produced which could not be sold, we could again conclude that the allocation was less than optimal.

A great deal of evidence can now be drawn upon for analyzing sources of inefficiency in the Soviet economy from both the theoretical and empirical points of view. Studies of the methods of price formation have directed our attention to the consequences of the use of average instead of marginal costs, of failure to account for interest and obsolescence (until very recently), of the complex system of multiple pricing, and so forth. We have also a considerable number of empirical studies of price and cost relations, of the consequences of physical planning with material balances, and of the results of the system of success indicators, and so on. It would

*_The American Economic Review_, vol. LIV:3, May 1964, pp. 480–89.

be a feasible approach to my topic to marshall all the evidence of inefficiency and present it as a sort of tally sheet. The trouble, however, is that there is no evident way of actually tallying it up. And short of a technique of tallying, it would remain nothing more than an anecdotal account, even though quantified in parts. However suitable such a technique might be for presenting a legal brief or a political tract, the amassing of pieces of anecdotal evidence is no substitute for a summary calculation. One wild price would serve as well as a thousand to establish that the system was less than perfectly efficient, but neither one nor a thousand would answer the question, 'How inefficient?'.

For I take it as evident that no real economic system is perfectly efficient. It is indeed of interest to analyze the peculiar sources of inefficiency in this or that economy, but such analysis can provide no summary evaluation of the performance of a system of economic organization. Rather than deal with the sources of inefficiency of the Soviet economy, I regard my task to be an evaluation of the overall efficiency of the system.

It would be possible to confine this task to the Soviet economy alone, but the results would be difficult to interpret. Suppose, for instance, we knew of a certain mechanical system that its efficiency was 20 per cent. Does it represent satisfactory performance or unsatisfactory? The answer will depend on the kind of machine and the efficiency of other machines designed for the same purpose. If it were a diesel engine, we would say it was a rather poor machine, for diesel engines have been developed with an efficiency of 40 per cent. If it were a thermo-electric generator, we would say that it was remarkably good, for existing generators operate in the range of 1 to 10 per cent. In like fashion, in order to interpret the significance of any indicator of the efficiency of the Soviet economy, we should have to have some notion of what is par for the economic course in general. For this purpose, I have selected the United States to serve as a standard of comparison.

One might be able to adapt a Paretian approach to a comparative study of efficiency, but there are certain difficulties. Pareto was, after all, an engineer, and it is not difficult to recognize the parentage of the production possibilities curve in the principle of the conservation of energy. Indeed, all engineering efficiency formulae are based on the notion that there is some absolute maximum quantum of output that can ideally be got out of a system. But the maximum output that can be got out of an economic system can only be established with respect to the assumptions one might wish to make about the ideal economic system, or indeed the ideal social system. For example, the production possibilities curve would have one position if we assumed a highly centralized planning system; another if we assumed a decentralized one; it would have one position if we took the present managerial incentive system as given; another if we assumed a different one. It would vary according to whether we assumed a better pricing system or the present one, greater freedom for private arbitrage activity or less, enlargement of the private household sector of agriculture or curtailment, and so forth. Depending on the assumptions one is prepared to make about the ideal system, the given system would turn out to have a number of different indices of efficiency. It would, moreover, be impossible to compare the efficiency of different types of economic systems, for the efficiency of each would be measured relative to its own ideal, and the ideals are not likely to be commensurable.

There is one final problem with an ideal output approach. One might find two economies perched precisely on their production possibilities curves, indicating that both were perfectly efficient in terms of their respective possibilities; and yet Economy I may produce a greater volume of output than Economy II for equivalent inputs. One might wish to interpret this as indicating that Economy II is getting as much out of its inputs as it can be expected to get under its present form of organization, but that if it were to change its organization to that of Economy I, it might get a greater output for the same inputs. The analysis of this case would require us to go well beyond the Paretian concept of efficiency.

Since the production possibilities approach is so protean to the grasp, I have decided to reject it in favour of a different attack on productive efficiency. The situation is this: An economy at (time or place) I produces a certain output P_I with certain inputs. At (time or place) II it produces a different output P_{II} with different inputs. The question to be asked is, what would the output at II have been ($\bar{P}_{II}$) had it been produced with the same efficiency as at I but with the inputs of II? The ratio of $\bar{P}_{II}$ to P_{II} will be our index of the relative efficiency of II compared to I. It is only productive efficiency that is to be measured here; the problem of allocative efficiency will be conspicuously ignored.

Before proceeding with the analysis, it would be well to turn to the data in Table 6.1. Value data are at 1955 prices, converted into roubles or dollars by 1955 conversion ratios. The capital stock figures are gross; that is, they constitute the 1955 cost of replacing the 1960 stock of physical assets by new but otherwise identical units. The US labour force data include employed and unemployed, while the Soviet figures are average annual employment. Involuntary Soviet unemployment is probably not large enough to make much difference (although involuntary Soviet employment may

Table 6.1   Outputs and labour and capital inputs, 1960

| | A. Basic Data | | | |
| | Original Prices | | Converted Prices | |
	USSR	US	USSR	US
1. GNP (billion roubles or dollars)	1,300 R (1,730 R)	$423 ($441)	$226 ($300)	4,870 R (5,080 R)
2. Capital stock (billion roubles or dollars)	2,546 R (2,965 R)	$1,400 ($1,513)	$509 ($593)	9,800 R (10,590 R)
3. Labour (million man years)	57.9 (95.7)	64.8 (70.7)	57.9 (95.7)	64.8 (70.7)

| | B. USSR as % of US | |
	At Dollar Values	At Rouble Values
4. GNP	53.5 (68.0)	26.6 (34.1)
5. Capital	36.4 (39.1)	26.0 (29.7)
6. Labour	89.3 (134)	89.3 (134)
7. GNP per unit of labour	59.9 (50.7)	29.8 (25.2)
8. GNP per unit of capital	147.0 (174.0)	102.2 (115.0)

Sources and Explanations: See appendix.
Notes: Figure in parentheses refer to the total economy. The others refer to the non-farm economy.

Soviet GNP at original prices is gross of turnover taxes and subsidies. An attempt was made to eliminate the effect of turnover taxes and subsidies in the converted values. See appendix.

make a difference from a welfare point of view). The figures in parentheses refer to the total economy; the others to the non-farm economy. Sources and details are discussed in the appendix.

Section B of the table presents the percentage relations between the USSR and the US for corresponding items. Because of the index number effect, the Soviet value magnitudes are larger relative to the US when both are valued at dollar prices than when rouble prices are used. For the non-farm GNP, the Soviet percentage is less than for total GNP, reflecting the relatively large proportion of Soviet output originating in agriculture.

The difference between the non-farm and the total capital stocks is not as great as the difference between the non-farm and total GNP. This reflects the relatively less capital-intensive organization of Soviet agriculture. The total Soviet labour force is 34 per cent greater than that of the US, but the non-farm labour force is only 89.3 per cent of that of the US, again reflecting the relative labour-intensity of Soviet agriculture.

Rows 7 and 8 of Table 6.1 present the single-factor productivity ratios implied in the basic data. Soviet labour productivity (row 7) is in all cases less than that of the US, although in the non-farm sector it is relatively higher as one would expect. The capital productivity figures reverse the picture (row 8). Since the Soviet capital stock falls short of the US by more than Soviet output falls short of US output, Soviet capital productivity is higher than that of the US. The Soviets get 47 per cent (74 per cent) greater output per unit of capital than the US in dollar terms and 2 per cent (15 per cent) more in rouble terms.

The nature of the task of computing relative efficiency is now clear. The USSR produces a smaller output than the US, but it does so by using considerably less capital and somewhat less labour (in the non-farm economy; in the total economy it uses more labour). The relative efficiency of the USSR therefore depends on the weights assigned to labour and capital. The choice of weights, which is the crucial decision, reflects the assumption one makes about the shape of the production functions.

Using John Kendrick's[1] method for our first set of computations, the weights are the relative factor shares of labour and capital. By assuming that the factors are paid the value of their marginal product and that these factor payments exhaust the product, Kendrick requires his production function to be homogeneous of degree one. By using constant product and factor prices, the production isoquants and the product transformation functions are treated as if they were linear. Hence the production function is of the form $P = aL + bK$. The relative efficiency of Economy II to Economy I is then given by the formula:

$$\frac{P_{II}/P_I}{(L_{II}/L_I)\cdot\alpha_I + (K_{II}/K_I)(1 - \alpha_I)}$$

where α_I *and* $1 - \alpha_I$ are the factor shares of labour and capital in Economy I.

In adapting the formula to our purposes, one must heed Moorsteen's caution that 'the input index employed clearly must refer to inputs that are both sufficient and necessary to produce the outputs measured by the output index'.[2] This condition is satisfied

Table 6.2   Soviet productive efficiency as % of US

	Rouble-valued Outputs, Dollar-valued Inputs	Dollar-valued Outputs Rouble-valued Inputs
$P = aL + bK$		
US weights ($\alpha = 0.8$	$E_1 = 33.8\ (29.8)$	
Soviet weights:		
$i = 8\%$ ($\alpha = .75$ non-farm, .8 total)		$E_2 = 64.1\ (60.2)$
$i = 20\%$ ($\alpha = 0.53$ non-farm, .60 total)		$E_2 = 90.0\ (73.7)$
$P = bL^{\alpha}K^{(1-\alpha)})$		
$\alpha = 0.8$	$E_3 = 35.6\ (32.3)$	$E_4 = 76.6\ (69.0)$
$\alpha = 0.7$	$E_3 = 39.0\ (36.5)$	$E_4 = 86.6\ (80.8)$
$\alpha = 0.6$	$E_3 = 42.6\ (41.4)$	$E_4 = 98.0\ (94.5)$
$\alpha = 0.5$	$E_3 = 46.7\ (46.8)$	$E_4 = 118.9\ (111.0)$

if the output index uses the prices of one country and the input index uses the prices of the other. (See Moorsteen for the proof.) Applying this condition to Kendrick's formula yields two indexes of relative Soviet efficiency:

$$E_1 = \frac{\dfrac{\sum p_{su}q_{su}}{\sum p_{su}q_{us}}}{\left(\dfrac{L_{su}}{L_{us}}\right)\alpha_{us} + \left(\dfrac{\sum k_{su}r_{us}}{\sum k_{us}r_{us}}\right)(1 - \alpha_{us})}\ ;$$

$$E_2 = \frac{\dfrac{\sum p_{us}q_{su}}{\sum p_{us}q_{us}}}{\left(\dfrac{L_{su}}{L_{us}}\right)\alpha_{su} + \left(\dfrac{\sum k_{su}r_{su}}{\sum k_{us}r_{su}}\right)(1 - \alpha_{su})}$$

where k refers to physical capital assets, r is the asset price, $\alpha_{us} = .8$, $\alpha_{su} = .8$ when return to Soviet capital is assumed to be

8 per cent, and α_{su} = .6 when return to Soviet capital is 20 per cent. See appendix for sources.

E_1 = 33.8 per cent (29.8 per cent); and E_2 = 64.1 per cent (60.2 per cent) with Soviet returns to capital at 8 per cent, and 90.0 per cent (73.7 per cent) with Soviet returns to capital at 20 per cent (Table 6.2).

Index E_1 has the following meaning: Assume that both countries have linear isoquants with slopes proportional to US factor prices, and linear transformation functions with slopes proportional to Soviet output prices; then if each country had used the inputs of the other, Soviet output would have amounted to 33.8 per cent of US output. E_2 has a similiar meaning, except that the input and output prices are reversed. The explanation of most of the large difference between the two results is to be found in the effect of pricing output at dollars or roubles.

The chief defect of a Kendrick-type of index for our purposes is that, like all fixed-weight indexes, it treats the underlying production and transformations functions as if they were linear. In fact the linearity assumption is only an approximation of the actual but unknown shape of the functions in the neighbourhood of the observed points. But one would probably be on safer ground to assume that the production function at least is characterized by a diminishing marginal rate of substitution among factors. Perhaps the least offensive way of incorporating this property is to replace Kendrick's production function by one of the Cobb-Douglas variety, $P = bL^{\alpha}K^{1-\alpha}$. The function retains Kendrick's assumption of constant returns to scale, but now the observed inputs can slide along nice convex isoquants instead of being forced to move along straight lines. It would be pleasant if some concavity could also be impressed on the product transformation functions, but linearity will have to continue to hold sway in that domain.

Assuming the Cobb-Douglas function, if we are given one observation on P, L and K, then for any assumed value of α the parameter b is determnined and the whole production surface defined. It is then possible to predict what the output would be, for any α, if a different set of inputs were used. Bearing Moorsteen's theorem in mind, we can thus construct two new indexes of efficiency, both of the form

$$\frac{P_{II}/P_I}{\left(\dfrac{L_{II}}{L_I}\right)^{\alpha I} \left(\dfrac{K_{II}}{K_I}\right)^{(1-\alpha I)}} .$$

E_3 uses Soviet price weights in the numerator and US factor prices in the denominator, while E_4 uses the prices in reverse:

$$E_3 = \dfrac{\dfrac{\sum p_{su}q_{su}}{\sum p_{su}q_{us}}}{\left(\dfrac{L_{su}}{L_{us}}\right)^{\alpha_{us}} \left(\dfrac{\sum k_{su}r_{us}}{\sum k_{us}r_{us}}\right)^{(1-\alpha_{us})}};$$

$$E_4 = \dfrac{\dfrac{\sum p_{su}q_{su}}{\sum p_{us}q_{us}}}{\left(\dfrac{L_{su}}{L_{us}}\right)^{\alpha_{su}} \left(\dfrac{\sum k_{su}r_{su}}{\sum k_{us}r_{su}}\right)^{(1-\alpha_{su})}}.$$

where the symbols have the same meaning and values as in E_1 and E_2 above.

The efficiency indexes have been computed, not only for weights corresponding to factor shares in the two countries, but for a series of values of α from 0.8 to 0.5. The indices are to be interpreted as indicating what percentage Soviet output would be of US output if either country had the indicated value of α and used the other country's quantities of inputs.

The results, in Table 6.2, indicate that for the same α the Cobb-Douglas index yields a somewhat higher value for Soviet relative efficiency than does the Kendrick-type index. With an α of 0.8, the Kendrick is 33.8 per cent, the Cobb-Douglas 35.6 per cent. With an α of 0.6 the two indexes (for the total economy) are 73.7 per cent and 94.5 per cent. Note that Soviet relative efficiency increases as the value of α declines (or as the capital exponent increases). The reason is that the use of US inputs by the USSR is equivalent to the substitution of capital for labour. The greater the contribution of capital to production, the more the Soviets benefit by undertaking the substitution (and the more the US would lose by shifting to Soviet inputs).

Our judgement about Soviet relative efficiency depends then on what the value of α actually is. Randomly collected estimates for various times and places confront one with a bewildering variety: 0.76 for the US in 1919, 0.64 for Australia in 1934–36, and 0.43 in Canada in 1937 (Douglas); 0.65 for the US (Solow); 40 for India (Divatia and Trivadi); 0.20 for the US (Valavanis); and so forth. It is difficult, however, to accept values of less than 0.5 for the USSR. It would surely require an increase of more than 10 per cent in the Soviet capital stock to compensate for a reduction of 10 per cent in the labour force. If one had to stab at a more or less reasonable set of values, they might lie in the range of 0.6–0.7 for the USSR and 0.7–0.8 for the US. At these values, the relative efficiency of the USSR ranges from 36–39 per cent of the US if the US used Soviet inputs and if outputs were valued at Soviet prices, to 87–98 per cent of the US if the USSR used US inputs and if outputs were valued at US prices.

Because of the index number problem there is probably not very much one can do to narrow the range of these indexes, short of cutting Gordian knots by splitting differences. But there is a great deal that could be done to narrow the range of items that contribute to the measured differences in efficiency. A substantial proportion of what has been registered here as relative Soviet inefficiency would be accounted for by the fact that the factors of production have not actually been held constant in all relevant and possible ways. Land has not been included at all, and a certain portion of what has been registered as US efficiency may be credited simply to a better natural endowment. Similarly, the factors are not homogeneous. The labour factor in the two countries is not homogeneous with respect to skills, hours of work per year, and other relevant respects. Capital is not homogeneous with respect to average age, wear and tear, or intensity of utilization.

Since factor differences are included in what is measured by the relative efficiency indices computed above, they should perhaps be referred to as 'gross' indices. They may be regarded as measuring the relative efficiency of total national economies rather than the efficiency of pure systems of economic organization. They tell us something about the gross result of the production efforts of two nations: the Soviets with all their poor agricultural resources and so forth; the US with all its unemployed and so forth. This is interesting to know. But the gross index can yield no conclusion about the relative efficiency, for example, of Soviet socialism and American capitalism as pure systems of resource allocation. One could approach an answer to this question, however, by cleaning up the data to render them more homogeneous and therefore capable of yielding a 'net' index of relative efficiency.

APPENDIX

Gross National Product

USSR   Bornstein's estimate[3] of USSR GNP at established prices in 1955 was 1,285.8 billion roubles. Assuming a 6 per cent rate of growth during 1955–60, the 1960 figure at 1955 prices would be 1,730 billion roubles. Bornstein estimated that 27.1 per cent of national income originated in agriculture in 1955. I assume that the figure fell somewhat by 1960, to approximately 25 per cent, yielding a non-farm output of about 1,300 billion roubles.

Bornstein's 1955 GNP of 1,285.8 billion roubles converted to a dollar figure of $212.4 billion, implying a rouble/dollar ratio of about 6. Applying this ratio to the 1960 estimates yields $288 billion for total GNP and $217 billion for non-farm GNP.

Since established Soviet prices are gross of turnover taxes and subsidies, they understate the dollar value of Soviet output relative to the US. Bergson estimated the extent of the understatement to be about 4 per cent.[4] Adjusting the converted figures by 4 per cent increases them from $288 billion and $217 billion to £300 billion and $226 billion.

US The 1960 GNP at constant 1954 prices was $440.8 billion.[5] The wholesale price index was virtually unchanged from 1954 to 1955. National income originating in agriculture in 1960 at 1954 prices was 4.1 per cent of total national income. Applying that percentage to the GNP figure above yields a non-farm GNP of $422.7 billion.

Bornstein's 1955 US GNP figure of $397.5 billion converts to 4,802 billion roubles, implying a rouble/dollar ratio of about 12.[6] Applying this conversion factor to the above results yields the figures of 5,290 billion roubles and 5,072 billion roubles.

Applying Bergson's correction factor of about 4 per cent to compensate for turnover taxes and subsidies in Soviet prices, the above figures are reduced to 5,080 billion roubles and 4,870 billion roubles.

Capital Stock

USSR In 1959 the USSR undertook a general capital inventory and revaluation. The results, as analyzed by Kaplan[7] are a 1 January 1960 total of 2,964.7 billion roubles at 1955 prices. The figure is gross of both wear and tear and depreciation; i.e. it represents the 1955 cost of replacing the 1960 stock of capital in place by new assets of the original type. It includes housing and livestock.

The agricultural component is reported to be 419.2 billion roubles, leaving a non-farm total of 2,546 billion roubles.

Bornstein's 'very rough' rouble/dollar ratio for investment end-items, with Soviet weights, is 5. Applying this to the rouble capital stock figure yields $593 billion for the total and $509 for non-farm.

US The basic figures are from Goldsmith.[8] For a coverage equivalent to that of the Soviet figure, I added structures, producers durables and livestock, for a total of $1,257.8 billion and a non-farm component of $1,162.2 billion. The figures refer to 1 January 1959, and are valued at the prices of 1947–49. I estimate 1959 gross investment less retirements to be $36.5 billion total and $34.3 billion non-farm. Applying the wholesale price index for 1955 of 117 (1947–49 = 100) yields a final estimate of $1,513 total and $1,400 non-farm, for the 1 January 1960 capital stock at 1955 prices.

The figures are taken from Goldsmith's 'gross' capital stock series, which were compiled by the 'perpetual inventory' method; i.e., gross investment less retirements. Like the Soviet figures, they are gross of both wear and tear and depreciation. They represent the 1955 cost of reproducing the 1960 capital stock in place with new assets equivalent to the original ones.

Bornstein's rouble/dollar ratio for investment at US weights is 7. Applying this to the dollar figures yields rouble figures of 10,591 billion roubles total and 9,800 billion roubles non-farm.

Labour

USSR The figures are those compiled by Weitzman, Feshbach and Kulchycka.[9] The figures correspond closely to average annual employment in man-years, and were designed for comparability with US data.

US Weitzman has also recomputed US employment data to make them comparable to Soviet data. His figures have been adjusted here in order to add the unemployed to the US data. The BLS unemployment data[10] of 5.1 per cent in non-agriculture and 3.0 per cent in agriculture were applied to Weitzman's 'constructed series' to obtain the final estimates.

Input Weights

USSR Bergson[11] gives the average annual wage in 1955 as 8,520 roubles. *Vestnik statistiki*, no. 5, 1961, reports that average money earning of wageworkers in industry rose 17 per cent from 1955 to 1960. I therefore assume the 1960 average wage to have been around 10,000 roubles. Applying this to the non-agricultural labour force of 57.9 million gives a total wage bill of 579 billion roubles.

I assume the real income in agriculture, including income in kind, to have been about 8,000 roubles. Applying this to the agricultural labour force of 37.8 million, gives a money income of 302 billion roubles.

Returns to capital are obtained by applying the arbitrary figures of 8 per cent and 20 per cent to the stock of capital in Table 6.1. The following are the resulting proportions of income going to labour and capital respectively: at 8 per cent return to capital, 0.74 and 0.26 for non-farm, 0.79 and 0.21 for total; at 20 per cent, 0.53 and 0.47 for non-farm, 0.60 and 0.40 for total.

US Kendrick[12] gives 0.79 and 0.21 for labour and capital shares, during 1948–53.

NOTES

1 John W. Kendrick, *Productivity Trends in the United States*, Princeton Univ. Press, 1961

2 Richard H. Moorsteen, 'On Measuring Potential and Relative Efficiency', *Quarterly Journal of Economics*, August 1961, p. 461.

3 Morris Bornstein, 'A Comparison of Soviet and United States National Product' in *Comparisons of the United States and Soviet Economies*, Joint Economic Committee, US Congress, 1959, Part II, p. 385.

4 A. Bergson, *The Real National Income of Soviet Russia Since 1928* Harvard Univ. Press, 1961, p. 295, fn. 9.

5 Bureau of the Census, *Statistical Abstract of the United States, 1962*, GPO, Washington, DC, p. 314

6 Morris Bornstein, op. cit.

7 Norman M. Kaplan, 'Capital Stock' in A. Bergson and S. Kuznets (eds.), *Economic Trends in the Soviet Union*, Harvard Press, 1963.

8 R. W. Goldsmith, *The National Wealth of the United States in the Postwar Period*, Princeton Univ. Press, 1962, pp. 123, 196–200.

9 M. Weitzman, M. Feshbach and L. Kulchycka, 'Employment in the U.S.S.R' in Joint Economic Committee, *Dimensions of Soviet Economic Power*, US Congress, GPO, 1962, p. 649.

10 US Bureau of Labor Statistics, *Employment and Earnings*, Annual Supplement, June 1962, p. 57.

11 A. Bergson, op. cit., p. 422.

12 John W. Kendrick, op. cit., p. 285.

7 The Economics of Overtaking and Surpassing*
1966

In the beginning there was England. And contentment vanished from the world. For the appearance of highly developed countries creates in others a condition of 'tension between the actual state of economic activities in the country and the existing obstacles to industrial development, on the one hand, and the great promise inherent in such development, on the other'.[1] The existence of such tension is the dominating fact in the economic and political programmes of many countries of the world. But although the basis of the tension is economic, economic theory has not proved conspicuously successful in providing guidance for the removal of the obstacles and the progress towards sustained economic development.

The reason is in part that the cultural, political and social characteristics of underdeveloped countries are usually very different from those in countries in which economic theory has flourished. But another reason is that economic theory has been concerned primarily with what might be called 'inner-directed' development. The tensions of backwardness, however, suggest that what is required is a theory of 'other-directed' development. In the former, the rate and pattern development are determined by the interaction of large numbers of producers and consumers each with his own product and time preferences; there is no particular social goal in view. In the latter, development is consciously directed towards

*Henry Rosovsky (ed.), *Industrialization in Two Systems: Essays in Honor of Alexander Gerschenkron* (1966), pp. 169–85. Reprinted by permission of John Wiley and Sons, Inc. The writer wishes to express his debt for the valuable criticism of an earlier draft to Herbert Levine, Peter Wiles, Abram Bergson, and other colleagues who were kind enough to comment on it.

the goal of imitating the attainments of other countries that are regarded as more advanced.

It is plausible to expect that, in principle, the character of self-generated behaviour ought to be different in significant ways from that of imitative behaviour. That there are differences in practice as well has been argued by Alexander Gerschenkron in his proposition that

in a number of important historical instances industrialization processes, when launched at length in a backward country, showed considerable differences, as compared with more advanced countries, not only with regard to the speed of development (the rate of industrial growth) but also with regard to the productive and organizational structures of industry which emerged from those processes.[2]

It is the purpose of this essay to demonstrate that imitation is a fruitful concept for exploring some old notions and generating a few new ones about the process of emergence from economic underdevelopment.

VARIETIES OF IMITATIVE DEVELOPMENT

Charles Lamb tells us that roast pig was first invented in China when a cottage burned down with a pig inside, and for centuries thereafter, his apochryphal Chinese roasted their pigs by building and burning down their cottages. Few would hold with a pure roast-pig theory of imitative development, although East European copies of the Soviet model during the Stalin period came astonishingly close. Part of the problem is precisely to discover what parts of the process to imitate without having to burn down a whole cottage.

The character of the process of imitative development depends on at least two policy decisions. First, one must establish precisely what aspects of the economy of the advanced country are to be imitated. And second, one must determine the desired time-rate of approach to the state of the imitated economy.

The Ends of Imitation
In his discussion of 'conspicuous consumption' Veblen introduced a decidedly imitative form of behaviour into social analysis. But the interdependence of consumer preferences implied in the behaviour of 'keeping up with the Joneses' was rather a nuisance for the main body of economic theory which was built upon the assumptions of 'inner-directed' rather than imitative behaviour. It

was not until Duesenberry developed a method for incorporating the 'demonstration effect' into demand theory that imitation found its way into formal theory.[3] Through the writings of Nurkse and others, the demonstration effect has now become a standard term of reference in the literature on underdeveloped countries.

Those who stress the demonstration effect identify high levels of consumption and economic security as the aim of the imitative process. Henry Wallich, indeed, argues that 'derived development' differs from the development of advanced countries principally in that the former is consumption-oriented, whereas the latter was production-oriented.[4] For the masses it is undoubtedly true that it is the consumer goods of the advanced countries that are the most potent source of tension leading to the urge for development. But to hitch a general theory of imitation exclusively to the consumer-goods cart would fail to account for another undoubtedly massive source of the tensions, at least in the case of certain of the larger socialist nations. The nature of the tension in the Soviet case was most forcefully stated by Stalin as early as 1931 in his famous speech, 'On the Tasks of Business Executives'. This was the speech in which he recited the long series of military defeats that Russia had suffered at the hands of her enemies, 'beatings she suffered for falling behind, for her backwardness.' Only by catching up with the capitalists could such defeats be avoided in the future. 'We are fifty or a hundred years behind the advanced countries. We must cover the distance in ten years. Either we do it or they crush us.'[5] To 'cover the distance' means to attain what they have, or at least their military production capacity, and even the time schedule is given. One could cite numerous other pieces of evidence to show that the concrete targets of the Five Year Plans were drawn up with the image of the capitalist countries prominently in view.[6]

Nor is Soviet development unique in this respect, at least among the socialistic countries. Thirty-three years after Stalin's speech to the Russians, Foreign Minister Marshal Chen Yi expressed the goals of communist China in the following words:

Whatever the major powers in the world can do, whatever level of technology they have reached, we want to catch up and arrive at the same level. We may be unable to catch up with a few very advanced powers in ten, twenty, or thirty years, but we will never give up the aspirations to catch up. If this is a strong attitude, it is because China is threatened. When the threat has been removed, we can take another attitude.[7]

The problem of establishing the aims of imitation is an instance of the general problem of assigning attributes to groups. Undoubtedly the aspirations of sub-groups differ, and one always flirts with the fallacy of reification in asserting that the 'aspirations of a people' are this or that. It is somewhat safer to distinguish at least the masses from the political élite. One could then assert with more confidence that the demonstration effect is probably the dominating source of tension among the masses.[8] Where the élite is heavily dependent on mass support for the maintenance of its power, consumer goods may also rank high as the objective of imitation, whatever the personal inclinations of the leaders. But if we are to capture faithfully the aims of the Soviet and Chinese élite then we must accord first place to military defence, and derivatively to heavy industry, as the aim of economic development. This assumption does not compel us to deny that in some ultimate sense material affluence is also their goal.[9] Moreover, as development proceeds, rising living standards may be regarded as necessary to elicit the desired quanta of effort and initiative. But for the explanation of the pattern of Soviet development during the Five Year Plan, as well as for recent Chinese development, the presumption is that the military and heavy industry attainments of the advanced capitalist countries are the principal goal towards which development has been directed.

The Time-Rate of Imitative Development
There is a certain optimism in evolutionary or stage theories, in the sense that latecomers will, and in some theories must, eventually move along the path traversed earlier by their advanced forerunners. However, such theories are not optimistic enough, certainly not enough to satisfy the imitative objectives of Stalin or Chen Yi, for whereas the underdeveloped country is assured that one day it will begin moving along the path of the forerunners, nothing is said about the time-rate of movement along that path. And without the specific inclusion of time-rates, nothing can be said about the possibility of overtaking and surpassing the advanced countries.

We may distinguish three requirements of successful imitation. The first and weakest requirement is that A commence a process of sustained development like that experienced earlier by B. The second is that at some future date A attain the level of development *presently* held by B. The third and strongest requirement is that at some future date A attain the level of development of B on the same date.[10] If for some reason B's development should cease, the last two requirements merge into one. Some underdeveloped countries may be content with an imitative process that satisfies only the first or second requirement. It is enough for them that per capita incomes begin an uninterrupted and modest rise; an evolutionary or stage theory, perhaps of the Marxian variety, would satisfy their aspirations. On the other hand, those who wish to overtake and surpass the leaders insist on the third requirement for which simple evolution will not do. Something must be added to an evolutionary theory, something which will support the possibility that the development of those who come later may be more rapid than that of those who came before.

Evolutionary and stage theories stress the similarity in paths of development, the principal differences among countries being found in the historical time periods in which they traverse the successive stages. But mere similarity of development does not necessarily imply that any conscious imitation occurred, any more than the similarity of physical development of successive generations of organisms implies that the offspring imitated the parent. The classical stage theory of cultural evolution (savagery to barbarism to civilization), for example, does not depend on savages imitating barbarians.[11] Marx, however, does suggest that the development of the lagging countries is conditioned by their awareness of the experience of the forerunners: 'The industrially more developed country presents to the less developed country a picture of the latter's future.'[12] By including some such notion as the forerunners 'holding up a mirror' to the followers, an evolutionary theory can be made to include a specifically imitative element. In pursuing the implications of the latecomers' opportunity to imitate, we can find the special features that create the possibility of 'overtaking and surpassing' the advanced countries.

One such feature emerged in the later debates among the Marxists about the possibility of skipping the stage of capitalism. Those who held to the purist position that stages could not be skipped were arguing, with a faint aroma of roast pig, from an organic model; children cannot skip the puberty stage by imitating the parent in the adult stage. Those who argued that latecomers could skip or foreshorten stages were presenting an instance of the case that imitative development may differ in a significant way from the development patterns of the forerunners.

Another special feature of imitative development was introduced by Veblen in his discussion of borrowing of technology. The imitator can adopt the most advanced forms of technology, which were not available to the forerunner when it was at the imitator's present position. It is therefore plausible that the imitator can cover the ground between its present position and that of the forerunner more rapidly than the corresponding ground had been covered by the latter in an earlier period.

Although the presence of such special features of imitation as stage-skipping and technology-borrowing is a necessary condition for overtaking the forerunner, it is not a sufficient condition. For if the forerunner continues to develop, the imitator will not necessarily ever catch up, even though his initial growth rates exceed those of the forerunner in the earlier period. To establish the sufficient conditions would require a double-dynamic analysis, that is, it would have to deal with the path of a moving point trying to catch up to a moving target. The analysis to be presented below has a more modest objective. We shall deal only with the second requirement of successful imitation, that the imitator attain the *present* position of the forerunner. Some part of Stalin's and Chen Yi's stated aims can be captured by adding the requirement that the target be attained in the minimal period of time. We decline the challenge of dealing with the pursuit of a moving target. Hereafter, the concept of overtaking and surpassing will be understood to mean the attainment of the present position of the forerunner in the shortest possible time.

We have now identified two possible commodity-objectives and two possible time-objectives of imitative growth. The commodity-objective may consist either of consumer goods or of military and heavy-industry goods; the time-objective may be merely to follow the path of the advanced country without specific regard to time or to overtake and surpass the present position of the advanced country. A general theory of imitative development would have to deal with processes described by all four combinations of these two sets of objectives. For the following discussion we shall be concerned with only one of the four combinations, that which characterizes the goals of Soviet-type imitative development set forth by Stalin and Chen Yi: to overtake and surpass the military-heavy industry attainments of the advanced countries.

SOME PATTERNS OF IMITATIVE DEVELOPMENT

The proposition to be investigated is that there are properties of the development process of an imitating economy which are different from those of the forerunner and which, moreover, make it possible for the imitator to overtake and surpass the military and industrial production capacity of the forerunner. In order to study structural growth patterns as well as aggregate growth rates, a model is required that lends itself to the analysis not only of the

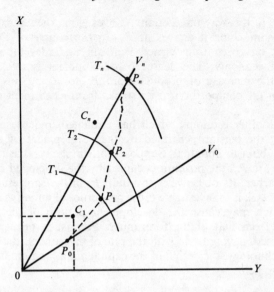

Figure 7.1 Base model of an imitative growth path

consumption–investment decision but also of a variety of substitution possibilities between factors and commodities. This could be accomplished by introducing several sets of variables representing different factors, consumer goods, and producer goods, but the number of variables would be awkwardly large. However, the same results can be obtained with only two variables by the ingenious device developed in the literature on efficient capital accumulation programmes, namely, by ascribing to the goods the properties of both consumption and investment. That is, the goods are both factors and commodities, and can either be consumed directly or combined to produce new stocks of the two goods (rather like coal or electric power). Goods of the more familiar kind that are used exclusively for consumption or investment may thus be treated as limiting cases.

We assume an economy, then, with two factors or commodities, X and Y, stocks of which are available initially in quantities represented by P_0 in Figure 7.1. The stocks are used up in the first period in the process of producing new and expanded stocks of X and Y at the point P_1 on the transformation curve T_1.[13] A certain portion of the new stocks, represented by C_1, is consumed, and the balance used during the second period for the production of new stocks at the point P_2 on the second-period transformation curve T_2. In this way the economy moves along the indicated path until at some time it arrives at P_n. In the course of the entire period it has been transformed from an underdeveloped to an advanced economy. The degree of development is reflected not only in the increase of product from P_0 to P_n but also in the change in the composition of its stocks from assortment ray OV_0 to OV_n.

Now another economy which has remained underdeveloped is seized by the tension generated by the development of the first, and sets about to imitate it. Suppose, for simplicity, that its stocks at time t are P_0, the position occupied by the developed economy t years earlier. Its objective is to attain P_n in the shortest possible time. Our task is to investigate those properties of imitative development which may cause the development pattern of the imitator to differ from that of the forerunner. Four such properties will be examined, having to do with the rate of investment, the borrowing of technology, the design of the capital plant, and the time-path of development.

The Rate of Investment
When the forerunner was at P_1, the amount of consumption C_1 was determined by the incomes, tastes, and time-preferences of that period. The location of the second period's transformation curve depended on how much was consumed of the first period's outputs. The smaller the consumption subtracted from P_1, the further to the north-east is the transformation curve T_2.

If the imitator at point P_1 is motivated by the 'demonstration effect' it will strive to imitate the consumption standards attained by the forerunner at time t. But the volume of consumption of the forerunner at time t is quite large, perhaps at the point C_n, well beyond the initial production possibilities of the imitator. Even if the consumption levels of the forerunner cannot be fully attained, consumer preferences and political necessity are likely to lead to a higher level of consumption than that of C_1 which was attained by the forerunner years ago when it was at the same stage of development. Hence, smaller stocks will be available for further production, and the second period's transformation function will lie below and to the left of T_2. It will therefore take the imitator more than t years to attain P_n.

But if the imitator is motivated by the desire to overtake and surpass the forerunner, it will keep consumption down to a level lower than C_1. Its second-period transformation curve will lie therefore to the north-east of T_2, and since the same argument will apply in successive periods, it will attain P_n in a shorter period than t years.

This second case describes the conditions of Soviet growth. During the Five Year Plans, consumption was held down to levels well below those in advanced countries at the same time, for the sake of rapid accumulation of production stocks. Indeed the harsh conditions of Soviet growth have sometimes been justified by pointing to the conditions under which industrialization began in the capitalist countries. Both the classical economists and Marx regarded it as an appropriate assumption that real wages were maintained at subsistence levels, and this is probably a fair approximation of Soviet conditions also, at least during the 1930s. Ignoring the fact that the conventional concept of minimal subsistence levels has changed, we may regard C_1 as the subsistence consumption level of both the forerunner at time 1 and the imitator at time t. How then can the rate of investment be higher for the imitator than for the forerunner?

Three factors provide the answer. The first is the fact that in the advanced countries the volume of consumption rose above subsistence levels as output increased. All that is required is that the imitator keep consumption from rising over time at the same rate as that earlier experienced by the forerunner. In fact, Soviet consumption per capita rose during the period 1928–55, according to Bergson's calculations at 1937 prices, at 1.7 per cent per annum, or at 2.0 per cent if one considers only the peacetime years. In the US during the periods 1869–78 and 1899–1908, the annual rate was 2.6 per cent at 1929 prices; it would have been appreciably greater at mid-period prices. Moreover, most of the Soviet growth occurred during the 1950–55 sub-period; in the 1928–40 sub-period per capita consumption declined at an annual rate of 0.6 per cent. Although consumption levels fluctuated in the United States also, there was no decline quite so extensive.[14] Hence by keeping the rate of consumption from rising as rapidly as that of the forerunner, the USSR was able to marshal larger proportions of its stocks for further production.

The second factor is that the imitator will mobilize its resources for a more intense rate of utilization than the self-generating economy did. The given stocks of labour or capital can thus be made to yield larger flows of factor services per period, and the transformation curve generated by a given set of stocks will therefore lie further to the north-east. Not very much evidence is available on capital services, but most analysts accept Soviet claims that the rate of utilization of capacity is greater in the USSR than in the United States.[15] With respect to labour, if the total population

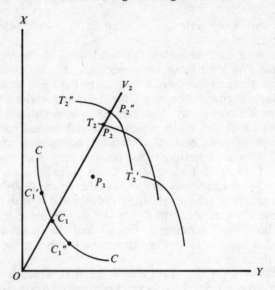

Figure 7.2 The optimal consumption mix

is regarded as the stock, 53 per cent of the Soviet population was in the labour force in 1939, compared wtih 32–33 per cent in the United States during the period 1870–1900.[16] However, Soviet workers probably worked fewer hours per month than United States workers did in the late nineteenth century.[17] In this case the 'demonstration effect' combined with socialist ideology to deprive the imitator of an advantage enjoyed by the forerunner.

The third factor deals with the commodity structure of consumption. Two baskets of goods, which may be equally satisfactory in terms of consumer preferences or subsistence levels, will leave different quantities of stocks available for production in the next period. Each such set of stocks will yield a different transformation curve in the next period. In Figure 7.2 CC is an indifference curve (representing perhaps the subsistence level) of consumption mixes that may be selected out of stocks P_1. If C_1 were consumed, the stocks left over would yield transformation curve T_2, but if C_1' or C_1'' were consumed, the transformation curves would be T_2' or T_2''.

Now, an 'inner-directed' economy exercising no control over the composition of consumption, would be led by consumer preferences to select some combination such as C_1 and to produce a second-period output such as P_2, whereas if the imitator has the power to control the composition of consumption, it has an additional degree of freedom. If it should wish to maximize output along the ray OV_2, it can provide consumers with a consumption-mix representing the same level of subsistence or welfare as C_1, but which would use up less of the resources that promote growth in the desired direction. It would thus adjust prices so as to induce consumption-mix C_1'', yielding transformation curve T_2'', and producing at P_2'', which represents a higher rate of growth along OV_2 than does P_2.

In the case of the Soviet economy the policy of restricting the consumption of residential housing and consumer durables may be interpreted as having had the purpose of reducing the consumption drain of those resources having the largest growth-inducing effect. Mr Khrushchev's intention to restrict the development of the Soviet automotive economy to dimensions more reasonable than those of the capitalist countries may have a similar effect.

Thus, even if the imitator were confronted with the same set of technological alternatives as the forerunner faced in the corresponding period, it may be expected to grow more rapidly because of its control over the rate and composition of consumption.

Borrowed Technology

However, the technology available to the imitator is not the same as that employed by the forerunner *t* years ago, and this is another factor enabling the former to maintain a higher rate of investment than the latter during its development period. The path of the forerunner is strewn with the rusted remains of innovations that hadn't worked but which had consumed resources in the process of being proved unworkable. The imitator is spared this waste of resources, which may not have been a 'waste' to the forerunner, since in the absence of perfect foresight, there is a necessary cost in discovering workable, to say nothing of optimal, forms of technology.

Consider a proposal by an imaginative engineer for an elaborate new process of mining coal. The obvious condition that the proposal must satisfy is that the production of one ton of coal will not require a direct input of more than one ton of coal. Less obvious is that the direct *and indirect* (in the input–output sense) requirement of coal should not exceed one ton. It is at least plausible that a technically elegant and complex process may consume a greater quantity of value than it produces. One way of testing the innovation is to apply the Hawkins–Simon condition in the context of an input-output model.[18] Another is to estimate costs on the basis of present and anticipated market prices. With less-than-perfect knowledge and foresight, one must expect that some estimates will be inaccurate, and innovations will be undertaken that should not have been. The market casts them off, and the forerunner has, in effect, borne the cost of eliminating the more grossly inefficient innovations that failed to satisfy the Hawkins–Simon condition.

Of the past innovations that did satisfy the minimal tests of economic efficiency, there is a larger sub-group that was invested in by unfortunate entrepreneurs only a short time before a more productive process was invented. These too clutter the historical path of the advanced country with costs of development that must be borne by the forerunner but are spared the imitator.[19]

The imitator thus has available to it a basket of technologies that have survived to time t and that have been preselected by the forerunner out of its historical experience. However, the forerunner's selection process has also eliminated other technological variants which neither consumed more value than they produced, nor were superseded by improved processes, but which were simply less efficient than the accepted ones, given the condition of the forerunner's economy. Some of these eliminated variants may be more efficient than the accepted ones under the conditions of the imitator's economy, and therefore, if the imitator confines the range of choice to the variants currently employed in the advanced economy, that imitation may take on the form of the roast pig. When the state of the imitator's economy is very far behind that of the advanced country, a direct imitation of the most advanced technology may result in a less-than-maximal rate of growth.

The argument is a variation of the factor–proportions problem.[20] In Figure 7.3, P_0 represents as before the current stocks of the imitator and the stocks of the forerunner t years ago, and T_n is the current transformation curve of the advanced country incorporating the most modern technology. If the imitator borrowed the most modern technological variants incorporated in T_n, with its initial stocks P_0 its transformation curve would be T_1''. Hence its output (P_1''), would be greater than that of the forerunner t years ago (P_1') and it would grow more rapidly. However, the most modern technological variants had been designed for a developed country, with stocks of factors available in the proportions OV_n. By redesigning and adapting the newest technology to its own factor proportions, the imitator can achieve a transformation curve that would yield a higher output such as P_1, greater than either P_1' or P_1''.

Was Veblen wrong, then, in ascribing Germany's success in overtaking England to the adoption of England's most advanced technology? Not if Germany's factor proportions were in the neigh-

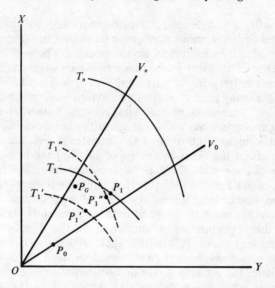

Figure 7.3 Optimal borrowing of technology

bourhood of England's, such as at P_G. In that case the direct imitation of England's most advanced technology would have been appropriate, for that technology had presumably been designed to maximize output with factor proportions in the neighbourhood of OV_n. Thus the closer the imitator's factor proportions are to those of the forerunner, the smaller are the differences in design of the optimal variants of the newest technology in both countries.[21] The existence of such differences between the more and the less developed imitator is suggested in Gerschenkron's proposition that 'the extent to which these attributes of backwardness occurred in individual instances appears to have varied directly with the degree of backwardness. . .'[22]

The evidence of Soviet practice in this respect is inconclusive. Granick has made a strong case for the view that, at least in the important instance of the metalworking industries, Soviet planners did adapt Western technology to their own factor proportions by substituting labour for capital wherever possible.[23] Even enterprises like the Gorky Automotive Plant, which was built on the direct model of the Ford River-Rouge plant and with the assistance of Ford engineers, was redesigned in significant ways in the light of special Soviet conditions.[24] Where Western technological equipment was used, the Soviets accommodated to their lower level of labour skills by redesigning job descriptions, so that several specialized Soviet workers performed tasks that in other countries were carried out by individual skilled workers. There is, moreover, the evidence of 'dualism' in the economy which suggests that something like a redesigning of borrowed processes did take place. For example, in many plants it is common to find basic processes highly mechanized whereas supplementary processes such as materials handling are carried out with large quantities of labour. The equivalent picture in agriculture is of the monstrous combine-harvester followed about the fields by troops of elderly peasant women. At least we can say that there is no roast-pig imitation here, and indeed Granick has shown that perfect imitation is quite impossible, if only because of large differences in social organization.

On the other hand, while the Soviets have evidently taken advantage of the opportunities of improving on the directly imitative transformation curve T_1'' in the light of their own factor proportions, it is unlikely that they moved to the fully optimal T_1. It is difficult, for example, to dismiss entirely the prolonged official criticism of what Stalin dubbed 'gigantomania' – the view that the best must be the largest. In the case of the huge Magnitogorsk works, the Soviet planners overrode the advice of their American consultants and designed their blast furnaces substantially larger than the largest their consultants thought prudent.[25] To some extent, the selection of capital-intensive designs reflects the absence of an interest charge for capital, which is itself evidence of insufficient awareness of the significance of factor proportions. There are also indications that equipment design, particularly that of imported equipment, was rather more advanced than was warranted by existing levels of technical skills. Stalin, however, operated on the basis of a singular learning theory that had a certain plausibility from the point of view of dynamic efficiency.

We proceeded openly and consciously to the inevitable outlays and over-expenditures associated with the shortage of sufficiently trained people who knew how to handle machines. True, we destroyed many machines at the same time, but at the same time we won the most important thing – time – and we created the most precious thing in the economy – Cadres.[26]

We may interpret Stalin's words as a decision to 'trade-off' scarce physical capital for even scarcer human capital. There is a basis in rationality for this decision for, as Gerschenkron has pointed out, 'Creation of an industrial labor force that really deserves the name is a most difficult and protracted process.'[27] If the length of the process can be reduced by introducing the raw labour to

the most modern of technological equipment, then the factor–
proportions argument for using less capital-intensive equipment
is somewhat weakened.[28] The argument is further weakened when
one considers another difference between self-generated and imitative growth that bears on the design of fixed plant.

Flexibility of Fixed Plant

We owe to George Stigler the distinction between the adaptability
and flexibility of fixed plant.[29] A given stock of capital is adaptable
if it can be combined with varying amounts of the variable factor,
like the ten shovels that can be combined with eleven ditchdiggers
by a suitable metamorphosis. The stock of capital is flexible, if
it approximates the best technology for a broad range of output,
although for no level of output does it incorporate the very best
technology; approximate efficiency over a broad range of output
is achieved at the cost of attaining perfect efficiency at no level
of output. Flexibility is built into plants to offset the consequences
of imperfect adaptability, for with imperfect adaptability any output
other than the optimum either would involve prohibitively high
marginal costs or would be highly unprofitable.

It is rational for an enterprise in a self-generating (market)
economy to pay the cost of building flexibility into the plant,[30]
for the characteristic of such an economy is uncertainty about the
future level and composition of output. To design a plant which
would give rock-bottom average costs only at the optimal output
would expose the plant to immediate collapse if economic conditions
should change and the optimum should shift to another level of
output. The firm in an imitating economy, however, need not have
the same concerns, in part because the imitating economy is likely
to introduce large doses of economic planning, which ideally should
be expected to reduce uncertainty. But more than the mere existence
of economic planning is involved, for a planned economy need
not be goal-oriented; it might be content to permit consumer
sovereignty to determine the compositon of the national product,
including the division between consumption and investment. The
crucial point is that the imitating economy has an end-in-view,
and therefore need have less concern for unanticipated and
uncontrolled variations in output or demand.

Consider an economy that wishes to change the composition
of its stocks in the shortest possible time from OV_0 to that of
the forerunner, OV_n. What will the shape of its transformation
curve be at the end of the process? The economy of the forerunner,
consisting of firms that have built flexibility into their plant, will
have a transformation curve like T_n in Figure 7.4, which is drawn

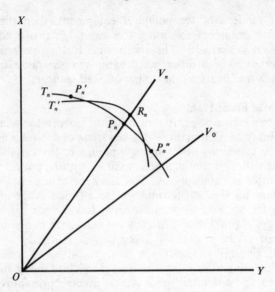

Figure 7.4 Optimal flexibility in plant design

with slight curvature to reflect a relatively high elasticity of transformation. The flexibility is necessary because the firms cannot know at the time their plant is designed whether the optimum will be P_n or at P_n' or P_n''. The imitator, however, knows precisely that the end-in-view lies along OV_n. Hence, it does not need to reduce its capacity to produce along OV_n for the sake of the relatively greater efficiency with which it might produce P_n' or P_n'' if it had to. Its transformation curve will have the shape of T_n' and its output will be R_n, greater than the output P_n which a non-goal-oriented economy would select. Therefore, the imitating economy ought to experience a more rapid rate of growth than the self-generating economy of the forerunner.

Have the Soviets taken advantage of this opportunity for catching up? Stigler notes that there are two principal techniques for building flexibility into plants: divisibility, and low fixed-to-variable cost ratios. The aforementioned practice of 'gigantomania' suggests that in the choice of the size of blast furnaces, for example, the Soviets preferred the productivity gains of an indivisible plant with a few large units, over the flexibility advantage of a divisible plant with many small units. It also suggests that they preferred the lower optimal-output costs that could be attained with higher fixed-to-variable cost ratios. In special instances, the Soviets did build flexibility into plants; in the tractor industry the possibility of conversion to military tanks was provided for, but the motive here was military rather than economic. By and large, however, the evidence seems to support the conclusion that the Soviets did take advantage of the imitator's opportunity to avoid the costs of flexibility.

Perhaps they went too far. Our proposition about the imitator's opportunity to avoid the costs of flexibility has abstracted from such nuisance considerations as imperfections in planning and changes in objectives. These unfortunate facts of the real world suggest that flexibility ought not be dispensed with as cheerfully as theoretical considerations direct. Nevertheless, the direction of the argument remains valid though its force is reduced from a bang to a whimper.

Imitation and the Turnpike Theorem

Suppose the imitator and the forerunner were alike with respect to all the factors discussed thus far; the consumption basket is fixed at the subsistence level in both (so that we may assume a 'consumptionless' economy), the same technology is available to both, and both start with the same production stocks. There is one final reason why the imitator may be expected to grow more rapidly. The argument is based on the conditions of efficient capital accumulation.[31]

Consider a self-generating economy with initial stocks P_0 and transformation curve T_1, as in Figure 7.5. Any point on T_1 is efficient in the sense that no other output could be produced that would contain more of both X and Y. Suppose that P_1 were chosen. After subtraction of the fixed consumption basket once more, T_2 is the second-period transformation curve and P_2 is an efficient point on T_2. Note that within each period production has been perfectly efficient. Nevertheless, the path may be an inefficient one for the whole time span. How can it come about that a path which is efficient within all periods may nevertheless be inefficient over the whole time span?

The argument is based on the fact that the position and shape of the transformation curve in any period depends on the choice of product mix of the preceding period. The position of T_2 is based on the choice of P_1 in the preceding period. But if P_1' (or P_1'') had been chosen instead, the transformation curve would have been T_2' (or T_2''). There are as many second-period transformation curves as there are points on T_1. By a familiar line of reasoning the locus of all second-period efficient points is the envelope E_2 to the second-period transformation curves. As can be seen in the figure, for example, if the economy wished its output in the pro-

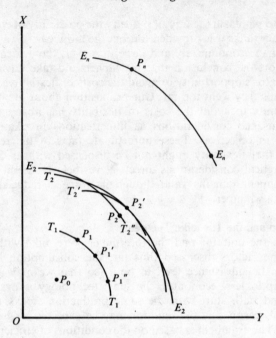

Figure 7.5 The optimal product mix

portions represented by P_2, it would have done better to produce at P_1' than at P_1. Then its second-period transformation curve would have been T_2' and its output P_2', greater than P_2. Therefore P_1 was not intertemporally efficient, even though it was located on the transformation curve.

Since the product mix at any time is the starting-point for the production of the next period, there will be a family of envelope curves for all succeeding periods. Of all possible paths of getting from P_0 to some subsequent P_n, 'only those paths which hop from envelope to envelope have any claim to efficiency'.[32] Two intertemporally efficient paths have been represented in Figure 7.6, paths 1 and 3. Between P_0 and any point on E_n one and only one (intertemporally) efficient path can be drawn. Path 2 is an example of a path which may be efficient within each period, but which is not intertemporally efficient. It would take longer to get from P_0 to P_n by path 2 than by path 1.

Now suppose we have given the historical data on the path actually traversed by a self-generating economy during the period in which it was transformed from P_0 to P_n. Is the path likely

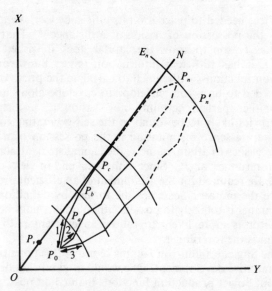

Figure 7.6 The turnpike growth path

to have been the unique efficient one? The answer depends, as in most economic theorems, on how 'perfect' the economy was. In this case, if there were perfect competition, and if there were constant returns to scale, and if there were perfect certainty (so that 'ex ante expected prices or rates of change of prices . . . corres- pond exactly to ex post observed prices',[33]) then competition would lead the producers inevitably along the efficient path. Competition would pick, out of all sets of prices over time, precisely that unique set of prices such that profit-maximizing entrepreneurs, producing with marginal rates of transformation equal to price ratios, would produce the appropriate product mixes on the envelope curves at all points. Any other set of prices could not endure, because arbitrage-through-time would restore prices to the optimal set, thus violating the assumption that ex ante prices always correspond to ex post.

The very strictness of the assumptions necessary to yield this result suggest the answer to the question about the self-generating economy. The likelihood that it was characterized by perfect cer- tainty is small indeed. Hence, even if perfect competition ensured that the economy was on its transformation curves at all times, it is most unlikely to have been on its efficiency loci as well. How- ever, perfect certainty is only one device that can guide an economy to the prices needed to place it on its efficiency loci. An alternative device is the possession of 'vision at a distance.'[34] That is, if the society has reason to know the capital stock it wished to attain at time t, it has sufficient information (given knowledge of the production functions) with which to calculate the prices or product mixes needed to hop from envelope to envelope along its efficient path. Neither perfect certainty nor 'vision at a distance' are characteristics likely to be found in the self-generating forerunner, but the very essence of imitation is the possession of a vision of what one wishes to attain, namely, the capital stock attained earlier by the forerunner at P_n. Since either an end-in-view or perfect certainty are required for the attainment of an efficient programme, and since the imitator possesses the former by definition whereas the forerunner is unlikely to possess either, other things being equal the imitator is more likely to follow an efficient path from P_0 to P_n than is the forerunner.

Did the Soviet economy in fact make use of this potential advantage of imitative development? One would need much more detailed data about Soviet production functions than could possibly be had if the properties of the optimal path were to be calculated. But if we make one more rather heroic assumption about the Soviet economy, then an important property of the optimal path may be deduced, which moreover can be subjected to a rough statistical test. It has been assumed in the preceding discussion that the economy is 'consumptionless' in the sense that consumption is fixed at the minimal level needed to sustain the labour force and provide for its natural growth. We now add the requirement that labour (and land), like all other commodity factors, be both an input and an output and that its rate of growth be proportional to the inputs used in its production. This additional requirement is not so unrealistic as it may seem at first glance, for if the labour unit is adjusted for levels of skill and incentives, then increased inputs of education and consumer goods may be expected to lead to an increase in labour so defined, though perhaps not proportionately. In like fashion, the 'output' of land will increase in response to increased quantities of quality-improving inputs.

To the extent that the Soviet economy satisfied the conditions specified above, if its growth path had been efficient, it should have exhibited a certain property. This property may be described by noting that a ray drawn at random from the origin would represent a 'balanced growth' path; that is, both stocks would increase at the same rate. Each of the one-parameter sets of rays would represent a different time-rate of growth. One such ray would represent the maximal growth rate that could be attained by balanced growth. Let that path, which has been named the von Neumann path, be represented in Figure 7.6 by *ON*. The von Neumann path is distinguished from all other balanced-growth paths by two properties:

1 by the aforementioned fact that it is the maximally rapid balanced-growth path, and
2 by the fact that although all other balanced-growth paths are intertemporally inefficient, it alone is efficient in both the intratemporal and intertemporal senses.

Thus, if by chance the initial capital stock happened to exist in the von Neumann proportions, such as at P_v, and if the economy wished to maintain these proportions indefinitely, the maximal time-rate of growth would be attained by shooting up *ON*.

In the general case, however, the initial stocks in the imitating economy are not likely to exist in von Neumann proportions, nor are the final stocks of the forerunner that the imitator wishes to overtake and surpass. The two stocks are more likely to be like P_0 and P_n, both off the von Neumann path. The interesting theoretical result is that even in this case the von Neumann path has a certain significance for the imitator. In the words of the inventors of the theorem:

... if the programming period is very long, the corresponding optimal capital program will be described as follows: The system first invests so as to alter its capital structure toward the special von Neumann proportions. When it has come close to these proportions, it spends most of the programming period performing steady growth at the maximal rate (more precisely, something close to maximal steady growth). The system expands along or close to the von Neumann ray *ON* until the end of the programming period approaches. Then it bends away from *ON* and invests in such a way as to alter the capital structure to the desired terminal proportions, arriving at $[P_n]$ as the periods ends.[35]

Let path 1 in Figure 7.6 represent the optimal path so described. The proposition has been termed the 'turnpike theorem' because the growth rate along *ON* is maximally rapid, like the speed rate on a turnpike highway. If one wishes to travel from one point to another, neither of which happens to be on the turnpike, it pays *under certain conditions* to drive out of one's direct path towards the turnpike in order to take advantage of the maximal speeds that can be attained. The conditions are that the initial and end points should be not too far from the turnpike, and/or that the distance between them should be relatively great. Without knowledge of the position of the Soviet economy's von Neumann path, one cannot judge whether the first of these conditions holds. But with respect to the second, one can presume that the Soviet programming period should or could have been great enough that the initial and end points ought to be satisfactorily far apart. Moreover, the Soviet economy can be regarded as an approximation of a 'consumptionless' economy in the sense described above, at least during Stalin's lifetime. Under these conditions, if the economy did capitalize on the imitator's advantage of having an end-in-view, then its growth pattern should have approximated a turnpike path.

If the Soviets did in fact succeed in attaining their turnpike path, then two characteristics of the growth pattern should be observable in the data (as necessary though not sufficient conditions). First, the degree of 'unbalance' should have diminished from period to period as the stocks moved from P_0 to P_c towards the turnpike, after which a period of balanced growth should have ensued.[36] Second, the rate of growth should have increased as the turnpike proportions were attained and the maximal balanced-growth phase achieved.

With respect to the first test, the turnpike theorem is sometimes interpreted in terms of the distribution of national product between consumption and investment. In these terms the theorem is supposed to mean that initially investment grows more rapidly than consumption in order to build up the capital stocks at a maximal rate, and that after a time resources are finally shifted back again in the direction of a greatly enlarged output of consumer goods. This interpretation, which corresponds roughly to the Feldman model,[37] deals with the rate of investment, and was discussed above in that context; it is not, however, a correct interpretation of the turnpike theorem. The turnpike theorem deals with a 'consumptionless' economy; the subsistence minimum is treated not as final demand but as intermediate product, like fuel or animal fodder. No conclusions can therefore be drawn which include consumption as final demand. The stocks of commodities or factors that constitute the variables are both inputs and outputs; they exist in certain quantities at the beginning of a period, and, after being used for production, they exist in larger quantities once more at the end of the period after intermediate flows (including consumption) have been netted out. The peculiar appropriateness of the turnpike theorem to Soviet growth is that it deals precisely with those commodities that Stalin and Chen Yi had in mind in their justification of the motive to overtake and surpass the advanced countries, namely, stocks of productive resources.

It is in relative rates of growth of different productive stocks,

then, and not in the difference between consumption and investment, that we should find our test of the extent to which an economy
is approaching balanced growth. Balanced growth is a process in
which the growth rates of X and Y are equal; that is, the ratio
of growth rates $(\Delta X/Y)/(\Delta Y/Y)$, is equal to unity (see appendix).
In an economy approaching balanced growth as in the turnpike
case, the value of the ratio in successive periods approaches unity.
What we require then are data on the growth rates of different
kinds of productive stocks for various periods.

The Soviets have recently published data which make it possible
to compute the growth rates of stocks of fixed productive capital
for seventeen industries, for the periods 1933–40 and 1940–55. Each
industry was compared with all the others, yielding 136 pairs of
industries in which relative changes in growth rates were observed;
the details are explained in the appendix. In only 21 of the 136
cases did the pairs of stocks behave in both periods as if they
were moving towards a balanced growth path. Moreover, the rate
of growth of capital stocks was slower in the later period than
in the earlier. Between 1933 and 1940 the capital stock increased
by 157 per cent, whereas in the period 1950–55 it grew by only
71 per cent. Thus, neither of the two characteristics one would
expect to find in an economy following a turnpike path is observable
in our data.

This conclusion is hardly likely to cause much surprise. For one
thing, the data are very crude; at the least, one would wish to
add inventories to fixed capital stocks. For another, even though
some of the conditions for the turnpike theorem were present (an
end-in-view, long-planning horizon, 'consumptionless' economy,
perhaps even constant returns to scale), others were not. Perhaps
the major conditions not satisfied by history are constant technology
and a fixed goal of desired stocks. In both instances, the fault
is with the forerunner, which continued to innovate and grow.
If the United States' economy had become stationary in the early
1930s, as some feared it might, the conditions for Soviet growth
along a turnpike path would have been fairly closely approximated.

The turnpike theorem, then, deals with an advantage available
to an imitator under certain conditions that are rarely realized.
If the theorem were generalized to deal with such conditions as
moving goals and changing technology, it would have more to
say about the behaviour of real imitators than it does in the present
form. In general, the usefulness of a theory of imitative development
like that presented here would be greatly extended if it were
equipped with the tools to handle the process of overtaking and
surpassing a moving goal.

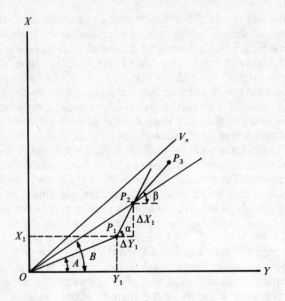

Figure 7.7 The approach to balanced growth

APPENDIX: THE APPROACH TO BALANCED GROWTH

Suppose an economy moves in one period from P_1 to P_2 (Figure 7.7). The ratio of the increments of X and Y is $\Delta X_1/\Delta Y_1$, or the tangent of angle α. The ratio of the initial stocks is X_1/Y_1, or the tangent of angle A. If the growth from P_1 to P_2 is balanced, angle α equals angle A, or $\Delta X_1/\Delta Y_1/X_1/Y_1 = 1$, or $\Delta X_1/X_1/\Delta Y_1/Y_1 = 1$. The numerator and denominator of the last fraction represent, of course, the growth rates of X and Y. If the ratio of the growth rates is not equal to unity, growth from P_1 to P_2 is unbalanced.

An economy approaching a turnpike would exhibit unbalanced growth initially; for example, α may be greater than A.[38] However, its movement in the next period from P_2 to P_3 would be confined within a certain range. P_3 would have to lie to the right of line P_1P_2 extended, since the turnpike must be approached asymptotically. In addition P_3 must lie to the left of OP_2 extended, else the direction of unbalanced growth simply reverses.[39] The condition that P_3 lie within the permissible range is $\alpha \gtrless \beta \gtrless B$.

The data are derived from the statistical handbook, *Industry in the U.S.S.R.* (Promyshlennost' SSSR), Moscow, 1957, pp. 16–17.

Table 7.1 Movement toward balanced growth of capital stocks in the USSR 1933–40 and 1940–55

Industries	Engineering	Food	Iron and steel	Electric power	Chemicals	Light industry	Lumber and woodworking	Petroleum	Non ferrous metals	Coal	Other building materials	Other fuels	Paper	Printing	Rubber and asbestos	Cement	Glass and china
Engineering	▓	*											*		*		
Food	*	▓			*								*		*		
Iron and steel			▓				*										*
Electric power				▓					*		*						*
Chemicals		*			▓	*									*		
Light industry					*	▓											
Lumber and woodworking			*				▓										*
Petroleum								▓			*						
Non ferrous metals				*					▓		*	*					
Coal										▓						*	
Other building materials				*	.			*	*		▓	*					
Other fuels									*		*	▓					*
Paper	*	*											▓		*		
Printing														▓			
Rubber and asbestos	*	*			*								*		▓		
Cement										*						▓	
Glass and china			*	*			*				*						▓

Note: The starred pairs of industries are those in which the changes in fixed capital stocks during 1933–40 and 1940–55 were in the direction of more balanced growth.

They consist of the percentage distribution of the stock of fixed productive capital in seventeen industries, at constant prices, for a series of years. Combined with the index of growth of all fixed capital in industry,[40] they made possible the calculation of growth indexes for the capital stock in the seventeen industries. The most appropriate time periods for investigation afforded by the data were 1933–40 and 1940–55. To satisfy the requirements of the turn-pike theorem, inventories should have been added to fixed capital, but the data were not available.

Ratios of the changes in capital stocks (α and β) and of the 1940 stocks (B) were calculated for all combinations of the seventeen industries taken in pairs. The data for each pair were examined to see if the condition formulated above was satisfied. Notwith-standing the 10 per cent margin of error allowed, the condition was satisfied in only 21 of the 136 pairs. The starred boxes in Table 7.1 are the pairs that moved together in a direction consistent with an approach towards a turnpike path.

Four industries (food, other building materials, rubber and asbestos, and glass and china) accounted for 15 of the 21 favourable cases. At the other extreme, printing moved towards balance with no other industries. The reason is that although its first-period growth rate was near the median for all industry (157 per cent), its second-period growth rate was lowest of all (50 per cent). Coal and cement moved towards balance only with each other. These two industries also exhibited erratic behaviour; they were the fastest growing industries in the second period (467 and 373 per cent), but among the slower in the first period (133 and 88 per cent). If these three industries, which accounted for 9.1 per cent of the capital stock in 1955, are excluded from Table 7.1, the total number of cases is reduced to 91, and the number of cases of movement towards balance is reduced to 20. The results convey no suggestion of any general movement towards balanced growth.

Finally, if the economy failed to fulfil the requirement of being 'consumptionless', one might wonder whether the consumer goods industries were disturbing the data. If food processing and light industry are removed from Table 7.1, together with the three erratic cases, the total number of cases is reduced to 66, and the number of movements towards balance is reduced to 14. Removal of the consumer goods industries thus fails to make a difference of any consequence.

NOTES

1 Alexander Gerschenkron, *Economic Backwardness in Historical Perspective*, Harvard University Press, Cambridge, Mass., 1912, p. 8.
2 Gerschenkron, p. 7.
3 James Duesenberry, *Income, Saving and the Theory of Consumer Behaviour*, Cambridge, Mass., 1959. Schumpeter, of course, assigned

a central place to imitation in his profit theory. The perpetual disappearance of innovational profit is due to the 'borrowing of technology' within the domestic economy.

4 Henry Wallich, 'Some Notes Toward a Theory of Derived Development' in A. N. Agarwala and S. P. Singh (eds.), *The Economics of Underdevelopment*, Oxford University Press, New York, 1963. Wallich's theory of derived development is a most suggestive approach to the analysis of underdevelopment as a distinctively imitative process. This paper is heavily indebted to Wallich's analysis.

5 Joseph Stalin, *Leninism – Selected Writings*, International Publishers, New York, 1942, p. 200.

6 Zaleski, for instance, notes the numerous instances in which Western techniques are cited in the First Five Year Plan. Eugene Zaleski, *Planification de la Croissance et Fluctuations Economiques en U.R.S.S.*, Paris, 1962, p. 57.

7 *New York Times*, 4 May 1964.

8 Provided that the tension exists at all. Accounts like Kusum Nair's *Blossoms in the Dust*, Praeger, New York, 1962, warn us that even in countries like India great masses of the peasantry have experienced scarcely any demonstration effect.

9 However, the consumption patterns in the future state of communist affluence are not expected to mirror those of the bourgeois countries. Mr Krushchev made it clear, for example, that if he had his way, the automotive economy would be based on the hire principle rather than on individual ownership. No roast-pig imitation here.

10 During the catching-up period, B may alter its path in a direction that A may choose not to follow. In that case A's growth is no longer 'imitative'.

11 The concept of imitation played a central role, however, in the great debate among anthropologists about the relative importance of 'diffusion' and 'independent invention' in explaining the similarity of culture traits in different societies. Diffusion is, of course, pure imitation. Imitation has also played a role in sociology (in child 'socialization') and in psychology (in learning theory). Economic theory is rather underdeveloped among the social sciences in its analysis of imitative behaviour, perhaps because innovative behaviour is so much more interesting.

12 Gerschenkron, op. cit., p. 6.

13 Commodities like machinery that outlast one production period may be handled by assuming 'that a machine tool produces not only fabricated metal products but also a one-period-older machine tool'. See p. 282 of Robert Dorfman, Paul A. Samuelson, and Robert M. Solow, *Linear Programming and Economic Analysis*, McGraw-Hill, New York, 1958, from whose work this model and the diagrammatic representation are adapted.

14 Abram Bergson, *The Real National Income of Soviet Russia Since 1928*, Harvard University Press, Cambridge, 1961, pp. 284–8.

15 See Alexander Erlich's remarks in Abram Bergson (ed.), *Soviet*

Economic Growth, Row Peterson and Co., Evanston, 1953, pp. 93–4. The statement does not necessarily apply to US capital utilization in the nineteenth century.

16 Warren W. Eason, 'Labour Force' in Abram Bergson and Simon Kuznets (eds.), *Economic Trends in the Soviet Union*, Harvard University Press, Cambridge, 1963, p. 57.

17 Janet Chapman, 'Consumption' in Bergson and Kuznets, op. cit., pp. 51–2; also Walter Galenson, *Labor Productivity in Soviet and American Industry*, Columbia University Press, New York, 1955, pp. 52–5.

18 Dorfman, Samuelson and Solow, op. cit., pp. 215–19.

19 See note 21.

20 Richard S. Eckaus, 'The Factor–Proportions Problem in Underdeveloped Countries', *American Economic Review*, September 1955. In Eckaus' Figure 4, process Oef may be regarded as the old technology and process Oab as the newest. If the existing factor endowment happens to be in the neighbourhood of Oef, then a greater output could be obtained by redesigning a new technology such as process Ocd, rather than employing the most capital-intensive process, Oab.

21 Veblen's chief point, however, is that Germany's transformation curve was superior to England's because the latter's capital stock consisted of units of various ages, whereas the imitator's capital stock consisted entirely of the most modern.

22 Gerschenkron, op. cit., p. 7.

23 David Granick, 'Economic Development and Productivity Analysis: The Case of Soviet Metalworking', *Quarterly Journal of Economics*, May 1957.

24 David Granick, 'Organization and Technology in Soviet Metalworking: Some Conditioning Factors', *American Economic Review*, May 1957.

25 M. Gardner Clark, *The Economics of Soviet Steel*, Harvard University Press, Cambridge, Mass., 1956, pp. 65–6, 84.

26 *Pravda*, 29 December 1934.

27 Gerschenkron, op. cit., p. 9.

28 Peter Wiles has commented that breaking an expensive machine would seem to be less efficient than 'not breaking a cheap one'. This would be correct unless (a) the expensive machine is more productive during its brief but noble lifetime than the cheap one during its long but humble lifetime, and (b) the worker's skill rises more rapidly in learning to operate and maintain the expensive machine than in the case of the cheap one.

29 George Stigler, 'Production and Distribution in the Short Run', *Journal of Political Economy*, June 1939; reprinted in William Fellner and Bernard F. Haley (eds.), *Readings in the Theory of Income Distribution*, Blakiston, Philadelphia, 1946.

30 'Flexibility will be added until the "accumulated" marginal cost equals the discounted marginal returns from savings due to that additional flexibility', ibid, p. 131.

31 The following discussion is based entirely on Chapter 12 of Dorfman,

Samuelson and Solow, op. cit. Needless to say, they bear no responsibility for this interpretation.

32 Dorfman, Samuelson and Solow, op. cit., p. 315.

33 Ibid., p. 319.

34 Ibid., p. 321.

35 Ibid., p. 331.

36 It may be assumed that the economy has not yet reached the point of development at which it is prepared to veer off the turnpike towards its 'final' destination P_n. A more general theory of imitation than that presented in this paper would deal with the problem of overtaking and surpassing a target that is moving. Such a theory would be more suitable to Soviet conditions, and the present theory dealing with an assumed fixed target would be a special case.

37 Evsey Domar, *Essays in the Theory of Economic Growth*, Oxford University Press, New York, 1957.

38 The argument would apply with all signs reversed if initially α were less than A.

39 Strictly speaking, the right boundary of P_3 is a line through P_2 parallel to OV_n. Since the position of OV_n is unknown, we have substituted the known OP_2. The effect is to extend the permissible range to include some growth patterns which are not consistent with movement towards the turnpike.

40 The index for 1932–33 was estimated as 125, in J. Berliner, 'Capital Formation and Productivity in the USSR.' *Special Publications Series*, no. 14, National Academy of Economics and Political Sciences, June 1958.

8 Bureaucratic Conservatism and Creativity in the Soviet Economy* 1971

When one alludes to bureaucracy in the modern economy, one frequently has in mind the structure of firms. The modern corporation, for example, is the organization to which most of the literature on economic bureaucracy alludes. It would therefore seem appropriate to discuss bureaucracy in the Soviet economy in terms of the organization of Soviet firms. It would be a fruitful discussion, for many of the problems of large-scale corporate organization are common to Soviet and non-Soviet firms.

But precisely because corporate bureaucracy is not distinctive of the Soviet economy, it is perhaps not the most instructive topic to deal with if our purpose is to illuminate the problem of bureaucracy in one-party systems. For there is a second bureaucracy that is unique to Soviet-type economies, and which may therefore provide an insight into the nature of bureaucracy that would not be afforded by the study of other economic systems. I refer to the set of organizations interposed between the firms and the Party leadership. To distinguish it from ordinary corporate bureaucracy, I shall refer to it loosely as the 'planning bureaucracy'. Its core is the set of organizations known as economic ministries for most of the Soviet period, and as national economic councils during Khrushchev's tenure. It includes also the organizations specializing in planning proper, finance, auditing, and those segments of the Party bureaucracy primarily charged with supervision of the economy.

*This chapter is based on a paper delivered at the annual meeting of the American Political Science Association in New York City, September 1966. Material in this chapter derives from the author's book, *Factory and Manager in the U.S.S.R.*, 1957, Harvard University Press, Cambridge Mass., and from a study in progress on innovation in the Soviet economy. This chapter is reprinted from Fred W. Riggs (ed.), *Frontiers of Development Administration*, © 1971, Duke University Press.

Three factors explain the presence of this kind of bureaucracy in Soviet-type economies. The first is social ownership of the nation's productive resources. The second is a central political authority with the power to direct the national economic enterprise towards the attainment of what it has defined as its social objectives. The third is the policy of directing economic activity by specific instructions to the individual firms. None of these three factors separately requires a planning bureaucracy; it is the three together that explain its presence. For example, socially owned enterprises might be organized by means of a market-type economy with a minimum of central direction. Even if the central political authority wished to determine the direction of economic activity, this might be accomplished by a variety of indirect controls, without requiring an extensive bureaucracy between the firms and the central government. The presence of the planning bureaucracy is the result of the specific policy decision to employ the method of direct instructions to firms for the purpose of attaining social objectives. It is the method variously known as central economic planning, or the 'command economy'.

To evaluate the role of the planning bureaucracy in Soviet economic development, one must compare it with some alternative organizational device for fulfilling that role. In discussion among economists, two alternatives are widely considered. The older one is the model of a decentralized form of socialist market system, first developed by Oskar Lange. The more recent alternative is a highly centralized system using mathematical programming models and electronic computers to issue instructions directly to the firms from the central planning organization. Both alternatives would eliminate or greatly reduce the size of the planning bureaucracy.

An analysis of these alternatives would shed some light on the relative merits of bureaucratic and nonbureaucratic structures for an efficient allocation of resources. But since our primary concern is not resource allocation but bureaucracy, I have chosen a different approach. I shall assume a planning bureaucracy as given, and ask rather whether the Soviet bureaucracy has operated as effectively as it might have, given the role assigned to it by the Party leadership.

I shall consider three issues that bear on the role of the planning bureaucracy as intermediary between firms and central planners: the problem of motivation, the determination of what will be produced, and the innovation of new technology. For convenience, I shall refer to the typical bureaucratic organization as the 'ministry', although the argument might apply to a national economic council or to such sub-units of a ministry as the chief administration. While the discussion will apply primarily to the planning bureaucracy, from time to time attention will be devoted to the bureaucratic structure of firms as well.

THE PROBLEM OF MOTIVATION

The planning bureaucracy, like the corporate bureaucracy, must be evaluated. Since the planning bureaucracy are not themselves directly responsible for the production of the planned output targets, they are evaluated by the performance of the firms for whom they are responsible. Hence, they are well motivated to root out incompetent enterprise directors and promote competent ones. While less is known about the internal operations of the ministries, one would guess that the motivational system, supported by the supervision of Party and other control organs, leaves little room for incompetence there. Nepotism and sinecures, although they undoubtedly exist, are not a serious problem either in the planning bureaucracy or in the management of firms.

In another respect, however, motivation does raise a problem. Like the directors of firms, the ministry personnel are evaluated according to the extent to which plan targets are fulfilled. Accordingly, their careers ride heavily on the level of the assigned targets. Sitting astride the main channel of information between firms and central planners, ministry personnel are in a position to influence the targets assigned to them. We do know that ministries tend to assign to their firms higher targets than are necessary in order to meet their own (ministry) plans; hence the pressure on firms tends to exceed that intended by the central planners.

This practice of 'clearance planning' by the ministries was for a long time illegal, but was subsequently legalized within specified limits. If the central planners construct their aggregate targets with the understanding that by the time the ministries allocate them to the firms the sum of the targets will have increased by some 10 per cent, there may be no excessive strain on the firms. But the entire process does introduce an element of uncertainty in planning that would not be present if the bureaucracy shared fully the objectives of the central planners, instead of guarding the interests of the ministry as a unit.

One of the most widely criticized practices of the corporate bureaucracy in the USSR is the understatement of the plant's productive capacity in order to secure an easy plan target. We know that the ministry has sought, without great success, to root out this practice in order to obtain for its own purposes a truer picture of the productive capacity of its firms. I know of no direct evidence that the ministry, in turn, tends to understate the aggregate productive capacity of its firms in its reports to the central planners. The practice, however, would be consistent with the tenor of Soviet bureaucracy, and there is evidence that the ministry does engage in analogous practices, such as the hoarding of scarce materials within the ministry's jurisdiction.

In summary, the motivational system that energizes the Soviet planning bureaucracy has succeeded in rewarding competence and eliminating the less able from responsible positions in both the planning and the corporate bureaucracy. At the same time, it has introduced certain inaccuracies in the flow of information and instructions between firms and central planners, which must have an unfavourable effect on the quality of economic planning.

It may be useful to pause at this point and restate our conclusion in general terms. We have been asked to evaluate bureaucracy as 'conservative' or 'creative'. Of the many ways in which one might interpret these terms, I propose one appropriate for the present discussion. The planning bureaucracy will be deemed creative if, in its relations with the firms, it makes precisely the decisions that would be made by Party leaders were they able to administer all firms directly. The planning bureaucracy will be deemed conservative, however, if its decisions tend to promote its own interests where they do not coincide with those of the Party leaders. The standard, then, is the degree to which the planning bureaucracy correctly interprets and promotes the objectives of the Party leadership. In these terms, our conclusion is that the bureaucracy is creative with respect to personnel practices but somewhat conservative in its contribution to efficient planning.

THE DETERMINATION OF THE PRODUCT-MIX

Let me now leave this general discussion of motivation and proceed to a more concrete field of behaviour. Perhaps the major role of the bureaucracy is to determine the composition of the national output, the so-called product-mix. It participates in this process by collecting and aggregating the data supplied by firms and transmitting them to the central planning board. It is on the basis of these data that the central planners compute the best combination of outputs to be produced the following year. The bureaucracy then receives gross output targets from the planning board, disaggregates them, and distributes them as specific production targets to the individual firms.

Viewed in this schematic way, the planning bureaucracy looks like little more than a data-processing system, which might indeed be easily computerized. And if planning were perfect, there would perhaps be no need for the planning bureaucracy. But plans are inevitably imperfect, for a variety of reasons. The data are not perfectly reliable, as was mentioned above. The process of aggregation leads to certain other errors. The 'coefficients of production' which are assumed by the central planners to be constant are in fact not always constant. The system of material balancing requires some firms to accept targets that are not always realizable. Unanticipated changes occur, such as the new capacity which was not ready for production at the expected time. For all these familiar reasons, the firms are not faced with the ideally simple task of merely executing the instructions transmitted to them in the plan. They are required to make decisions not specifically provided for in the plan. If the planned product-mix cannot be fulfilled, the firm must decide which products to underfulfil. Or if the resources are available for overfulfilling the plan, the firm must decide which products to produce in excess of plan.

If there were no bureaucracy interposed between firm and central planners, the firm might consult the planners directly in each such case, in order to assure that the decision would be made so as to conform to the objectives of the central political authority. But in an economy of hundreds of thousands of firms such continuous consultation is impossible. The role of the planning bureaucracy is to guide the activities of the firms so that decisions conform to the objectives of the Party leadership.

The evidence is clear on the results. Firms make their decisions on the basis of the criteria of success established by the planning bureaucracy. The chief criterion for most of the Soviet period has been 'value of output'. Accordingly, firms have tended to select those product-mixes that yield a value of output greater than the planned target, thus overfulfilling the plan. Nevertheless, they are frequently charged with 'violating the assortment plan', that is, underfulfilling the targets for certain products while overfulfilling the targets for others. Violation of the planned product-mix is one of the longest standing charges against Soviet firms. It is unlikely to have persisted so long without some support from the planning bureaucracy. Has this bureaucracy acted creatively or conservatively, then, in this aspect of its role as intermediary between Party leadership and firms?

The ministry has the power to end the practice of assortment violation. Systematic dismissal or punishment of enterprise directors who make such decisions would yield results. That the ministry has not used this power may be explained by several factors, two of which merit discussion here. One is the motivation of ministry officials. The second, and more significant, is the difficulty of interpreting the Party leaders' objectives.

In the general discussion of motivation above, we noted that the planning bureaucracy, like the firms, tends to make those decisions which contribute to a higher score on the standards by which they own work is evaluated. In some cases, this leads to creative behaviour; in others, to conservative behaviour. The crux of the issue is the standard of evaluation. The same conclusion may be drawn here. In assessing the practice of assortment violation by firms, ministry officials are guided by the effect of that practice on their own record of performance. And like the firms, ministry officials are evaluated generally by the standard of plan fulfilment, the chief index of which is value of output. There is no more favourable report that the head of a chief administration can present to a minister or to the head of a national economic council than that his organization has overfulfilled the monthly plan.

Where the consequence of a strict insistence on assortment is underfulfilment or bare fulfilment of the plan, the ministry has been inclined not to insist. A creative response by the planning bureaucracy would be to insist that firms concentrate on those products that it knows to be more important to the Party, even if the consequence is that both firms and ministry might underfulfil the gross output plan and be deprived of the month's bonus; that is, to follow the spirit of the plan instead of the formal criterion of performance. Instead, it chooses the conservative path of following the formal rules.

OBSTACLES TO BUREAUCRATIC CREATIVITY

But even if the bureaucracy were motivated to respond creatively, there is a major difficulty it would face in trying to do so. The problem is that of determining the relative importance, or value, of different commodities, and its solution lies at the core of the economic theory of resource allocation. Briefly stated, in order to respond creatively, the planning bureaucracy must somehow know what product-mix the Party leaders would have chosen, were they able to make all the decisions that must in fact be made by the directors of firms. But the Soviet economy does not provide a satisfactory mechanism for informing either the planning bureaucracy or the corporate bureaucracy of the decisions that would best satisfy the objectives of Party leadership.

The point requires elaboration, for it is central to the economist's appraisal of the role of the planning bureaucracy in the Soviet economy. The output of a nation's enterprises consists of two major types of goods: final product and intermediate product. Final product is the end result of the economic process, the things that are desired for their own sake, so to speak, such as consumer goods and military hardware. Intermediate product consists of those things that are desired not for their own sake but because they are needed to produce final product; copper wire, for example, which is produced not in order to be used directly, but because it is needed to produce television sets or radar equipment. At any point in time, the nation's economy is capable of producing a large number of different combinations of television sets, radar, copper wire, and millions of other commodities. The task of national economic planning is to arrange for the production of that combination, or product-mix, which best satisfies the objectives of the central Party authority.

In the process of drawing up the plan, the central planners, in a rough sort of way, select the optimum combination of products. At this stage there is no need, theoretically speaking, for either the corporate or planning bureaucracy to know the objectives of the top leadership. Party leaders and central planners sit down together, pick out the optimum combination, and then assign the appropriate targets to the producing firms via the planning bureaucracy. Firms and ministry have no other role than to provide the central planners with accurate information on what they are capable of producing and then simply producing what they are told to. There is no scope for creativity in the planning bureaucracy, for all decisions have been premade by the Party leaders and hence there is no need to know what the Party leaders' intentions are.

The problem of creativity arises when we return to the real world and recognize that plans are not perfect. Consequently, decisions must be made by the planning bureaucracy. Perhaps the overall plan was too high: the targets for two commodities cannot both be fulfilled, and one must decide how much of each to produce. Perhaps the overall plan was too low: the targets for both commodities can be overfulfilled and one must decide how much of each to produce in excess of the plan. One cannot refer each such decision to the central planners, and hundreds of such decisions must be made, both by the firms and the planning bureaucracy. If the planning bureaucracy is to respond creatively, it must make the decision which would be made by the Party leaders. But how are they to know what the Party leaders would choose?

Suppose a given volume of resources could produce either one unit of copper or five units of aluminium. Which would contribute more to the objectives of the Party authorities? Or, in other words, which has the greater value? The answer depends on many things. It depends on how much copper and aluminium are required to produce television sets and radar. And it depends on whether the Party authorities wish to stress consumption or defence this year. A change in Party policy will alter the relative values of copper and alumnium. If military goods require more copper than alumi-nium, then a shift in policy towards defence will increase the relative value of copper.

What I have described is the so-called duality principle of economic theory. To any given technology and preferences, there corresponds a unique set of relative values, called 'shadow prices', of all commodities. Changes in technology and in Party policy lead to changes in the shadow prices of all commodities. If the planning bureaucracy knew the shadow prices, then they could make their decisions creatively if they were so motivated. They would devote their resources to copper or aluminium according to whether the one or the other yielded a greater value when measured at the shadow prices. Their production decisions would then correspond to what the Party leaders would have chosen were they able to make the choices themselves.

The trouble, however, is that the shadow prices are not known in the Soviet economy, either by the central planners themselves or by the planning bureaucracy or the firms. Prices are announced, but it is well known that Soviet prices do not at all correspond to the true shadow prices. Soviet prices are used primarily not as a guide for resource allocation but, among other things, as an instrument of control and evaluation of production performance. Since it is in terms of these prices that performance is evaluated, and since there are no other clear indicators of the Party's prefer-ences, production decisions tend to be made in terms of those prices. Hence the practice of selecting output combinations which, at the ruling prices, contribute most to overfulfilment of the planned value-of-output targets.

The planning bureaucracy is not entirely devoid of guides to the Party's preferences. For one thing, the Party's own bureaucracy forms part of the planning bureaucracy, providing certain crude indicators of Party policy. If a troublesome shortage of fuel has developed, or if a major construction project is being held up because of a deficit of cement, the signal will be effectively communi-cated to the relevant producing firms and ministries, and the pro-duction decisions will be made in accordance with the Party's preferences.

THE PRIORITY PRINCIPLE

The so-called priority principle also works in the same direction. The detailed production instructions contained in the plan are supplemented by a set of general directives regarding the relative importance of certain industries. In some cases the priority is informally stated and widely understood, such as the prime importance of filling the orders of military goods producers. In other cases, the priority is indicated in formal Party pronouncements, such as the decision to expand the chemical industries in order to increase the production of fertilizers, synthetic fibres, and plastics. In yet other cases, specific campaigns are conducted, such as that for the expansion of corn production in place of other grains.

The employment of general priority instructions does provide the planning bureaucracy with some crude guides for decision-making in the instances when the plan is not sufficiently specific. And there is evidence that the planning bureaucracy does respond creatively in these cases. We know that plant directors would rarely underfulfil an order destined for military use in order to overfulfil some other target that would count for more in total value of output. We may infer that, if the planning bureaucracy were aware of a transgression in this regard by a firm, it would quickly take measures to remedy it. Even if the planning bureaucracy might be disposed to ignore a general priority rule, the fact that priorities and campaigns become the focus of attention of Party and government control organizations would deter it from a conservative response.

The priority principle serves another important function from an economic point of view. It acts as a 'stabilizer' of the economic process. Stability refers to the capacity of an economic system to restore balance in production after an incipient imbalance has begun to develop. It is conceivable, in the Soviet economy, that a decision might be taken somewhere in the system to expand the production of some commodity that either uses large amounts of copper, or uses other inputs that use large amounts of copper, while no corresponding provision was made to expand the production of copper and of the things needed to produce copper. In a market economy, the incipient imbalance would automatically lead to a rise in the price of copper, which would in turn lead to a reduction in the demand and an increase in supply of copper, thus restoring balance. It is sometimes argued that the stabilizing property of a market system is a more important advantage than its efficiency in allocating resources. Without automatic stabilizers, a centrally planned economy might suffer large and growing imbalances.

The priority system is a device for restoring balance once a major imbalance has been detected. If the developing copper shortage became large enough to attract the attention of the central planners, a campaign would be undertaken to expand the production of copper and to reduce its use in those cases where substitutes may be employed. Thus, the bureaucrat motivated to act creatively can take the priority system as a crude guide to the objectives of the Party.

But the trouble with the priority system is that it is too crude. The knowledge that copper now ranks high in the values of the Party is of some use to the bureaucrat, but not very much, for it is clearly not higher than everything. Should the Ministry of Non-ferrous Metals allocate more resources to fulfil the plans of copper mines if the result is that the tin mines may underfulfil their plans? And if so by how much should tin production be allowed to fall? If the general instruction is to replace copper with substitutes, should this be done regardless of the cost of the substitute? In some cases, it would be technically possible to replace copper by iron, but the quality of the product would deteriorate and the cost may be high. Should the substitution nevertheless be made on the basis of the general priority now assigned to copper?

Because of the crudity of the priority principle, the planning bureaucracy has tended to adhere literally to the injunctions of a campaign, to a point beyond what economic rationality would have dictated, or the central planners would have wished. The fiasco of the corn-growing campaign of Nikita Khrushchev may be interpreted in these terms. There may well have been regions in which natural conditions were such that the substitution of corn for other grains would have promoted the objectives of the Party, but it is now clear that the process went far beyond the bounds of rationality, even in terms of the Party's own objectives.

The fault should not be ascribed entirely to the character of the planning bureaucracy, for in large measure it was the policy itself that was wrong. But if we assume that the policy was not simply to grow corn under all circumstances, but rather where it would increase the net value of grain output, then we may regard the response of the bureaucracy as conservative rather than creative. It was concerned with its own record of performance as that record was evaluated by the Party leadership, and not with making those decisions which would best satisfy the objectives of the Party leaders.

We may now generalize the nature of the difficulty. A priority system is a method of ranking or ordering things according to their importance or value. But ordinal indicators of value are not sufficient for economic decision-making. The economic process requires cardinal indicators of value, which we call prices. The shadow prices discussed above are ideal quantitative indicators of the relative importance of commodities according to the values of the state. Were such indicators available, the bureaucracy could make and enforce all decisions not previously made by the central planners in precisely the way the central planners would have made them. In the absence of such indicators they have no way of knowing the extent to which one or another decision would further the Party's objectives. Deprived of the information needed to respond creatively, they fall back on a conservative solution. They base their decisions on those formal or informal criteria used by their supervisors for evaluating their work. They shift the product-mix, where possible, towards products the prices of which are such that they count for most in the computation of plan fulfilment. They pursue the priority principle to such a point as will earn them recognition as effective leaders.

Let me briefly conclude this discussion of the product-mix. The Soviet planning bureaucracy, like the corporate bureaucracy, tends to act conservatively, in the sense that their decisions are usually made according to the standards of evaluation applied to them and not by reference to what the Party leaders would have decided in their place. The reason is partly due to the motivational system, which places heavy emphasis on certain formal and informal criteria of performance. But conservatism is fostered by the absence of a satisfactory set of indicators of the relative values of goods implied by the Party's preferences. Having no precise way of knowing the Party's preferences even if they were motivated to act creatively, the bureaucracy tends to make decisions favouring their own organization's performance record. Thus, if a culprit must be found, a major candidate for the cause of bureaucratic conservatism is the absence of an adequate pricing system.

QUANTITATIVE VERSUS QUALITATIVE CRITERIA

This conclusion suggests a distinction that may prove useful in the analysis of bureaucracy. There are two types of social organization for which a bureaucratic structure might be designed. In one, the typical decision that must be made is of an 'either-or' kind. The Passport Office of the State Department must decide either to issue a passport or not to issue it. In the second, the typical decision is of the 'how much' kind. The Internal Revenue Service must decide not whether to tax the citizen or not, but rather how much to tax him. The difference corresponds to that between quality and quantity.

Now the problem of bureaucracy, as I see it, is that an organization's leaders cannot specify in complete detail the decisions they would wish the bureaucracy to make in all possible instances. They therefore specify certain detailed rules to be applied to those categories in which most of the decisions are likely to fall and, for the rest, define the general principles to be followed in making decisions for those categories not specifically identified. The conservative bureaucracy is one that interprets all cases literally and insists on following the detailed rule even when the general principles suggest that the case is not one to which the rule was intended to apply. A creative bureaucracy takes the general principles as a guide to the leader's objectives and departs from the specific rule when it believes the category is not one to which the rule was intended to apply.

I should like now to present two propositions relating to the likelihood that a bureaucracy will behave creatively. The first is that the more clearly and unambiguously the general principles are presented, the more likely is the bureaucracy to respond creatively in terms of those principles. The second is that general principles covering qualitative categories are more difficult to formulate clearly and unambiguously than those relating to quantitative magnitudes. If these propositions are true, it follows that bureaucracies that deal primarily with qualitative categories are more likely to act conservatively, and bureaucracies that deal primarily with quantitative decisions are more likely to act creatively. A ministry of foreign affairs is likely to be more conservative that a ministry of finance. (The point, of course, applies not to the policies of the ministries but to the manner of their implementation by the bureaucracies.)

The first proposition will probably be regarded as fairly reasonable. Given a choice between following a clear rule and a fuzzy one, most people are surely likely to follow the former. The second proposition is rather harder to defend. Suppose there are two organizations. The objective of one is to issue passports to all citizens except when the issuance of a passport would not be in the national interest. The objective of the second is to attain a maximal output with given resources from the joint efforts of those who comprise the organization. My contention is that a set of general instructions to the bureaucracy designed to attain the objective of the first would be much less clear and unambiguous than would the instructions to the second bureaucracy. In the first case, one would rely heavily on a listing of all the qualitative characteristics one can think of at the time of persons whose travel abroad might endanger the national interest. This detailed listing, and not the more amorphous notion of national interest, is likely to become a literal guide to decision-making. In the second case, 'maximization of output with given resources' is a fairly unambiguous guide (given prices and certain other parameters), and the bureaucrat would have no difficulty applying this kind of principle to the problem of how much labour should be allocated to copper or to tin.

If these propositions are true, then one would expect economic bureaucracies in general to be more creative than others that deal primarily in qualitative matters. The conclusion of our discussion of the product-mix problem, however, was that the Soviet planning bureaucracy tended towards conservatism. Does the Soviet case disprove the generalization? On the contrary, the problem there is precisely that the system has not taken advantage of the potential creativity of an economic bureaucracy. The planning bureaucracy has been given only qualitative rules for decision-making, such as a priority rule of the form 'copper is more important than tin'. But the problem is not to issue passports to copper and tin; it is rather how much copper and how much tin.

The instructions are simply not clear enough for making the kinds of quantitative decisions the planning bureaucracy is called upon to make. What is required is a set of shadow prices that express the relative values of the Party leaders, and a general rule for allocating resources in the light of these prices. Deprived of the quantitative instructions needed to respond creatively, the Soviet planning bureaucracy is obliged to act conservatively. The potential creativity of an economic bureaucracy is lost because it is managed like a bureaucracy designed to make qualitative decisions.

INNOVATION OF NEW TECHNOLOGY

I have thus far discussed bureaucratic creativity in terms of a standard appropriate to the current operation of the economy, without regard to economic change. It is time to shift to the discussion of change. Here we might expect to find stronger evidence of bureaucratic creativity, for it is here that the economy has demonstrated what is probably its most signal success. The Soviet economy has broken few world records for efficiency of resource allocation, but it has compiled an impressive record in its rates of economic transformation.

In assessing the role of the bureaucracy in promoting economic development, there are at least two facets of the development process upon which we might focus. The first is the mobilization of savings in order to generate a high rate of investment. The second is the promotion of technical innovation. While the system has probably been more successful in the first than in the second, I propose to discuss the second because it directs our attention to more interesting problems of bureaucracy in general and of the Soviet economy in particular.

There is little doubt that the system has been effective in generating an enormous volume of new technology. One need only compare the technological status of the economy today with any earlier period to be persuaded of the fact. To be sure, much of the advance has consisted primarily of expansion of existing forms of technology: a new steel mill is an innovation even if its technology duplicates that of existing steel mills. But much of the advance consists of genuinely new and improved technology, although unfortunately we have no quantitative measures of the magnitude.

However, effectiveness is not the same thing as efficiency. Effectiveness refers to a system's capacity to attain certain results, without regard to the effort and resources employed in attaining those results. Efficiency refers to the relationship between the magnitude of the results and the magnitude of the effort and resources invested. I assume that it is efficiency rather than effectiveness that one ought to have in mind in assessing the creative or conservative role of bureaucracy. Therefore, as an approximate indicator of efficiency, I shall define conservatism and creativity in roughly the same way as the terms were used in the preceding discussion. A creative bureaucracy is one in which the rate and pattern of technological change, given the resources available, is the same as that which would have been achieved by the system's leaders had they been able to make all the decisions made in fact by the bureaucracy. A conservative bureaucracy, at the opposite extreme, introduces none of the changes that would have been introduced by the leaders. We may expect that most bureaucracies would fall somewhere between these polar opposites.

Where does the Soviet bureaucracy fall in respect to technological change? We cannot, of course, know what rate of technological change would be generated if the Soviet leaders could make all the decisions. But we do know that they regard the present rate as quite unsatisfactory. In every major Party or government review of the economic state of the nation, one may expect to find criticisms like Mr Khrushchev's complaint a few years ago:

In our country some bureaucrats are so used to the old nag that they do not want to change over to a good race horse, for he might tear away on the turn and even spill them out of the sleigh! Therefore, such people will hold on to the old nag's tail with both hands and teeth.[1]

Some quantitative evidence is also available. It is reported that the rate of fulfilment of the union-level plan for the introduction of new technology is normally in the range of 50–60 per cent.[2] There are, moreover, many reasons for regarding even these figures as an overstatement. The percentages refer to the number of projects successfully completed, without regard to the size of the projects. Accordingly, officials tend to select for completion smaller projects requiring little effort, in order to compile a favourable record.[3] The figures also include exploits of imaginative Soviet officials of the sort *Izvestia* criticized: 'The enterprise merely changes a button, and the management claims an innovation.'[4]

FACTORS INHIBITING INNOVATION

The evidence is clear that there is fairly widespread resistance to innovation in the economy. Most of the evidence, however, deals with the practices of firms. We know much less about the attitude toward innovation of the planning bureaucracy, which is the central concern in this paper. But since the firm ultimately determines whether or not an innovation will be introduced, we must devote some attention to the factors influencing the firm's decision.

The major incentive for innovation is a system of special monetary bonuses. Equipment and machinery producers, for instance, receive bonuses based on the cost savings of the firms that use the new equipment. Under the bonus scheme in use between 1956 and 1961, innovation bonuses amounted to about 1 per cent of the total wages and salaries of equipment-producing firms.[5] In addition to monetary awards, a record of successful innovation is likely to enhance the reputation of a manager and promote his career.

Were these the only factors involved in managerial decision-making, one might expect a reasonably creative response to innovation opportunities. The evidence indicates however, that the positive incentives for innovation tend to be dominated by more potent factors tending toward conservatism. The most important of these others factors is the primacy of current production plan fulfilment as the indicator of general managerial performance. Plan fulfilment is the first objective of management, not only because it is the principal criterion of performance, but because a large portion of the manager's monthly take-home pay is tied to it. Plan fulfilment adds approximately 20–50 per cent to one's base salary, compared to the average of about 1 per cent earned for successful innovations.

However, the primacy of current plan fulfilment would not tend to inhibit innovation, despite the large differences in potential monetary awards, if there were no conflict between the two activities. Managers do not resist innovation out of a primal urge, but because the effort and resources devoted to innovative activity may cause the current production plan to be underfulfilled.

A number of reasons may be cited for the conflict between innovation and plan fulfilment. First, a major innovation often requires several years before the kinks are ironed out and it begins to operate successfully. During that period the planned output, which would have been attained under the old technology, is not likely to be attained while the new technology is being mastered. Second, even if in the long run the new technology justifies itself many times over, the tenure of office of Soviet officials is relatively short, and their planning horizon tends to focus on the short run. A record of several successive periods of underfulfilment of plan may lead to loss of bonuses and perhaps demotion, leaving the eventual benefits of the innovation to be enjoyed by the next manager.

Third, new technology often requires considerable new resources and new suppliers. Given the difficulties of obtaining supplies in a tautly planned system, innovations tend to aggravate the already tight supply situation. Fourth, the prices of new products are often set at a level that provides a lower rate of profit and counts for less in computing plan fulfilment, than do the older standard products. Hence, if plan fulfilment is threatened, the tendency is to shift away from the new products toward the safe old ones.

Fifth, the customers of new equipment must rely on the producer for servicing and for spare parts. Since the shortage of spare parts is one of the perennial problems of Soviet management, firms are cautious about installing new equipment and increasing their dependence on the services of other firms. The strategy of minimizing dependence on other firms has led to a number of costly 'autarkic' practices, such as the construction and equipping of large machine shops for the purpose of producing one's own spare parts and rebuilding old equipment rather than taking the chance of installing new models.

Sixth, the introduction of new models involves the firm in extensive testing and negotiations with research institutes and other official agencies whose approval is required before the production is authorized. Seventh, Gale Johnson has noted that a long history of agricultural campaigns for innovations which proved to be ill-advised has undermined the confidence of agricultural officials in new techniques and equipment, at least those imposed upon the farms by industrial firms and the bureaucracy. The consequence has been a 'hostile environment for technical change'.[6]

This set of factors has generated a widespread tendency to avoid risk-taking. As summarized by the *Economic Gazette*:

Frequently a person who never makes mistakes is the man who never shows any personal initiative and never takes risks upon himself; and such people are good managers. The whole world will come loose on the head of the innovator who is courageous and not afraid of risk or mistakes that may accompany research and change.[7]

We have established that the corporate bureaucracy of the firms tends to be conservative rather than creative with regard to innovation. Our concern, however, is with the role of the planning bureaucracy. What can one say about its behaviour? As in our analysis of the product-mix problem, one would expect that the behaviour of the planning bureaucracy must be in part responsible for the character of the firm's behaviour. Since less is known about the planning bureaucracy, the precise pressures under which it operates cannot be described in as great detail. But enough is known to suggest that in important ways it supports, or at least does not positively discourage, conservatism in the firms. This generalization, which emerged from earlier studies of the Soviet economy, is supported by the most recent investigation, by Barry Richman. His conclusion is as follows:

It is evident from Soviet sources and interviews with Soviet managers that in most instances, no significant penalties are imposed for failure to fulfill innovation assignments. In general, *sovnarkhoz* officials and enterprise party officials are reluctant to compel managers to innovate unless they themselves have received firm orders and are subject to pressure from their own bosses. The personal status of these officials hinges on the criterion used for evaluating and rewarding enterprise management. For this reason innovation assignments often have little operational significance for enterprise managers.[8]

The view that the source of the conservatism of firms is to be found in the planning bureaucracy is supported by many hints in the literature. Alec Nove, for instance, quotes the following comment in a Soviet literary periodical:

Suppose the director desires to bring into production a new (plastic) powder ... he would have to wait endlessly in ministerial reception rooms. There is a risk here. The risk is not that millions might be lost. He might take up these powders and, God forbid, the quarterly plan will be messed up, and the ministry will show up badly in the statistical report.[9]

The planning bureaucracy – ministry or national economic council – is the 'home office' of the firms. It is they who evaluate the firms, who determine the bonuses of managerial personnel, and who either promote or retard the careers of directors. Hence, it is the interests of the planning bureaucracy, as perceived by plant managers, that govern the decisions of firms. The bureaucracy is held to account, above all, by fulfilment of current-plan targets. And, since innovation often threatens plan fulfilment, both bureaucracy and firms tend to respond conservatively to it.

FACTORS ENCOURAGING INNOVATION

We have emphasized thus far the factors that inhibit innovation. This, of course, is only part of the tale, and we must also account for the fact that innovation does take place and the economy has progressed technologically. A number of factors help account for the fact that, despite the tendency towards conservatism, innovation does occur.

First, commercial secrecy as practised in private enterprise economies does not prevail in the Soviet economy. Hence, the stock of technological knowledge from which innovations might be drawn is rather wider, other things being equal, than it would be in a market economy. Second, as a relatively underdeveloped economy, the Soviet Union has been able to draw on the vast body of advanced technological knowledge available in the West. The volume of translated and published technological information available in the USSR is perhaps the largest in the world. Third, it is likely that the introduction of borrowed technology is both easier and less risky than the introduction of technology that has never been tried before. Moreover, in the 1920s and 1930s, a substantial portion of the new technology was introduced into the USSR by Western firms under contractual arrangements.

Fourth, given the high rate of investment, much new technology was introduced in the form of entirely new enterprises. Since in such cases there are no established production lines that may be upset if a new process is introduced, the sources of resistance are not present. Fifth, in such high-priority industries as aerospace and defence-related industries, the bureaucratic distance between firms and central planners is very small. These are what Nove calls 'naturally centralized' production processes. Since very little bureaucracy is interposed between central planners and firms, bureaucratic conservatism does not arise to inhibit innovation. Moreover, these high-priority industries are run by the most highly trained and least replaceable of managerial and technical personnel, who are more likely to regard innovation as a fulfilling challenge and as a mode of advancement, rather than as a threat to their positions.

Sixth, innovations vary greatly in the degree of risk associated with their introduction. The least risky are presumably adopted first, in order to satisfy the minimal demands for fulfilling the new technology requirements, and they contribute to the record of technological progress. The risk is further reduced by managers who use such familiar devices as stockpiling supplies in anticipation of trouble and understating the output capacity of the new process. There are, moreover, innovations which increase productivity so quickly that they promote rather than retard the short-run interests of managers in current plan fulfilment.

Seventh is the fact that within the bureaucracy interests often conflict, and the conservative behaviour of one bureaucratic group may be resisted by the pressure from another. A research institute that has developed a new process may have a strong professional and personal interest in seeing the process widely introduced and will exert pressure in the ministry to overcome the foot-dragging by chief administrations and firms. Members of the Party bureaucracy, moreover, may be operating under specific instructions that impel them to push on occasion for innovations that the production bureaucracy might have preferred to postpone; or one ministry's plans may be dependent on the production of certain new equipment by another ministry. If the stakes are high enough, the latter will exert pressure on the former through the Council of Ministers. This is perhaps the chief source of the pressure on firms from their own planning bureaucracy, which ordinarily gives tacit support for resistance to innovation that threatens current plan fulfilment.

Eight, and finally, somewhere near the top of the hierarchy the line between 'Party leadership' and 'planning bureaucracy' is blurred. Many of the most important ministers are members of the highest Party councils and also head bureaucratic establishments. They are part of the group who generate the very preferences we have employed as the standard for determining whether the planning bureaucracy will take those decisions which are or are not in accord with Party preferences. They are more judges than judged, and however one might evaluate their performance, it is surely not by the same kinds of criteria as are used for officials located further down the hierarchy. They are a major source of continuous pressure for innovation that helps explain the rate of technological progress the system has achieved.

The factors promoting innovation in the Soviet economy then, have led to a substantial rate of technological progress. But the rate has been less than it would have been had the Party leadership been in the position to make the decisions to innovate. The reason may be ascribed to certain conditions making for conservative rather than creative behaviour in the planning bureaucracy interposed between Party leaders and firms. As in the case of product-mix decisions, the primacy of fulfilling current production plans as a criterion of performance militates against the creative response of assuming those risks which Party leaders would if they were able to make all decisions.

SOME SUGGESTIONS FOR REFORM

It may be useful to conclude the discussion by considering some ways the system might be changed so as to increase its creativity. Since it is the planning bureaucracy whose behaviour is under analysis, I shall exclude from consideration those proposals that would do away entirely with that bureaucracy. I shall assume that a planning bureaucracy will continue to be interposed between central planners and firms and consider ways in which the conservative tendencies of this bureaucracy might be modified.

The analysis has identified two major sources of conservatism. One is the absence of a satisfactory set of quantitative indicators of the relative values of commodities as implied in the Party's preferences. The other is the fact that the incentive system is tied to a criterion of performance that motivates behaviour not consistent with Party preferences. These sources of conservatism might be modified by the introduction of three types of measure. First is a pricing system designed to approximate more closely the true shadow prices of commodities and factors of production. Second is the use of a criterion of performance better designed to lead to decisions consistent with the Party's preferences. And third is a set of incentives which, given a satisfactory measure of performance, will maximize the efforts of managers to make decisions consistent with the Party's preferences.

A voluminous literature has now developed on the problem of price formation in the Soviet economy, and I shall not comment on it here. The regime has announced its intention to introduce a major reform, and we may expect a new pricing system to be introduced eventually. Informed as it is likely to be by the extensive development of economic theory in recent years, the new pricing system is likely to serve more successfully than past policies as a guide to the relative values of goods as implied by the preferences of the Party leaders. If the bureaucracy is authorized to accept these prices as a basis of decision-making, we may expect more creative behaviour. Instead of such vague guides as an instruction to 'substitute aluminium for copper whenever possible', firms and ministries could decide on the appropriate substitution in each case on the basis of the announced prices. If the central planners discover that, with given prices, the demand for copper still exceeds the supply, they can then raise the relative price of copper. This will serve as a precise quantitative guide to users of copper to press the use of substitutes still further and to producers of copper to shift resources to copper production still further. 'Violation of the assortment plan' will cease to be regarded as an act of bureaucratic conservatism, but rather as a signal to the central planners that certain prices should be adjusted.

A satisfactory system of prices would provide a clue to the Party's wishes needed by those firm and ministries who happen to be motivated to behave creatively. But we have seen that there are certain defects in the structure of bureaucratic motivations. In particular, the dominance of value of output as the criterion of performance focuses decision-making on that at the expense of a variety of other considerations, such as cost of production and innovation. The defect of this criterion has long been known to Soviet economists and has most recently come under the vigorous criticism of Professor Liberman.

His well known remedy is the use of profit rather than value of output as the principal criterion of performance. Given a satisfactory set of prices, decisions which would increase profit would at the same time be consistent with the objectives of the Party's leaders. Firms and ministries motivated to respond creatively would no longer face the prospect of showing a poorer record of performance as that performance has been evaluated in the past. Since costs of production affect profit, they would devote the same attention to cost-minimization as would the Party leaders, were the latter able to make all decisions. If the period over which profit is calculated were lengthened, the motivation for innovation would be increased, since short-run losses due to innovation may be offset by long-run profits. Thus, the use of profit rather than output as the criterion of performance would motivate more creative behaviour in the bureaucracy.

The two reforms proposed above would be expected to channel decision-making in a direction more consistent with the objectives of the Party's leaders. But the success of these reforms would depend on one more factor, namely, the incentives determining the intensity with which managers promote the Party's objectives. The prime incentive in the past has been income, particularly the monetary bonuses for successful effort in excess of that provided for in the plan. The evidence suggests that the system of monetary incentives has been highly successful in eliciting a high level of effort; the problems have arisen from the misdirection of effort rather than its intensity. The shift from value of output to profit as the criterion of performance would not eliminate income as the primary reward; the only change is that the income would be earned on the basis of the profit made rather than the output produced.

But the success of the income incentive depends not only on the criterion of performance, but also on the size of the incentive. The evidence of the past suggests that the size of the income payments to successful managers has been sufficient to attract into the occupation a competent group of officials and to motivate them to work hard at their jobs. There is one aspect of endeavour, however, in which the incentive system has not seemed to work. I refer to effort directed towards innovational activity. One of the causes of the conservative attitude towards innovation was identified above as the primacy of short-run plan-fufilment targets. With a shift to profit as the criterion, resistance to innovation might be reduced, especially if the time period for evaluating profitability is extended.

However, a question may be raised whether the size of the incentive income is sufficient to motivate the desired degree of innovative activity. One may distinguish the task of current management of the economy from the task of introducing technological change. It is a plausible conjecture that incentives adequate to the first task may not be adequate to the second. If so, the promotion of a more creative response to innovation by both the planning and the corporate bureaucracy may require a substantial increase in the size of the incentives for successful innovation.

In the analysis of the private enterprise economy it has been found convenient, especially in the writings of Schumpeter, to distinguish the 'wages of management' from the 'profits of entrepreneurship'. The distinction has lost some of its force in the modern corporate bureaucracy, but the point undoubtedly still applies. It requires a relatively modest income prospect to motivate a firm to continue with the production of a long-tested product or with the use of a proven process, but it requires a much larger set of income possibilities to motivate the firm to take on a new product or process. If the income opportunities available for the second are no greater than those available for the first, the volume of innovative activity is likely to be much less.

There is reason to believe that the same principle may apply to the Soviet economy. Innovation involves risk and it also involves a great deal more effort than does the successful management of an ongoing production operation. Salaried officials are likely to think many times before risking the respectable income they earn from successful current operations for the sake of an innovation that would not bring substantially greater rewards. To pose the problem in this way is to suggest a possible solution. If the structure of incentives were such as to hold out the possibility of very large rewards, commensurate with the social profitability of the new product or process, the willingness to respond creatively might be greatly enhanced.

What is needed is an incentive system that will allow for the creation of Soviet millionaires. It might seem as if the proposal conflicts with a basic ideological precept of an acceptable socialist income-distribution policy. But the history of the Soviet economy attests to the ideological flexibility of the system in the face of economic pressures. Moreover, the proposal is not a radical departure from present income policy; it is rather an extension of that policy. For one thing, there may already exist millionaires, among the most successful writers and artists who earn very large incomes on the basis of royalties. Secondly, the incomes will be earned not from exploitative or monopoly power, but from the promotion of the interests of the socialist state.

Third, present income policy is based on the proposition that persons should be rewarded in proportion to their contribution. This policy is applied to the incomes of labour and of management. The one major area to which it is not applied is entrepreneurship or innovation. If it were applied there, then the persons who conceive and implement a successful innovation that contributes many millions to the socialist economy would be awarded some portion of those millions for their pains. Failure to do so is in fact inconsistent with present policy. Innovators are perhaps the most exploited group in the economy as measured by the gap between the value of their contribution and the size of their rewards.

The point of the proposal, however, is not equity but efficiency. If the rate of innovation is indeed less than it would be were the Party leaders themselves able to make all the decisions, then bureaucratic conservatism involves a loss to the society. Each year's national product is less than it could be, and the gap between actual and potential product grows over time. If the gap could be closed by offering to the innovator a substantial portion of the gains from innovation in the form of personal income, the objectives of the Party's leaders would be more fully attained. The creation of a class of socialist millionaires may be the price of eliminating this major locus of bureaucratic conservatism.

NOTES

1   *Pravda*, 2 July 1959.
2   *Pravda*, 22 November 1962.

3 Gregory Grossman, 'Innovation and Information in the Soviet Economy', *American Economic Review*, vol. 56, May 1966, p. 126.
4 30 August 1963.
5 Barry M Richman, *Soviet Management: With Significant American Comparisons*, Englewood Cliffs, NJ, 1965, p. 194.
6 D. Gale Johnson, 'The Environment for Technological Change in Soviet Agriculture', *American Economic Review*, vol. 56, May 1966, pp. 148–9.
7 *Ekonomicheskaia gazeta*, 23 November 1963.
8 Richman, *Soviet Management*, op. cit., p. 197.
9 Alec Nove, *The Soviet Economy*, New York, 1961, p. 169.

9 Some International Aspects of Soviet Technological Progress*
1973

The rate and direction of technological advance in any country depend primarily on its domestic institutions and policies. The structures of the economy and of the educational and scientific institutions are of predominant importance. Policies regarding the distribution of income and the allocation of funds for research and development also play a major role. While a country's technological attainment is accounted for primarily by these internal factors, it is also influenced to some substantial degree by the country's relationships with the rest of the world. The objective of this study is to present some thoughts about the effect on Soviet technological progress of the nature of its international relations.

THE EFFECTS OF ISOLATION

A fundamental feature of modern science and technology is its international character. One need only imagine what the present level of world technology would be if in the past fifty years each nation had sought to develop its science and technology solely on the basis of its own intellectual resources. Even such leaders as the United States have depended heavily upon advances in other countries. In his book, *The Sources of Economic Growth in the United States and the Alternative Before Us*, Edward Denison estimates that over half of the advance in knowledge that affects our growth originates in other countries. Because of the international

*Warren Lerner (ed.) 'The Development of Soviet Foreign Policy: Studies in Honor of W. W. Kulski' special issue of *South Atlantic Quarterly* 72:3, pp. 340–50. Copyright Duke University Press.

nature of technological advance, any country that does not participate fully in that international intercourse suffers a disadvantage
in the promotion of technological progress. That has been the case
with the USSR. The international flow of technological knowledge
takes place through the movement of publications, products, and
persons. The Soviets have relied most heavily on the first, less
on the second, and least on the last. The effectiveness of technological transfer, however, is in the reverse order. They have therefore
not benefited from international technological development to the
same extent as more open societies.

Publications

The Soviets have sought to keep abreast of technological developments in the non-socialist countries primarily through the extensive
purchase of foreign scientific and technical literature and by a
massive programme of translation and dissemination. One has the
impression that the major research centres and enterprises have
fairly good access to these materials. They have undoubtedly been
of benefit and account for a significant part of Soviet technological
advances. But there are certain problems in relying upon publications as a major source of information. For one thing, outside
of the major centres they do not seem to be generally available.
The practical consequences may be seen in an account by an
engineer in an industrial design institute – the establishment that
is responsible for the design of new plants and the choice of the
technology included in them. The engineer is under instruction to
make sure that the plant's technology is equal to the best available
in the world. 'However,' he writes, 'how am I supposed to know
what the best technology is that is available in the world? I have
very few catalogues of foreign firms, and besides, most of them
are a number of years old.' The same problem of knowing the
current level of world technology must also arise in programmes
such as the recent efforts to upgrade quality levels by the procedure
known as State Quality Certification. Under this procedure, enterprises are encouraged to submit their latest models to a commission
of experts, and if they pass the test of equivalence to the best
world technology, the producers are entitled to charge a higher
price. But in the absence of a full knowledge of the state of world
technology, neither the product designers nor the experts can carry
out the jobs assigned to them. Further evidence of the problem
is the occasional published reviews of the work of the industrial
research and design institutes. One often reads that products are
presented as new that have long since appeared elsewhere, not

only in other countries but sometimes in other research and design institutes and enterprises in the USSR.

More significant, however, is that even at best, published materials are a poor way of keeping abreast of current developments. This is particularly true in the high-technology industries and in products undergoing rapid technological advance. Generally by the time a development appears in the scientific, engineering and industrial journals, the horizon of development work has moved forward, and reliance on those sources is an invitation to premature obsolescence.

Products

A second source of technological transfer is international trade in products that incorporate advanced technology. Here too the Soviets have not benefited from this source to the same extent as have other countries. For one thing, Soviet trade has, until recently, accounted for a smaller portion of the national product than has been the case in capitalist countries. Moreover, about four-fifths of their trade has been conducted with other socialist countries, none of whom have been leaders in the development of world technology. In the post-Second World War period, part of the explanation of the low level of technological transfer through trade has been the consequence not of Soviet policy but of the Western embargo. To some extent, however, it has been due to Soviet policy as well. Even in the case of commodities that were not on the embargo lists, Soviet purchasers for a long time made a practice of purchasing a few models as prototypes for copying, preferring to substitute domestically produced equipment for imports. Hence, even in the absence of the embargo, it is not likely that foreign trade would have led to a massive presence of foreign equipment and components in Soviet factories, or of foreign-manufactured consumer goods in Soviet markets. The reasons for the self-exclusion from international trade with capitalist countries are largely political. They reflect in part considerations of national defence, and in part a desire to avoid excessive dependence on capitalist economies that might lead to political pressures. The policy of autarky was strongest and most explicit in Stalin's lifetime and has only slowly given way since – primarily, we may suppose, as a result of economic considerations.

The limited presence of foreign products of advanced design on Soviet markets affects the level of Soviet technology in various ways. For one thing, it removes what would otherwise be a source of competitive pressure on Soviet enterprises to upgrade the quality of output. One can see this competitive pressure at work in a socialist country like Yugoslavia, where the shops carry a full range of products from a great number of countries. The presence of these products must serve as a stern source of production discipline on Yugoslav enterprises that are obliged to compete against them. The price- and quality-competition of foreign products acts in the same way in the markets of capitalist countries. Soviet foreign trade policy provides an umbrella of protection to Soviet producers, with a corresponding reduction in the pressure for quality of output. The policy also limits the knowledge available to Soviet designers and producers regarding the current quality standards in the rest of the world. American embassy people in Moscow have expressed the view that one of the reasons for the keen Soviet interest in promoting international trade expositions in the USSR is to give their engineers an opportunity to study the models of foreign technology presented in the exhibitions. They report that large numbers of engineers from all over the USSR come to Moscow on these occasions on special travel allowances and virtually crawl in and out of the equipment, taking notes on its technical properties.

A greater degree of participation in international trade would, for these reasons, serve to advance the level of Soviet technology. This indeed may prove to be the major gain from the current expansion of trade with the United States. Trade, however, like publications, has certain limitations as an instrument of technology transfer. The technology incorporated in manufactured products and even in the import of manufacturing plant like the Fiat automotive works in Togliatti, tends to lag behind the most advanced technology still in the development process. Moreover, in many of the high technology industries, the manufacturing technology is not reproducible simply on the basis of the physical product. In the production of transistors and integrated circuits, for example, neither chemical nor mechanical analysis provides a clue to the precisely controlled manufacturing techniques. In such technologies only the purchase of a manufacturing licence provides the knowledge of the technology. This is probably the reason for the growing Soviet interest in the purchase of foreign licences and in joint production arrangements.

Foreign Travel

A case could be made for the view that the chief source of international transfer of technology is not the movement of publications or products but the movement of persons. In this connection one thinks first of international meetings and conferences, and they are an important part of the process but probably not the most important part. The movement of individual students and scientists among universities and research centres in different countries is perhaps more important. In both of these activities, Soviet citizens participate only to a limited extent. The institution of the 'cultural exchange agreement' is a reflection of the political problems which such exchanges present to the Soviet leadership.

Perhaps the chief agent of technology transfer is the industrial sales engineer with his catalogue and sample case. It is not accidental that Japanese businessmen account for so rapidly growing a share of the commercial passengers in international aircraft. If we had data on the nationality composition of international commercial travel, I would guess that it would be highly correlated with national technological levels. In this kind of travel, Soviet citizens play a very small role.

The commercial traveller transfers technology in two ways. First, in the process of sales promotion, he informs producers in other countries of the newest technology available abroad. With a keen interest in selling his products, he informs potential adopters about the technical parameters and operating characteristics of his products. This personal approach in international sales activity has contributed significantly to the transfer of technology. The second contribution of international sales travel is to inform sellers about the technical attainments of foreign firms. A commercial agent selling to a foreign firm will necessarily become familiar with the firm's facilities, in order to judge the manufacturing guarantees he is prepared to make, or to adapt his product to the requirements of the firm. In the process he learns the properties of the competing foreign technologies. In this and other ways, progressive firms engaged in international sales keep informed of the changing technological levels in other countries.

On both of these counts, Soviet engineers are deprived of the benefits of the international flow of technological information. Because of the inaccessibility of Soviet enterprises to foreign industrial sales personnel, Soviet managers and engineers do not gain the information on foreign advances in their own technology that is available to firms in more open societies. Soviet purchasing is done by the foreign trade corporations, the representatives of which cannot be expected to have a detailed knowledge of the specific technical requirements of the firms for which they are purchasing. The sellers are unable to redesign their equipment to the technical requirements of the unknown users, nor are they able to service their products in the ways they normally do in other countries, and are therefore reluctant to offer performance guarantees. Moreover, Soviet enterprises do not benefit from the information imparted by the stream of foreign sales engineers who visit the enterprises of other countries. More significant, however, is the fact that Soviet engineers do not travel about the world on business as do sales engineers and businessmen of other countries. Development work and product improvement are conducted with a very constricted flow of information on what has been accomplished by progressive industry in the rest of the world.

There are indications that some of these restrictions will be relaxed in the wake of the political accommodation between the USSR and the United States. Foreign firms are to be allowed to maintain offices in the USSR, and foreign sales personnel may be allowed greater access to Soviet firms. Soviet engineering and management personnel are travelling abroad in greater number, and joint research projects will enable Soviet scientists and engineers to reside abroad for extended periods. This relaxation may be expected to contribute to technological advance in Soviet Russia.

Political Implications

There is a widespread dissatisfaction among Soviet political and industrial leaders with the rate of technological progress. A great many measures have been introduced in the economy in recent years designed to encourage innovation, and the spurring of technological progress was one of the major gains hoped for from the general economic reform of 1965. The focus of the effort, however, is on the reform of internal economic arrangements and policies. In this, Soviet leaders are surely right, for the economic system does contain a number of substantial obstacles to innovation. Moreover, it is the reform of internal institutions and policies that holds the greatest promise of accelerating technological progress. Whatever the internal arrangements, however, the international factors discussed above will continue to act as a drag on the attainable rate of technological advance. Although these international aspects of technological progress are not widely discussed in the published literature, they must surely be on the minds of some Soviet observers, particularly the sophisticated officials in the State Committee on Science and Technology and in the Academy of Sciences. The public silence must reflect, not oversight, but the political delicacy of the subject. For if the foregoing analysis is correct, it means that the Soviets have paid a heavy economic cost for the political controls on the movement of products and persons. It means that the price of joining the international technology club is a massive expansion of the right of Soviet industrial, scientific, and engineering personnel to travel abroad, and of foreign businessmen to travel more easily in the country and to visit Soviet enterprises in search of new business. The current steps taken in this direction suggest that the Soviet leadership may be willing to pay the price, at least in part. The interesting question is whether the traditional system of political and social controls can accommodate itself to a growing traffic of persons across the country's borders.

THE EFFECT OF WESTERN ECONOMIC GROWTH

The capitalist West serves as a source of advanced technological knowledge for the USSR. But it serves also in another way that affects Soviet policy. It sets the standard by which the Soviet leaders evaluate their own economic and technological performance.

At the time of the Revolution, no article of Bolshevik faith was stronger than the belief that capitalism had entered the stage of general crisis and that the socialist society would fairly rapidly overtake and surpass the economic level of the advanced capitalist countries. That faith was strengthened during the depression of the 1930s. But the unexpected vitality exhibited by the West in the post-war years, and the remarkable performance of capitalist Japan, must have shaken the confidence of the Soviet leadership. The decline in the Soviet growth rate since the late 1950s has compounded the sense of trouble.

One cannot overstress the role of the West in the formulation of Soviet policy. On the face of it, Soviet economic and technological performance has not been at all bad. The growth rate of GNP even now is in the range of 4–6 per cent. The annual growth rate of total factor productivity is in the neighbourhood of 3 per cent, which is well within the range of the capitalist West, although in the low part of the range. The sense of crisis and the surge of economic reforms must be accounted for on the basis of the relative rather than the absolute performance of the Soviet economy. Imagine for example that the stagnation of the 1930s had persisted in the capitalist countries throughout the post-war period. The performance of the Soviet economy would then have been regarded by the Soviet leaders as a cause for celebration rather than a source of concern. There would have been no occasion to question the effectiveness of Stalinist economic arrangements, no massive territorial decentralization of economic management under Khrushchev, no audience for the reformist proposals of Liberman and no impetus for the 1965 economic reforms. The rate of technological progress generated by the economic system would have been regarded as entirely satisfactory, and there would have been no motivation to tamper with a system that produced those results.

Viewed in this light, the future of Soviet society depends not so much upon what happens in the USSR as what happens in the West. The present rate of Soviet technological progress is probably the maximum that may be expected in a system in which the economy is centrally planned and the political organization of which requires the restriction of personal travel. A substantial acceleration of technological progress is not likely to occur in the absence of some considerable economic decentralization and political liberalization. Those in the USSR who argue for such policies base their case in part on the need to promote technological progress. And the strength of their case depends on the continued vitality of economic growth and technological progress in the West. If for some reason Western economic and technological performance should slow down, the pressures for liberalization within the USSR will diminish. The present system will have proven itself to be entirely satisfactory, and those political authorities whose power derives from that system will be more firmly entrenched. This is not to say that the pressures for liberalization will be irresistible. The Party leadership can go on for a long time tinkering with the system without introducing any substantial changes. If my judgement is correct, however, such tinkering will not be successful. That judgement is based on the view that modern technology advances most rapidly under conditions of economic decentralization and political liberty. The major international consequence of modern technology may therefore be to tip the balance somewhat in favour of political liberalization. If that is so, then the greatest friend of freedom in the USSR may prove to be IBM.

In the absence of a more radical change in economic organization than can reasonably be expected, the general level of Soviet technology is likely to continue to lag behind that of the West. There are two principal areas of technology, however, in which Soviet advances have approached and sometimes exceeded those of the West. These are first, fields in which technological advance has not been rapid in the West, and second, fields in which advance is based on mission-oriented projects rather than economy-oriented innovation.

In the first group are such industries as steelmaking, large-size turbines, and machine tools. I would guess that research and design expenditures in these fields are a larger proportion of total R & D in the USSR than in the West. Soviet products in these areas have competed successfully against those of other countries for large orders in Japan and Finland. Even in these cases, however, the greater the component of high technology, the less successful Soviet products have been. Some of their general machine tools have succeeded, but in numerically controlled tools I am not aware that they have entered foreign markets. Their capability in these fields, moreover, continues to be weakened by the effects of internal economic organization. A good illustration of the problem is provided by the development of the petroleum turbo-drill, as Robert Campbell shows in his book, *The Economics of Soviet Oil and Gas*. Despite the abundant engineering skills manifested in the tool, it appears not to have been an economic success, and Soviet efforts have now been redirected to the development of the conventional rotary drilling technology.

By mission-oriented development, I mean the kind of work that in all countries is organized in large-scale centralized organizations, like aerospace and military technology. In such projects, the mission is defined primarily by technological parameters, and the economy of resources is secondary. The quality of performance, therefore, depends primarily on the scientific and technological skills of personnel, and in this respect Soviet scientists and engineers are surely the equal of those in other countries. Such projects are insulated from the operation of the normal economic processes. To the extent that the exploration of these mission-oriented, advances requires that they move through the economic system, their quality diminishes. The TU–104, for example, was the world's first commercial jet aircraft put into operation by Aeroflot. In purely technological terms, it was quite successful, but its economic characteristics, such as payload, were such that it could be employed only under subsidized arrangements. One of the Western airline executives invited to visit the first demonstration in the USSR remarked. 'It's a beauty. I wish we could afford a plane like that in our country.' Western evaluation of the new supersonic jet is of the same order. The performance of Soviet commercial aircraft on the world market will provide a good indicator of the extent to which future economic reforms succeed in improving the innovativeness of the economy.

It is in the fields of rapidly advancing high technology such as electronics and chemicals that the gap is greatest between the scientific and engineering talent of the society and its capacity to transform advances in knowledge into economically competitive innovations. Computers provide the most celebrated case. As more resources are allocated to computer technology – and it is a puzzle why the field has been relatively neglected – the prospect is that in software and in basic hardware they will come abreast of the pace of world development; but in the general quality of mass-produced basic equipment and peripherals a gap is likely to persist.

One course would be to import equipment on a large scale. But such a course would run counter to general foreign economic policy; and indeed, Soviet officials have not demonstrated any eagerness to do so. Another would be to purchase entire foreign manufacturing plants and to produce under foreign licence, a course in which they have shown the greatest interest. The evidence is not yet in, however, on the magnitude of the gain from production under foreign licence. The case of the Fiat plant offers some indication that production under foreign licence is not a way of escaping fully from some of the innovation-depressing properties of the domestic economy. Production start-up is running behind schedule, and there are reports that the labour input is running substantially higher than in the corresponding plants in Italy and elsewhere. Hence licensed production may not provide a key to the effective incorporation of foreign technology into products for export.

The foregoing observations have certain implications for Western economic policy towards the USSR. The export of advanced technology to the USSR (especially when accompanied by credits) will help advance the level of Soviet technology in a variety of fields. It is most likely to be accomplished by the purchase of foreign plants and by licenced production arrangements rather than large-scale import of products. Soviet gains, however, will be of the same order as those accruing to other countries that purchase import licences; the licenser rarely gives up his technological leadership. The Soviet gains will be somewhat reduced, moreover, because of the drag of the internal elements of economic inefficiency. Hence the relaxation of controls on the export of Western technology may help the USSR reduce the gap, but is not likely to project the Soviets into a position of equality or leadership. The decisive limiting factor in Soviet technological advance, relative to that of the West, is likely to continue to be the internal organization of the economy.

10 Technological Progress and the Evolution of Soviet Pricing Policy* 1981

The basic structural features of the Soviet planned economy emerged in the period following the termination of the New Economic Policy (NEP) and the launching of the First Five Year Plan. With respect to the structure of prices, three principles were formulated as a guide to the formation of industrial wholesale prices. The first is the principle of average cost pricing; the price of a product is based on the average cost of its production in all the enterprises in that branch of industry, plus a normal profit mark-up of 4 to 5 per cent over cost. The second is the principle of permanent prices; once the price is assigned to a product, it endures without limit of time, although from time to time prices are revised. The third is the principle of uniformity; the price of a given product is the same for all sellers and all purchasers. For decades these three principles have been presented in the general literature as the basis of price formation. In fact, certain departures were introduced in the very first years in which they were being formulated, but in the course of time the departures became increasingly massive, and the three principles have become less and less useful as a guide to the actual basis of price formation.

A variety of considerations have contributed to the evolution of price policy. There is, however, one common thread that unifies much of the history of that evolution. That thread is the effort

*Reprinted, with permission, from Steven Rosefielde (ed.) *Economic Welfare and the Economics of Soviet Socialism: Essays in Honor of Abram Bergson* (1981), © Cambridge University Press.
I am grateful to Barney K. Schwalberg for his careful reading and insightful criticism of an earlier draft of this paper, and to the editor, Steven Rosefielde, for his valuable comments.

to grapple with the problems encountered in the promotion of technological progress.

ASSUMPTIONS REGARDING TECHNOLOGICAL PROGRESS

A structure is normally designed with certain functions in view. With the termination of NEP, there were two functions for which the new economic structure was designed. The first was to serve as a resource allocating mechanism, to replace the market mechanism that had served that function in the past. The second was to facilitate the attainment of the government's objective of generating a high rate of growth. It was in that context that the structural features of the new economic system took shape.

The choices of structural arrangements that were made for the purpose of promoting economic growth are those that are now thought of as the distinctive features of the Soviet economy: collectivized agriculture, for the purpose of generating a large and secure marketed surplus; an exceptionally high rate of investment; the predominance of heavy industry; and so forth. One can detect in this set of choices the predominance of the view that the source of rapid growth is the building-up of the capital stock. At the same time, one finds little evidence in these early structural choices that much thought was given to the second source of growth, technological progress.

That technological progress contributes to growth was, of course, widely appreciated at the time. If that appreciation did not find reflection in the economic structure then taking form, the reason may lie in the current views about the nature of technological progress and its relationship to socialism.

The architects of the structure of the Soviet socialist economy approached their task from two perspectives: that of the Marxian conception of the nature of capitalist development and that of the government of an economically underdeveloped country. From these perspectives one may identify four assumptions that characterized their views about the nature of technological progress under socialism. Those assumptions are expressed somewhat starkly below, but they do capture the thrust of widely held views.

The Superiority Assumption
It was generally assumed that the rate of technological progress

would be higher under socialism than under mature capitalism.[1] That view follows from the Marxian theory of the contradictions of capitalism. In its progressive stage, capitalism releases a great flood of technological advances, but as the system matures technological progress slows down under the influence of growing contradictions. With increasing concentration of industry, for example, the spur of competition no longer compels capitalists to seek new technologies for invading each other's markets, and monopolies are increasingly successful in suppressing inventions that threaten the loss of capital values. In the most advanced stage, technological progress virtually ceases, which hastens the arrival of the general crisis. Following the revolution technological progress flourishes again, at a rate limited only by the scientific and technological prowess of the population, and unimpaired by the contradictions inherent in the preceding social system.

The Investment Assumption

The basis of Marxian growth theory is the model of expanded reproduction. That model was generally accepted as the basis of the controversies during the Industrialization Debate of the 1920s, and the growth process with which it dealt underlay the structural design of the economy in the early 1930s. The purpose of the model was to illuminate the structure of the growth process, the crux of which was the requirement that the capacity of the capital goods sector exceed the replacement rate of the total capital stock. But to the extent that it established the terms of the analysis, its effect was to focus attention on investment as the primary source of growth.

And although the Marxian model taken by itself did not yield any policy recommendations one way or another, people whose minds were set on industrialization at the greatest possible speed could derive from the construct a powerful support for their contention that in order to secure a rapid and smooth advance in the future a discontinuous jump was needed now.[2]

The promise of technological progress also figured prominently in the debate. But in the context of the times, that term referred not to advancing the frontiers of knowledge, but to equipping the economy with the kind of technology currently employed in the most advanced countries. Technological progress was therefore synonymous with investment, and the higher the rate of investment, the more rapidly an economy could appropriate the fruits of technological progress. Hence, the first order of business in designing the planned economy was to provide for a high rate of investment.

The Product Innovation Assumption

From a Marxian perspective, the decline of technological progress under capitalism is a consequence of the structure of the system. Private ownership, production for profit, and competition result in a squandering of resources devoted to innovation; commercial secrecy leads to a wasteful multiplication of research efforts in competing firms; and scientists in different industrial laboratories work in ignorance of the results produced elsewhere. Since these practices are consequences of the capitalist structure, once that structure is replaced by socialism, these sources of inefficiency and restraints on technological progress will be removed. Instead of several small research units in the individual firms in each industry, a single centralized research institute could be established in each industry, thus taking advantage of economies of scale and eliminating the waste of duplication. The abolition of commercial secrecy will further spur the growth rate of new technological knowledge. Hence, new products will be developed at a rate never before attained under capitalist conditions. And in the absence of monopolistic restrictions the socialist enterprises, producing for use rather than for profit, will readily introduce into production those new products certified as ready for production by the central planning agency.

The essence of the Product Innovation Assumption, then, is that the process of new product invention and innovation proceeds more or less automatically under socialism. The only structural provision that needs to be made is the establishment of the centralized research and development institutes. Once they are in place, the rate at which new products appear is limited only by the quality of the nation's scientific and engineering manpower and the volume of resources placed at their disposal. No other special provision needs to be made in the economic structure – incentives, or prices, or organizational arrangements; or otherwise put, the rate of product innovation under socialism is invariant with respect to economic structure. As that rate depends primarily on the volume of resources allocated for the purpose, and the planning agency controls the allocation of resources, the rate of product innovation is uniquely determined by central planning policy.

The Soviet leadership was not so naive as to expect that all managerial officials were devoid of personal ambitions that might on occasion present obstacles to product innovation.[3] But such manifestations were very likely thought to be transitory, and in any case not of such magnitude as to require any major attention in the overall design of the structure of the economy.

The Process Innovation Assumption

The argument with respect to new processes is substantially the same as that regarding new products. There are no elements of socialist economic structure that would deter enterprises from changing over to improved production processes that have been certified by the planning agency as ready for application. Hence, new processes will move fairly automatically from the laboratory into the production operation. The rate of process innovation is therefore also invariant with respect to economic structure and is uniquely determined by the planning agency.

It followed from the foregoing assumptions that the primary function of the new economic structure was allocative. The static allocative task was to manage the mobilization and direction of resources towards the production of the desired outputs, for which the planning method of material balances was developed. The dynamic allocative task was to direct the flow of output so as to attain a high rate of investment. It was for the fulfilment of these allocative tasks that the elements of economic structure were designed. As for technological progress, all that was required was that appropriate provision be made for the establishment of centralized research and development institutes adequately supplied with trained personnel and materials and equipment. Beyond that, no special provision needed to be made in the design of economic structure for the promotion of technological progress. Given the assumptions about technological progress under socialism, once the allocative mechanism was securely in place, the rate at which new products and processes would be incorporated into the economy would be limited only by the availability of resources for investment.

It was in that context that the basic decisions regarding the new economic structure were made and that the principles generating the price structure were formulated. In the course of time, however, the pricing system underwent an extensive evolution. It is our thesis that a central feature in the explanation of the evolution of price policy is to be found in the continuous effort to come to grips with the accumulating evidence that the assumptions are not valid. Each of the major changes in price policy discussed below reflects the abandonment of one or more of those assumptions.

SUBSIDIES FOR NEW TECHNOLOGY, 1930–36

The massive investment programme launched under the First Five Year Plan led rapidly to the emergence of inflationary pressures. Industry felt the pressure initially from the rising wage payments that resulted from enterprise efforts to attract and hold the labour requirement to meet excessively high production targets. Rising wage costs reduced profit margins and enabled enterprises to press for higher wholesale prices. Rising wholesale prices added further to production costs and the wholesale price level began to spiral upwards in typical inflationary fashion.

It would have been possible for the state to respond to the inflationary pressures by authorizing price increases just large enough to maintain all prices at the average-cost level. That was not done, however. Instead, prices were permitted to rise at differential rates in such manner as to produce different profit rates. Some prices were permitted to rise to levels required to return a normal profit. But others were either held constant or permitted to rise slowly at a rate insufficient to maintain normal profit levels. Enterprises producing the latter kinds of products received subsidies from the state budget to cover the difference between their prices and their rising costs.

The episode was the first major departure from the formal principle of average-cost pricing. The inflation itself, of course, violated the principle of permanent prices, but the cause in this case was not related to the matter of technological progress. It was in the policy of subsidies that one finds the first effort to cope with that issue. The major reason for that departure was to encourage the adoption of new technological processes.

The massive investment programme of the early 1930s entailed the production of large quantities of new types of materials and equipment and the appearance of new production processes. One would not be surprised if, under capitalist conditions, such rapid technological change would meet with some resistance, particularly by workers and lower-level managers threatened by the obsolescence of their skills and possible redundancy. But the Process Innovation Assumption led the Soviet leadership to expect that there would be no significant structural basis for such resistance to appear under socialism. In fact, the evidence mounted that such resistance did appear, and was sufficiently widespread to require a response. In view of the state of overfull employment in labour markets, it may be thought that workers had no serious reason to fear technological displacement. But the loss of a job nevertheless involved considerable private costs to workers. A certain amount of time was required for job search, especially since the labour exchanges had been abolished. Having to leave one's friends – the 'collective' – and perhaps move to another city, is still identified in the sources as one of the bases of resistance to technological redundancy.[4] As regards foremen and lower-level management, the introduction of complex new mechanical and electrical equipment of which they had little understanding undermined their authority and weakened their competence to manage their section. They were, moreover, increasingly dependent on the new young servicing technicians, who knew so much more than they did. Senior management had the same concerns, and in addition had to face the difficult problems of production start-up. Under the best of circumstances, start-up operations are uncertain, unexpected problems arise, and unanticipated costs are incurred. Under the specific Soviet conditions of the 1930s, when the major political slogan was 'tempo', the uncertainty was all the greater.

Under the pressure of mounting evidence of resistance to the adoption of new technology, the Process Innovation Assumption had to be abandoned. Once it was acknowledged that the rate of process innovation is not invariant with respect to economic structure, the task was then to introduce the appropriate structures. In the case of price structure, prices were now to serve a new function that would not have been required had the Process Innovation Assumption been valid – as an incentive to motivate process innovation.

During the period covered by the First Five Year Plan it was necessary in the interest of industrialization to maintain low prices for the production of heavy industry. Low prices for metal and coal meant low prices for machines, thus creating an additional stimulus to the adoption of machinery in all branches of the national economy.[5]

The decision to maintain low prices on such products as coal, metals, and machinery constituted the first major departure from the principle of average-cost pricing. As costs rose, the losses sustained by the enterprises that produced those products were covered by state subsidies. The intent was to encourage other enterprises to replace their older technology by new, with the prospect of lower cost of production and larger profits. Since the principal criterion of enterprise performance and reward was not financial performance but rather output plan fulfilment, the subsidization of input prices was not the strongest incentive that might have been designed. Profit, however, was an important secondary criterion of performance, and it also served as a source of working capital, which greatly increased management's ability to acquire resources for fulfilling output plans.[6] Hence, a manager who would hesitate to mechanize a production process because it would reduce output plan fulfilment in the short run, during the start-up period, might nevertheless proceed with the innovation if it promised a sufficiently large profit in the long run.

As the general price level continued to climb, the volume of subsidies required to maintain the low-price policy on machinery, coal, and metals grew continuously. At the same time, as the experience with subsidized pricing accumulated, the negative effects of large-scale subsidies became increasingly evident. In April 1936 the government decreed that subsidies be phased out and prices restored to average-cost levels. The major reason for that decision was the growing magnitude of the distortions in relative prices that developed as the effects of subsidized inputs percolated through the price system. In some of the other criticisms levelled against subsidies, however, one can see the growing awareness that, contrary to the Product and Process Innovation Assumptions, managerial behaviour is highly responsive to variations in economic structure.

The system of budget subsidies fostered, on the one hand, an irresponsible attitude among certain managers of economic organs... Budgetary subsidies encouraged some managers to be irresponsible and negligent about finance: on the principle 'that anyway the budget will refund'.[7]

Following the decree of April 1936, the government launched a process of price reform designed to restore the average-cost principle as the basis of the price structure.[8] The process of reform was interrupted by the outbreak of the war. During the war, subsidies again grew to very large magnitudes, and in 1949 the government once again undertook an extensive price reform to eliminate subsidies. The task proved to be more complicated than anticipated, and it required several subsequent price reforms to accomplish that end. The last of that wave of reforms occurred in 1955, and the prices finally established at that time are thought to constitute a close approximation of average cost.[9]

TEMPORARY PRICES, 1955–64

The restoration of average-cost pricing in 1955 concluded the first episode in the evolution of pricing policy. The elimination of subsidies, however, generated a new set of problems that launched a second wave of changes in pricing policy. In this case the changes consisted of departures from the principles of permanence and of uniformity of prices. The source of the changes was again the incompatibility of those pricing principles with the requirements of technological progress. In particular, the accumulated evidence required the abandonment of the Product Innovation Assumption.

The principle of permanent prices is that once a price is established, it is regarded as undated, in the sense that it is expected to endure for a long period of time. The principle of permanence is the source of the stability of Soviet prices, which was thought to demonstrate the superiority of a planned socialist economy over a capitalist market economy, in which prices fluctuate continuously in response to the 'anarchy of the marketplace'. Price stability also eases the tasks of economic planning and of the evaluation of enterprise performance.

The specific problem that arose derives from a special feature of the cost behaviour of new products. In all economies the real cost of production of new products tends to decline over time following the first production run. Among the reasons for the high initial production costs are the small scale of output and the costs of start-up and learning. As production experience accumulates, start-up costs decline because of learning-by-doing and because of economies of scale. In the course of time, average cost declines until it levels off and stabilizes thereafter at what may be regarded as long-run average cost. Given this pattern of cost behaviour over time, if the price of a new product is set at its initial average-cost level and is unchanged thereafter, the earned profit rises as the product grows 'older' and cost approaches its long-run minimum. Hence, an enterprise that drops an older model from its product line and starts up the production of a new model suffers a decline in both its total profit and its average profit rate. If the new product is added without reducing the output of older products, total profit increases but the profit rate declines, and profit rate is one of the indicators of performance. A mass of empirical evidence has been published by Soviet analysts showing that profit rates are higher on older products than on new, and that the more innovative the enterprise, as measured by the proportion of new products in its total output, the lower its rate of profit.[10]

Had the original assumptions about the nature of socialist technological progress proven to be valid, the post-1955 price structure would have posed no serious problem. In particular, if the Product Innovation Assumption adequately described innovative behaviour, the rate of product innovation would not have responded to the new price structure. New products would have been introduced at a rate predetermined as optimal by the central planners, irrespective of the penalty that the price structure placed upon product-innovating enterprises. In fact, evidence abounded that the price structure did exert a significance influence on product-innovation decisions of enterprises. New products were referred to by such terms as 'disadvantageous' and 'non-competitive', and managers did in fact discriminate against the introduction of new products in the many ways, both formal and informal, in which they were able to exercise that choice. When it became clear that the rate of product innovation did in fact vary with the price structure, contrary to the Product Innovation Assumption, the task at hand was to modify that structure in such ways as to eliminate the source of that bias.[11]

The modification that was selected was the rejection of the principle of permanent prices in the case of new products and the substitution in its place of the principle of 'temporary' prices.[12] The new principle was first introduced in the engineering industries and later extended to others. Under the new principle, products first introduced into production after 1955 were assigned not permanent prices that endure without limit of time, but temporary, or 'dated' prices. The temporary price was to be high enough to cover the high initial costs of production plus the normal profit rate for the industry. After a period of time, however, when the new product's average production cost had declined and had begun to approach its long-run level, the temporary price was to be dropped and a lower permanent price assigned. The assignment of the permanent price transformed the product, as it were, from the category of 'new' to 'old'. This new pricing method was designed to eliminate the high profits that would otherwise have been earned by older products and thus to reduce the bias against the introduction of new products.

One of the reasons for the original formulation of the principle of permanent prices was its convenience as an instrument of central planning and control. That there was merit in that view was demonstrated by the events that followed the discarding of that principle in favour of temporary prices for new products. It was anticipated that the number of products eligible for temporary prices would be relatively small and the system therefore easily administered. In fact, enterprises seized upon the temporary price arrangement with enthusiasm and the number of products selling at temporary prices expanded rapidly, far beyond what was intended. In 1964, 40 per cent of the output of mining machinery, 41 per cent of textile machinery, and 47 per cent of forging and pressing equipment were selling at temporary prices. In some enterprises the percentage reached 70 per cent and higher.[13] In 1966 the price catalogues, which list only permanent prices, contained price listings for only about half the value of all equipment output.[14] The prospective customer or project designer who needed a price quotation on the unlisted equipment had to call the producing enterprise to find out what the temporary price was.

One reason for the explosion of temporary prices was administrative complexity. The agencies of price administration were unable to process all the applications for temporary prices and to monitor the conversion of temporary prices to permanent prices. Consequently, many products continued to sell at their high temporary prices long after they should have been replaced; they were 'simply transformed into permanent prices, in effect'.[15] A second reason was that enterprises took advantage of the temporary-price regulations to secure higher prices for those of their older products that earned low profit rates.[16] By making some minor modifications in an older product, it could be represented to the price administration agency as a 'new' product, and if the application was successful it could receive a new high temporary price, higher than the old permanent price. The increase in the volume of 'simulated innovation' was one of the serious consequences of temporary pricing.

The discussion has concentrated on the influence of technological progress on the principle of permanent prices. Temporary prices, however, also led to extensive incursions into the principle of uniform prices as well. The objective of that principle is that the same price should be paid for the same product by all purchasers. That objective clashed, however, with the objective of the temporary-price regulations, which was to encourage new product innovation. There was no problem in the case of a product that was new in the sense of not having been produced before in the USSR. The problem arose, however, in the course of the diffusion of that product among other producers. In the case of the second, third and later enterprises to introduce the same new product, the question was whether each of them should be entitled to apply for new temporary prices. According to the principle of uniform pricing, they should not; their prices should be the same as that of the identical product innovated by the pioneering producer. If the objective is to promote the diffusion of the production of new technology, however, they should be; for each enterprise faces its own start-up costs, even in the case of new products already produced elsewhere. Again, it was under the impact of the requirements of the technological progress that the principle of uniform prices was abandoned. The temporary-price regulation was interpreted to mean that a product was 'new' if it was produced for the first time in a given enterprise, and was therefore entitled to a temporary price based on the initial average cost of production in that enterprise. The result was a growing number of instances in which the same product was selling at different prices.[17]

Thus, the realization that the Product Innovation Assumption could not be counted on to promote technological progress led to departures from both the principle of permanent prices and the principle of uniformity. The cure, however, proved to be worse than the disease, and the price administration agencies virtually lost control of the price system as the number of temporary-priced commodities spread far beyond what was originally intended. The price structure that had been put together with such difficulty between 1949 and 1955 had begun to come apart once again, and it required another major price reform in 1967 to put it back together. To prepare the ground for that reform, a decree of June 1966 required that the use of temporary prices be greatly restricted.[18] They could be used, for example, only for products that are new in the strict sense of having been 'introduced for the first time in the USSR'. That requirement restores the principle of uniformity, but the use of temporary prices continues to exclude a certain range of new products from the principle of permanent prices.

A more significant legacy of the episode, however, is that the terms in which the discussion of price policy are conducted have been greatly modified. Price stability, which was seen originally as one of the advantages of the planned economy, is now generally conjoined with price flexibility as a desideratum of price policy. In the interest of greater flexibility the current policy is to conduct more frequent general price revisions and partial revisions of groups of prices. New instruments of price flexibility such as stepped pricing have come into vogue. Under stepped pricing a new product is assigned not a single temporary price but a schedule of prices that decline in predetermined steps at specified future dates.[19] Thus, the requirements of technological progress have dislodged the principle of permanent prices from its paramount position and replaced it by the notion of an optimal combination of stability and flexibility.

THE NEW PRODUCTS FUND, 1960

The decline in cost over time is one respect in which the cost behaviour of new products differs from that of established products. There is another respect, however, in which the cost behaviour of new products is distinctive. Because of this latter feature, it proved to be impossible to maintain the average-cost principle that was restored in 1955 after the elimination of subsidies.

Soviet analysts distinguish two stages of production start-up of new products. The first, called the production-preparation stage, consists of costs incurred before the first full production run. It includes enterprise-financed design and development, labour training, prototype construction, sometimes the acquisition of specialized equipment, and testing. The second, called the break-in stage, consists of costs that are incurred after production has commenced and that diminish in time and eventually vanish when the technique for producing the new product is fully mastered. These are primarily the aforementioned learning costs. It was the learning costs of new-product production that led to the temporary-price episode. It was the production-preparation costs that led to the next period in the evolution of price policy.

The intention of the elimination of subsidies was that the price be high enough to enable the enterprise[20] to recover all costs of production out of sales revenue. That requirement poses no particular problem for the producer of established products because in an ongoing production operation, current outlays can be covered out of current sales or out of short-term commercial credit. The product innovator, however, incurs production-preparation costs in the period before production begins. During that period there is no sales revenue out of which those costs can be defrayed.

Before 1955 the problem was dormant because start-up costs were presumably covered by the subsidies for new technology. After subsidies were eliminated, however, start-up costs were to be included in the price of new products by capitalizing them over a specified number of years; two to three years in the case of machinery products, for example.[21] Thus, production-preparation costs, the first of which might be incurred months or years before the first production run, would not be fully recovered until two or three years after the first production run. During that long period of time those expenses had to be financed either out of the enterprise's working capital or by bank credits. Because of the inherent uncertainty of the innovative process, product innovators often faced the prospect of running up unanticipated debts or having to deplete their working capital, with potentially serious consequences for their main lines of established products.[22] One consequence of these financial pressures was that managers contrived to recover their outlays more rapidly by reducing the capitalization period of start-up costs, often to one year, and in some reported cases they were loaded on to the cost of the first few production runs.[23] The shortening of the capitalization period is one of the reasons for the sharp increase in the relative prices of new products during the temporary-price period.

As the nature of the problem began to emerge in the writings of Soviet analysts, it became evident that both product innovation and process innovation were adversely affected. The financial difficulties that production-preparation costs entailed tended to bias management against product innovation, and the sharp rise in new-product prices due to the elimination of subsidies and the excessively rapid capitalization of start-up costs biased management against the adoption of new machinery and equipment for incorporation into their own production processes. Hence both the Product Innovation Assumption and the Process Innovation Assumption proved again to be deficient as guides to managerial behaviour with respect to technological progress.

Once it is clear that behaviour is responsive to economic structure, one can proceed to search for that structural arrangement that would elicit the desired behaviour. The change in price structure that was eventually introduced in this case involved a return to subsidies. Thus, the principle of average-cost pricing gave way again in response to the imperatives of technological progress.

A decree of 1960 authorized selected ministries to establish a New Products Fund (*fond osveniia novoi tekhniki* – literally, 'fund for the mastery of new technology').[24] The fund is financed by what is essentially a tax on the ministry's enterprises, amounting to 0.3 to 3.0 per cent of the enterprise's total cost of production. Enterprises preparing to introduce new products apply to the ministry for a subsidy to cover production-preparation costs. The subsidized costs are not included in the producer's full cost of production, nor in the average unit cost of the new product on the basis of which the price is established. The subsidies cover roughly 15 per cent of the production costs of new machinery products and to that extent the fund has contributed to a reduction in the wholesale prices of new products.

The fund has very likely succeeded to some degree in its twin objectives. By reducing the strain on the enterprise's working capital in financing start-up costs, it has reduced one of the sources of bias against product innovation.[25] And by reducing the prices of new products, it has increased the returns to process innovators who purchase those products for incorporation into their own manufacturing processes. The structure of prices is therefore now somewhat more supportive of technological progress, but at the cost of the abandonment of the principle of average-cost pricing in the case of new products.

PRODUCTIVITY PRICING, 1965

The use of subsidies is a modification of the principle of average-cost pricing in the sense that some costs are excluded in determining what the price should be. Subsidization does not, however, violate the broad principle that the cost of producing the product should be the basis of price determination. In 1965, however, a major decree of the government authorized a new set of pricing principles that virtually dislodged cost of production as the basis of new-product pricing.

The source of the problem is that when prices are based solely on cost of production, relative prices cannot reflect differences in productivity. A typical instance of technological progress, however, is the development of a new model of a product that is more productive than an older model in some or all of the uses in which the latter had been employed, after the cost of production of the two models is taken into account. Relative prices, however, will reflect only the difference in their costs of production, not the larger difference between their net marginal productivities. The significance of this consequence of cost-based pricing depends upon the extent to which decision-making with respect to product innovation is influenced by economic structure – specifically price structure in this instance. In a world of perfect planning, for example, the omniscient planners would increase the output of the new model from year to year and correspondingly reduce the output of the older model. As the output of the new model increased, it would replace the older first in those uses in which its net marginal productivity was highest, and then in successively less productive uses. The new model would continue to replace the older one at the optimal time rate, until in equilibrium the ratio of the marginal productivities of the two models was equal to the ratio of their costs. Throughout this process the prices of the two models serve only to establish the financial terms at which products are transferred from those who produced them to those who purchased them. In particular, producers are not deterred from introducing the new models into their product lines by a price structure that conveyed to them none of the 'fruits' of their innovativeness; none, that is, of the quasi-rent generated by the higher productivity of the new models.

The four assumptions about technological progress held by the designers of the Soviet economic structure appear to refer to a world substantially like that described above. The Superiority Assumption provided reason to expect that whatever the potential for technological progress in the state of the art, it would be fully exploited in a socialist planned economy in which the capitalist barriers to technological progress had been eliminated. Under the Investment Assumption it could be taken for granted that the technology incorporated in the rapidly growing new capital stock would be the world's most advanced, although suitably adapted to Soviet factor proportions and other special conditions. And the assumptions regarding product and process innovation sustained the view that such elements of economic structure as the structure of prices are unlikely to restrain the innovative enthusiasm of socialist managers.

Although it may have been possible to accept these assumptions in the early 1930s, it was no longer possible to do so in the 1960s. The several episodes in the evolution of price policy set forth above reflect the fact that the Product and Process Innovation Assumptions had already been called into question in the pre-war period and had been further undermined later. The other two assumptions, however, did not face serious challenge until the post-war period. The history of the 1930s gave no reason to challenge the Superiority Assumption; on the contrary, the juxtaposition of the capitalist depression against the rapid expansion of Soviet industry appeared to strengthen it. It was the remarkable post-war technological advances in the capitalist world that made it increasingly difficult to accept that assumption. By the 1960s no responsible Soviet official could continue to believe that the laws of history could be counted on to project the Soviet economy into technological superiority. If superiority were to be attained, something had to be changed within the economy and the society. As for the Investment Assumption, it was dealt a mortal blow by the development in the 1950s of econometric techniques for measuring the contribution of technological progress to growth, relative to the contribution of increasing capital and other inputs. The cumulating research made it clear that technological progress has accounted for a much larger proportion of the growth of capitalist countries than had formerly been guessed. During the period 1955–70, for example, gross domestic product grew in the USSR at an annual rate of 5.7 per cent, about the same rate as that of France (5.4 per cent), West Germany (5.4 per cent), and Italy (5.6 per cent). Abram Bergson has calculated, however, that real national income per worker, adjusted for capital stock, grew at an annual rate of 2.4 per cent in the USSR, substantially less than in France (3.9 per cent), West Germany (3.4 per cent), and Italy (4.4 per cent).[26] The findings suggest that over half of the growth of those countries has been due to technological progress, and that the rate of technological progress in those countries has been 50 to 100 per cent more rapid than that in the USSR. The implication is that the thing the Soviet economy does best – mobilizing capital and other factors of production – is not that decisive after all in promoting modern economic growth. The weight of the accumulating evidence demanded the rejection of a policy that was based on the assumption that a high rate of investment was a sufficient condition for the task of promoting rapid growth. The new attention given to the independent role of technological progress can be seen in the growth of a large volume of Soviet writings seeking to understand the nature of what has been called the 'scientific–technical revolution'.

With the abandonment of all four original assumptions about technological progress, the way was clear for that general review of the structure of the Soviet economy that is referred to as Economic Reform, one of the chief purposes of which is to promote technological progress. All the major elements of economic structure have come under review; incentives, organizational arrangements, and prices. It was in that context that criticism finally turned to the central principle that prices should be based solely on cost of production.[27]

The 1965 pricing statute established a complex set of procedures for incorporating productivity into the pricing of new products.[28] Two such procedures will serve to illustrate the new approach.

The first procedure is applied in the pricing of a new product that was designed as an advance over an older product, called the 'analogue', and was intended to serve as a partial substitute for the analogue. The procedure in analogue pricing involves three steps. The first step consists of the calculation of an 'upper-limit' price, which is the price at which a user would be indifferent between purchasing the new product or the analogue.[29] The method involves the calculation of the maximal increase over the price of the analogue product that a purchaser would be willing to pay for the new product because of its greater productivity. The formula consists of the present discounted value of the stream of additional net output produced by the technological advances incorporated in the new product (durability, reliability, fuel economy, etc.).

The second step involves the calculation of a 'lower-limit' price, which is the price at which a producer would be indifferent between producing the new product or the older analogue. This price is calculated in the traditional manner; it equals the sum of average cost of production plus the normal profit rate in the industry.

The third step involves the determination of the final wholesale price. The general instruction is that the wholesale price is to be set somewhere between the upper- and lower-limit prices in such manner that the quasi-rent produced by the innovation is divided 'equitably' between the producer and the user of the new product.

Since the instructions skirt the question of what an equitable sharing should be, that question has generated an extensive controversy. The indecisiveness of the authorities on this crucial issue opened the way for efficiency-minded economists to urge that the wholesale price be set at the market-clearing level.[30] Under this operating rule, at the start of production when the rate of output of the new product is still low, the wholesale price would be set close to the upper-limit price in order that the restricted supply be allocated to the product's most productive uses. In the course of time output expands and the wholesale price would be gradually reduced as the new product is allocated towards successively less productive uses. Finally, when the long-run optimal rate of output is attained, the wholesale price would approach the lower-limit price. Thus, the quasi-rent generated by the new product would be appropriated initially by the product innovator in the form of above-normal profit, but the profit rate would diminish over time, falling finally to the normal-profit level when the new product ceased to be 'new'.

Critics of this market-clearing rule regard as inequitable an arrangement in which all the quasi-rent accrues to the producer of the new product and none to the user. They have proposed as an equitable rule of thumb that the wholesale price be set at a level at which the producer receives 30 to 50 per cent of the quasi-rent and the user receives the balance.[31] The authorities appear not to have taken a position on this issue. Evidently, the market-clearing rule is used in the case of new products that are regarded as in very short supply, but the equity rule seems to be the most widely employed. Meanwhile, the price administration agency has been grappling with a series of complicated administrative problems that analogue pricing entails. One such complication is that in the case of major technological advances, the spread between the lower- and upper-limit prices is very large and both the market-clearing and equity rules yield very large profits to producer or user or both. The authorities appear to hold the view that, beyond a certain level, above-normal profits cannot be justified, regardless of the nature of their origin. Accordingly, a regulation has been introduced which limits the wholesale price to a level that would yield the producer an earned profit rate no larger than 50 per cent more than the normal profit rate for the industry.[32]

That strong limitation serves as a reminder that although the authorities are prepared to make structural changes in the interest of technological progress, some structural changes are still regarded as out of bounds even though they may contribute to technological advance.

The second pricing procedure in the 1965 statute applies to new products that involve no significant technological advance but are designed to fill in or extend an established product line. Suppose that a certain type of pump is produced in three sizes, capable of delivering 10, 50 and 100 gallons per minute. It has been decided that there is a sufficient number of uses in which it would be economical to produce a pump of the same type with a capacity of 30 gallons per minute. Under the traditional pricing principles, the new pump would be priced at its average cost plus normal profit, without regard to the prices of similar models with varying technical parameters. The 1965 statute requires that new products that are part of a 'parametric series' be priced not at their cost but in a manner consistent with the prices of other models having different technical parameters.

Several methods are employed for calculating parametric prices, the principal one being a form of hedonic index. Price is regressed statistically upon the major technical parameters, such as capacity, durability, and weight, with data derived from the established line of products. The multiple regression coefficients then measure the economic value, as it were, of each of the parameters. Applying the regression equation to the parameters of the new product yields the price. Thus, parametric pricing ignores entirely the cost of producing the new product; the price depends solely on its productivity relative to that of the other models in the product line.

Neither analogue pricing nor parametric pricing are entirely new in the USSR. Abram Bergson has pointed out that 'while average cost pricing did become the rule with the latter reform [1949], the government again and again has departed from it'. One such departure was the pricing of different grades of iron ore, in which production costs were subordinated to ore content and other qualities in the manner of present-day parametric pricing. A second was the pricing of close substitutes such as the major fuels. The price of petroleum has been disproportionately high not only in relation to its cost but also to its caloric content relative to that of other fuels. The reason was that the productivity of petroleum to the user was so much higher than that of other fuels that the implicit demand would have greatly exceeded the supply at a cost-based price or even at a parameter (caloric content)-based price.[33] The pricing of petroleum on the basis of its productivity resembles the current procedures of analogue pricing, including the market-clearing rule for allocating the quasi-rent. These earlier departures from cost-based pricing, however, were the exception rather than the rule; they were employed only in those cases in which the static inefficiency of average-cost pricing was exceptionally large. The pricing statute of 1965, however, mandated the adoption of productivity-based pricing as the normal rule in the case of new products generally. Hence, in the domain of products that are central to technological progress, relative prices have ceased to bear any relationship to cost of production.

The argument of the chapter may be summarized by imagining that, contrary to fact, the original assumptions about technological progress had proven to be valid. Had enterprises adopted new processes at the optimal rate even though the social benefits exceeded the private benefits (or losses) accruing to them, there would have been no reason to undertake the subsidy policy of the 1930s. Had enterprises been willing to introduce new products at the optimal rate even at the cost of a decline in their profit rates, there would have been no resort to the use of temporary prices in 1955 or to the New Products Fund subsidy programme of 1960. Suppose, in addition, that technology had indeed stagnated in the post-war capitalist world and that technological advance had contributed very little towards economic growth relative to capital investment. Under these conditions it is unlikely that the USSR would have undertaken that critical and no doubt painful re-examination of its economic structure that led to the introduction of productivity pricing in 1965. Thus, had all four assumptions proven to be valid, the Soviet price structure today might very well be based on the principles first adopted four decades ago.

This chapter has examined the influence of technological progress on the evolution of only one aspect of economic structure – that of prices. A similar examination of the evolution of organizational structure and incentives structure would very likely support the view that the need to accommodate to the requirements of technological progress has been a major influence in the shaping of the Soviet economy overall.

NOTES

1   On the Superiority Assumption during the Industrialization Debate, see Alexander Erlich, *The Soviet Industrialization Debate, 1924–1928*, Harvard University Press, Cambridge, Mass., 1960. p. 19. The assumption was also widely held outside the USSR. For example, Alexander

Bavkov wrote in *The Development of the Soviet Economic System*,
Cambridge University Press, Cambridge, 1946:

> The abolition of proprietary rights over inventions and of secret
> patents and improvements in manufacturing processes, together
> with the mutual exchange of industrial information among enter-
> prises, cannot but contribute to a fuller and more timely use of
> the creative initiative of those actually working for industrial pro-
> gress, and remove anomalies in the utilization of industrial
> inventions which often occur under the competitive system...
> [p. 302]

2 Erlich, op. cit., p. 147.

3 The experience with price administration in the 1920s provided the
   first evidence that managers of socialized enterprises find it advantageous to raise their prices far above normal profit levels when they
   can (R. F. D. Hutchings, 'The Origins of the Soviet Industrial Price
   System', *Soviet Studies*, 13 July 1961, pp. 2–5, 11). At that time,
   however, prices were not set by higher government organs and that
   price behaviour was not illegal, nor was the economy yet controlled
   by overall central planning.

4 *Ekonomicheskaia gazeta*, no. 46, 1967, p. 30; *Voprosy ekonomiki*, no.
   10, 1969, p. 38.

5 *Planovoe khoziaistvo*, no. 5, 1936, pp. 76–7, quoted in Baykov, op.
   cit., p. 294.

6 Joseph S. Berliner, *Factory and Manager in the USSR*, Harvard
   University Press, Cambridge, Mass., 1957, ch. 5.

7 *Planovoe khoziaistvo*, no. 5, 1936, pp. 76–7, quoted in Baykov, op.
   cit.

8 The continued upward wage drift after 1936 led again to a rise in
   the volume of subsidies. In 1939–40, prices were increased once more
   to restore average-cost prices (S. G. Stoliarov, *O tsenakh i tsenoobrazovaniia v SSSR* (Prices and Price Formation in the USSR), Statistika,
   Moscow, 1969, p. 57).

9 Richard Moorsteen, *Prices and Production of Machinery in the Soviet
   Union, 1928–1958*, Harvard University Press, Cambridge, Mass., 1962,
   p. 10.

10 Joseph S. Berliner, *The Innovation Decision in Soviet Industry*, MIT
   Press, Cambridge, Mass., 1976, pp. 249–54.

11 David Granick found that during the First Five Year Plan there was
   little evidence of managerial resistance to the introduction of new
   Western product designs into production in Soviet plants. He explains
   this in part by the fact that many of the plants in that period were
   newly built and produced only a few complex products. In enterprises
   that produced both the old and new products, he suggests that such
   resistance may have been possible (*Soviet Metal Fabricating and
   Economic Development*, University of Wisconsin Press, Madison, Wis.,
   1967, p. 236. This explanation is consistent with the evidence that
   not until the post-war period did the problem of resistance to product
   innovation come to the fore. In the later period new product designs

were primarily of Soviet rather than Western origin, and the proportion of new products produced by newly built enterprises was much smaller; hence, more managers confronted the issue of the conflict between new and old products.

12 Temporary prices were employed during the 1930s as well (Hutchings, 'Soviet Industrial Price System', p. 20). That they did not become a matter of serious concern until the 1950s was due to the availability of subsidies. It was only after the 1955 price reform, which finally eliminated branch subsidies, that temporary prices were given a formal place in the pricing system. A. I. Komin, *Problemy planovogo tsenoobrazovaniia* (Problems of Price Formation), Ekonomika, Moscow, 1971, p. 150.

13 Komin, op. cit., p. 150.

14 *Planovoe khoziaistvo*, no. 10, 1966, p. 3.

15 Komin, op. cit., p. 150.

16 Permanent prices were reviewed from time to time, to eliminate the disparities in earned profit rates that arise when relative prices are constant but relative costs change. On these occasions some permanent prices were revised downwards, to restore the normal profit level for the industry. It was these products whose prices had been reduced to normal profit levels that are referred to in the text, not those older products that were still selling at their original permanent prices and therefore earning large profits because of the reduced production costs.

17 Berliner, op. cit., 1976, pp. 280–1. Certain departures from uniform pricing have been permitted in activities in which variations in natural resource endowment greatly influence unit costs of different producers, as in petroleum extraction and agriculture. In those cases, different producers receive different prices for, say, a ton of oil or a ton of wheat, but all purchasers of oil or grain pay the same price, except for regional differentials. In the case of temporary prices, however, purchasers could buy the same product from different producers at different prices.

18 K. N. Plotnikov and A. S. Gusarov, *Sovremennye problemy teorii i praktiki tsenoobrazovaniia pri sotsializma* (Current Problems of Theory and Practice in Socialist Price Formation), Nauka, Moscow, 1971, pp. 124–8.

19 Berliner, op. cit., 1976, pp. 293–8. The problems of administering stepped prices are also discussed by Gregory Grossman, 'Price Control, Incentives and Innovation in the Soviet Economy' in Alan Abouchar (ed.), *The Socialist Price Mechanism*, Duke University Press, Durham, NC, 1977, pp. 163–4.

20 More precisely, it is the branch of industry that is expected to cover the costs out of revenues. Hence, it is the average cost of the branch that serves as the basis of price. Enterprises whose costs are above the branch average continue to be subsidized by the branch ministry out of the profit earned by lower-cost enterprises. These subsidies, however, do not appear in the state budget. Abram Bergson, *The*

Eonomics of Soviet Planning, Yale University Press, New Haven, Conn., 1964, p. 162.

21 Plotnikov and Gusarov, op. cit., p. 371.

22 Innovation is often characterized by cost overruns and by scheduling delays. Among the reasons are imperfections in the working drawings prepared by the research and development staff, requiring redesign of the product; production engineering problems that arise in the course of start-up; unfamiliarity with new materials and components; procurement problems because relationships have not yet been established with new suppliers; and marketing problems because of user resistance to untested technology.

23 P. S. Mstislavskii, M. G. Gabrieli, and Iu. V. Borozdin, *Ekonomicheskoe obosnovanie optovykh tsen na promyshlennuiu produktsiiu* (The Economic Basis of Wholesale Pricing of New Industrial Products), Nauka, Moscow, 1968, pp. 113–14.

24 Berliner, op. cit., 1976, pp. 198–204, 217–24.

25 The size of the fund is not sufficient to cover all the production-preparation costs of all product innovators. The balance continues to be financed primarily out of the enterprises' own working capital. *Planovoe khoziaistvo*, no 3, 1971, p. 36.

26 Abram Bergson, *Soviet Post-war Economic Development*, Wicksell Lectures, Almqvist & Wiksell, Stockholm, 1974, pp. 70–8.

27 Several other lines of development in Soviet economics converged around this time, all tending to discredit the principle of cost-based pricing. Gregory Grossman noted that in the post-1956 theoretical debates on pricing in general, virtually all the participants rejected the average-cost-plus-normal-profit formula ('Price Control', op. cit., pp. 129–30). The earlier debate on the choice among investment alternatives also contributed to the rejection of that principle and provided the basis for the analogue-pricing method discussed below (Berliner, op. cit., 1976, pp. 306–7).

28 The 1965 statute was supplemented in 1969 by a more detailed document entitled *Manual for Determining Wholesale Prices on New Industrial Products*. The following description is based on the latter document as presented in Berliner, op. cit., 1976, ch. 11. Further analysis of the new procedures may be found in Grossman, 'Price Control', op. cit., pp. 158–64 and in Michael J. Lavelle, 'The Soviet "New Method" Pricing Formulae', *Soviet Studies*, vol. 26, January 1974, pp. 81–97.

29 The procedure assumes that there is a single use for the product, and does not deal with the case in which the product has alternative uses in which its productivity differs. That more general case underlies the views of the proponents of the market-clearing rule discussed below.

30 For example, *Voprosy ekonomiki*, no. 5, 1967, pp. 34–5.

31 *Ekonomicheskaia gazeta*, no. 31, 1969, p. 11.

32 Plotnikov and Gusarov, op. cit., p. 372. This maximum may be the reason for the finding reported by Grossman ('Price Control', op.

cit., p. 161) that in the case of most new products the producer gets no more than 10 to 12 per cent of the quasi-rent. Although this limit on the wholesale price places a ceiling on the profit that the product innovator may earn, in essence it merely shifts the profit to the purchaser of the new product, who captures the balance of the economic rent. It is not clear why that is regarded as less objectionable. The policy is consistent, however, with a long standing tendency to regard the encouragement of the adoption of new products and processes as more important than the encouragement of the production of new products and processes. See Granick, op. cit., p. 235.

33   Bergson, op. cit., 1964, pp. 163–4.

11 Prospects for Technological Progress* 1976

PROSPECTS FOR TECHNOLOGICAL PROGRESS

The structure of the Soviet economic system was designed with a particular strategy of industrial growth in view. That strategy was the maximal rate of mobilization of labour and capital into industrial production. The structure adopted was that of centralized economic planning, and the historical record supports the conclusion that it was a reasonably successful structure. It enabled the Soviet government to generate very high rates of investment, to manage the transfer of unparalleled millions of workers from agriculture to industry, and to attain an impressive rate of economic and industrial growth during the first 35 years of the plan period.

However successful that growth strategy had been in the past, its appropriateness to the conditions of the present-day Soviet economy has been increasingly called into question by the Soviet leadership. The principal stimulus to reconsideration is, of course, the decline in the rate of the growth that dates from about a decade ago. The Ninth Five Year Plan set a target annual growth rate of 6.7 per cent, but the economy managed to achieve a rate of only 5.1 per cent. The Tenth Five Year Plan[1] now sets the target at the annual rate of 4.4–5.1 per cent, which is unprecedentedly low for the USSR.

*Soviet Economy in a New Perspective, US Congress, Joint Economic Committee, (1976) Washington, DC, pp. 431–46.

DEMISE OF THE CLASSICAL GROWTH STRATEGY

In addition to the concern that the classical growth strategy is not working as well as it did in the past, there is evidence that it is becoming increasingly difficult to implement that strategy on the same levels as it was implemented in the past. The signs of that difficulty are evident in the pages of the Tenth Plan. The annual increase in the supply of labour is expected to diminish during the next five years, continuing a trend that has been operating for some time. Hence, if nothing else changed, the rate of growth would be expected to decline on that account. Moreover, the agricultural sector no longer contains large reservoirs of labour that could be drawn off into industry to maintain the growth of the industrial labour force, as had been the practice in the past.

The classical strategy could nevertheless be maintained if the rate of investment could be augmented sufficiently to offset the decline in the growth of the labour force. Far from increasing, however, the growth rate of investment is also expected to decrease during the next five years, and by an astonishingly large amount. Capital investment, the volume of which grew during the last five years at the annual rate of 6.9 per cent, is scheduled to grow during the next five at only 4.4–4.7 per cent. Since the growth rate of investment has been declining for some time, though not at this sharp rate, the growth rate of the capital stock must be expected to decline as well.

Unlike the growth rate of the labour force, which is determined largely by demographic factors that are outside the control of the government, the growth rate of investment is a policy decision of the government. The decision to reduce the growth rate of investment reflects the pull of other claimants on the nation's output, particularly defence and consumption. The Tenth Plan reveals very little directly about the government's intentions with respect to defence expenditures, but there are a number of indications of the pressures upon the government to maintain consumption. Among the 'basic tasks' set forth for the next five years is the intention 'to increase the incentive role of pay and the dependence of each worker's income on his personal labor contribution.'

The classical growth strategy was originally designed for a society in which levels of living were extremely low and the coercive apparatus of the state was overpowering. While monetary incentives have been employed since the inception of the plan period, in the conditions of the time relatively small annual increases in consumption levels were thought to be adequate to the task. Labour discipline was maintained by such coercive means as imprisonment for excessive absenteeism or lateness to work. With the diminution of the extent of coercive controls following the end of the Stalin's rule, the incentive system was obliged to bear a greater burden in controlling the behaviour of the labour force. The smaller the stick, the larger the carrot has got to be. And indeed, per capita living levels have been increasing steadily in the past two decades, following a long period in which they were virtually unchanged. The shift in the relative importance of coercion and incentives may well have been the beginning of the decline in the potency of the classical growth model, although it was probably not recognized as that at the time. For when the population becomes accustomed to expect increases in income as the reward for effort and risk-taking, the regime is increasingly constrained in the extent to which it can channel resources into investment instead of consumption. The Polish food riot of 1970 is widely regarded as the event that drove home to the leaders of the USSR the limits within which they now have to operate in deciding on the distribution of output between investment and consumption.

The pressures for increasing consumption are compounded by another feature of recent economic policy that finds sharp reflection in the Tenth Plan – the accelerating development of the Eastern regions of the USSR. The document specifies that the Eastern regions are to provide 'the entire five-year-plan increment in the extraction of petroleum and gas and in aluminium production, more than 90 per cent of the increment in coal extraction, roughly 80 per cent of the increment in copper production', and so forth. To provide the labour to man these extensive increases in production facilities, the government will have to continue the process of inducing large numbers of workers to leave their homes and migrate to the cold and relatively underdeveloped frontier communities scattered throughout Siberia. To attract the required labour force, the government has found it necessary to pay the moving costs of workers and their families, and to offer premium wage rates, substantially higher than those in other parts of the country. Thus, to the general increase in the consumption requirements of the population, there has been added the supplementary consumption requirements of inducing the labour force migration to the East. That supplementary cost itself is now to be further increased. The Tenth Plan provides for the introduction of 'length of service pay increments for workers and office employees in the regions of the Far East'. The reason for this new measure is that high as the premium wage rates have been, they have not been sufficient to compensate for the harsh frontier living conditions experienced by the migrants, and many of them returned to their original homes after their first contract was ended. The length-of-service increments should help to hold some of the migrants in their jobs for a longer period of time, but it represents one more obligation assumed by the government to provide the necessary flow of consumer goods.

TOWARD A NEW GROWTH STRATEGY

The signs of the growing ineffectiveness of the classical growth strategy began to emerge towards the end of the 1950s. At about the same time there began to develop in the West a body of economic research that called into question the foundations upon which that strategy had been built. The classical strategy sought to promote economic growth by bringing into production each year larger and larger quantities of the factors of production – land, labour, and capital. That method of expanding output had, of course, always been practised by nations that had experienced economic growth. It had always been known, however, that the economic growth of nations was due not only to the annual increase in the quantities of the factors of production but also to the steady improvement of their quality; and particularly by improvement in the quality of the materials, equipment and technological processes; that is, by technological progress. What was new in the research referred to was not the fact that technological progress had always accompanied factor-of-production increases, but the discovery that technological progress accounted for a much larger proportion of the growth that had been achieved than had previously been imagined, and that factor-of production increases were a less important source of growth than had been thought. The discovery was followed by a veritable explosion of research designed to measure the contribution of various forms of technological progress to economic growth and to understand the social and economic forces that promote technological progress.

The general conclusion of Western research on Soviet growth is that technological progress has proceeded considerably more slowly there than in the advanced capitalist countries. In the period 1950–62, for example, in the United States and in all the countries of Western Europe technological progress was a more important source of growth, and in many cases much more important, than increases in labour and capital inputs. In France technological progress was the source of 79 per cent of the achieved growth of output, while in Italy and Norway it accounted for 78 and 77 per cent. In none of the major countries did it fall below 50 per

cent. In the USSR, by contrast, technological progress accounted
for only 42 per cent of the growth of output during that period.
The USSR alone depended on the classical growth strategy – additions of labour and capital – for over half of its economic growth.[2]

The new appreciation of the significance of technological progress
in the promotion of economic growth offered the Soviet leaders
an alternative strategy to the increasingly less effective classical
strategy. If it was no longer possible to generate new annual supplies
of labour and capital at the rates of the past, the rate of economic
growth need not decline if the rate of technological progress could
be increased. That is, growth would be generated not primarily
by more and more machines but by better and better machines.
Quality of inputs would substitute for quantity, with no less output
resulting, it may be hoped. The classical Soviet growth strategy
would be replaced by what may be called the modern strategy.

About a decade ago the Soviet literature began to devote growing
attention to the analysis of what is called the scientific–technical
revolution. Official pronouncements began increasingly to stress
the importance of technological progress in the management and
planning of the economy. The Tenth Five Year Plan is the capstone
of this trend. Mr Kosygin has referred to it as the Plan of Quality,
a formulation that has been widely picked up and used to encapsu-
late the main thrust of the plan.

How does one implement a strategy of accelerating technological
progress beyond the rates achieved in the past? Two approaches
may be identified. One is to import large quantities of foreign
technology in those fields in which it is most superior to domestically
produced technology. The other is to find ways of augmenting
the domestic rate of technological progress beyond that achieved
in the past. Both approaches have in fact been adopted.

THE ROLE OF IMPORTED TECHNOLOGY

The import of advanced foreign technology is, of course, the foundation of the policy of detente. In view of the wide publicity given
to this policy in the West, it is remarkable how little reflection
one finds of it in the text of the Tenth Plan. The plan does call
for 'measures aimed at the broader participation of the Soviet Union
in the international division of labor and at enhancing the role
of foreign economic ties in the accomplishment of national
economic tasks and the acceleration of scientific and technical progress'. It foresees an increase of foreign trade turnover by 30–35
per cent, and calls for measures to improve the efficiency with

which foreign economic ties are conducted. One does not get the impression that the import of foreign technology is the dominating approach adopted by the Soviets for implementing the new strategy of economic growth.

If that is indeed so, the Soviets have probably made a wise choice. Foreign technology can certainly make a contribution both to the level of Soviet technology and to the rate of growth. All countries gain from trade based on comparative advantage. The Soviets as well as the other centrally planned economies have tended to 'under-trade', in the sense that their volume of trade has been less than that of market economies at equivalent levels of economic development.

They have sought to produce by their own effort a much larger range of products than have market economies, and as a consequence they have denied themselves some of the benefits of the international specialization of labour. Even if the technological level of Soviet production were on a par with that of the advanced capitalist countries, it would have paid them to import more than it was their policy to do in the past. The growing volume of Soviet trade with those countries is therefore bound to provide the Soviets with benefits in the form of the gains from trade that they had formerly forgone. Imported technological equipment will also contribute to the general elevation of the quality of the Soviet capital stock and therefore to an increase in the rate of technological progress.

It is nevertheless to be doubted that as an approach to the adoption of the new growth strategy, the import of foreign technology could prove to be satisfactory. If the domestic economy should remain no more capable than in the past of generating its own technological progress, it is hardly likely that the economy could generate in the future the rate of technological progress required by the new growth strategy. For one thing, the economy is so large that the overall impact of imported technology is likely to be marginal. The overwhelming proportion of the nation's annual increments in capital equipment will have to be of domestic manufacture. Hence unless the general level of domestic technology improves, the contribution of technological progress to overall growth is likely to remain small. Secondly, the technology of the advanced capitalist countries is adapted to the level of technological and managerial skills and knowledge of their own or of equivalent countries. Unless the broad level of technological and managerial skills and knowledge in the USSR attains that level, the imported equipment is likely to operate at a lower level of productivity than is found in the host country, thus losing some of the gains from trade.

But third, and most important, a country that relies on imports for a broad range of its advanced technology cannot expect to project itself by that means into the ranks of the leaders in the generation of new technology. Particularly in the fields of the most advanced and rapidly changing technology, the lead times are such that by the time a new enterprise outfitted with imported equipment is in full production, that equipment and its products have already begun to obsolesce. In short, the import of foreign technology cannot serve as a substitute for a technologically innovative economic system. Only the second approach, the augmentation of the domestic innovativeness of the economy, can provide a suitable basis for the new strategy of economic growth.

ORGANIZATIONAL STRUCTURE

In all systems, social no less than physical, the structure bears a certain relationship to the functions that the system performs. If an engine is designed to attain a maximum speed, a certain structure is appropriate; but if it is designed to minimize fuel consumption, a different structure would be employed.

The function that the Soviet economic system was designed to support was the classical strategy of economic growth. The structure that was designed for this purpose was that of centralized economic planning. Now the system is being called upon to perform a different function, to generate a high rate of technological progress. The old structure, however successful it was in supporting the function for which it was designed, is simply not well designed for carrying out the new function. If the Soviets are serious about shifting to the new growth strategy a new economic structure will have to be designed, appropriate to the new task. The process of economic reform, initiated by Mr Khrushchev, is the term applied to the search for this new economic structure.

The Tenth Plan is replete with references to the importance of accelerating the rate of technological progress and of improving the effectiveness of the R & D (research and development) institutes and the other organizations whose work is crucial to that goal. Section VII of the Plan, for example, which is titled. 'The Development of Science', proposes 'to increase the efficiency and improve the quality of scientific research. . . . To accelerate the introduction of scientific achievements in the national economy. . . . To improve the system of management of research and design organizations and the planning and financing of scientific research.' These are statements of aspiration, however, and not programmes. The Plan does, however, allude to a number of specific reforms in economic structure that are designed to help attain those aspirations. The question is whether they are equivalent to the new type of economic structure that is required to support the new strategy of promoting growth through technological progress.

Soviet analysts have devoted a great deal of attention in recent years to the subject of technological innovation. The obstacles to innovation have been discussed fairly candidly in the published sources and we have a reasonably firm understanding of where the problems lie. They may be grouped into three categories that constitute the basic structural elements of the economic system; organizational structure, price structure, and the structure of incentives.[3] Each of these three elements exerts a strong influence on the kinds of decisions made by Soviet managerial officials as they conduct the daily business of the production units for which they are responsible. The crucial decision with respect to technological progress is the innovation decision – whether to introduce a new product or process, or to continue producing an established product by means of an established manufacturing process. The general problem with the old economic structure is that it gave maximal encouragement to decision-makers to favour established products and processes, and to discriminate against innovations 'as the devil shies away from incense', in Mr Brezhnev's words.[4]

The nature of the anti-innovation bias may be illustrated in the case of each of the three elements of economic structure. Consider first the organizational structure of the economy, which refers to the kinds of organizations (enterprises, R & D institutes, ministries, state planning committee) that have been established to conduct the nation's economic activity, and the range of responsibilities assigned to each of them. It is the organizational structure that governs the process whereby the production units receive the inputs of goods and services required for their production activity and dispose of the products they produce. Consistent with the principle of centralized economic planning, the organizational structure is such that the central government agencies bear the major responsibility for providing the enterprises with their inputs and disposing of their outputs; in contrast to a market economy, for example, in which the enterprises bear the responsibility for carrying out these two functions. The government says to its enterprises, in effect, 'We will give you the things you need with which to produce, and we will take care of selling the things you produce. Your job is to concentrate on the task of producing the maximal output of the things we instruct you to produce.' That way of organizing the inter-enterprise flow of goods and services makes a great deal of sense in a centrally planned economy, and it deserves much of the credit for the high rates of output that the economy has achieved in the past. The trouble with it, however, is that it orients managerial officials to concentrate on doing those things they have learned to do well and to shy away from doing new things. Many reasons for this anti-change bias may be set forth, but two will serve.

First, it is inevitable that the effort to plan centrally the supply of all the inputs needed by all enterprises cannot be entirely successful. In fact, it has been done rather badly, and most enterprise managers regard the problem of getting the supplies they need to be the most difficult aspect of running a Soviet enterprise. It is perhaps the principal reason that enterprises often run into difficulty meeting the production targets that are assigned to them. Consequently enterprises seek out ways of minimizing the risk of failure due to supply shortages, like hoarding labour and materials, or producing their own components at high cost rather than relying on the uncertainties of subcontracting. In view of the centrality of the supply problem, it is understandable that any decision-maker contemplating an innovation will ask how the decision to innovate will affect his supply situation. Unfortunately, the decision to innovate is likely to increase the intensity of the supply problem. The innovation of new products or processes often requires the enterprise to use materials with which it is not familiar, and to be assigned to new suppliers who are not yet familiar with the enterprise's quality requirements and with whom no personal relations have yet been established. Changes always involve unanticipated difficulties, a certain amount of wastage until the new technology is mastered, and sudden needs for supplies that could not have been foreseen a year earlier when the enterprise's supply plan was first forecast. Hence the risk-minimizing decision is to avoid changes. Supply problems are minimized by producing the same product by means of the same process as long as possible.

The second problem of organizational structure also involves the matter of supply. The decision to innovate obliges the enterprise to provide itself with a supply of something that is not required at all by non-innovators – the supply of R & D services. That greatly expands the range of supply problems with which the enterprise must cope, and compounds the risk of failure. There are many reasons for the peculiar set of difficulties associated with the supply of R & D services, but one has commanded central attention. When the organizational structure of the Soviet economy was established a half century ago, it was designed with the purpose, among other things, of avoiding what were regarded as the wastefulness and irrationality that characterized the 'anarchy of the capitalist marketplace'. One such element of waste was the commercial secrecy of capitalism, and the consequent duplication of R & D facilities in competing enterprises. The abolition of private property made it possible to avoid the waste of duplication and secrecy and to benefit from the economies of scale. The organizational form that incorporated this view was the establishment of centralized R & D facilities, one for each branch of technology. All R & D work on mining machinery, for example, would be concentrated in a single large institute, which would establish a uniform technological policy for the industry. The new products and processes developed by that institute would be submitted for approval to the ministry, which would then assign them to the appropriate enterprises to be put promptly into production.

Again, this organizational device has been responsible for a good proportion of the new products and processes that have over the years made their way through the R & D process into final production. Yet it has long been known that the process suffered from many defects, largely due to the dissociation of R & D institutes from the producing enterprises. The responsibility of the R & D people tended to end when a new design was officially approved by the ministry; what happened to it thereafter was the responsibility of the ministry people and the enterprises. Enterprises, for their part, often found that the design work had to be redone, because it was originally executed without knowing which enterprise eventually would be assigned the task of first introducing it. The institutes developed an unfortunate reputation of producing shoddy work and enterprise managers exchanged horror stories of the troubles they ran into after having been assigned the task of introducing a new technological process designed by the people in the R & D institute who had no knowledge of their own production and technological conditions. In an interesting analysis of the problem, Academician Trapeznikov concluded that the central issue was the 'monopolistic' nature of the R & D organizations.[5]

If scientific and technological monopoly takes shape, the result is the stagnation of ideas. The customer can only say to the design organization, 'Please, do at least slightly better.' And the monopolistic design organization will answer, 'We can do no better; if you don't like it, do it yourself!' And the enterprise will have to content itself with this answer.

If the objective of accelerating technological progress is to succeed, features of the old organizational structure like these will have to be changed. The Tenth Plan provides some clues about the kinds of structural changes that the government is relying upon to accomplish the desired result. With respect to the general problem of supply, the Plan calls for the completion of a programme to establish 'direct and continuous ties based on long-term economic contracts' between suppliers and purchasers of mass-produced commodities. This refers to an effort to end the past practice in which the suppliers assigned to an enterprise would be changed frequently and arbitrarily by the central planners, leading to interruptions in the flow of supplies and to changes in the quality of materials supplied. The purpose of the new measure is to introduce greater stability in the flow of inputs and to reduce the risks associated with supply.

This is to be done by building into the central planning system a network of long-term planned flows of supplies between specified suppliers and purchasers, which the central planners are obliged to honour. The measure may improve the supply situation for enterprises that require a large and steady supply of a mass-produced commodity, like an electric powerplant that requires a steady flow of coal. It is not likely to have much impact on innovating enterprises, particularly in the machinery industry, which do not deal in such mass-produced inputs to the same extent. Moreover, the very stability of the direct ties established between suppliers and users may have the effect of discouraging change. If an enterprise has estabished a satisfactory long-term relationship with a supplier of a copper part, it will be relatively riskier to undertake an innovation substituting a cheaper plastic part for that copper part, especially if the plastics supplier has already established a set of long-term contracts with large users of plastics who are more important to his business than the prospective new purchaser. This reform will provide some improvement in the supply situation of enterprises producing established products with the same inputs year after year, but by reducing the degree of flexibility in the system, may actually increase the riskiness of innovation.

The Plan also anticipates the continuation of 'work on the development of wholesale trade'. This passage alludes to a reform that is designed to introduce a genuine degree of flexibility into the supply system and may therefore significantly encourage innovation. Under the old organizational structure the supply system operates by a materials-allocation method. Virtually all important materials and equipment are handled by the central agencies of government, who issue materials allocation certificates to the enterprises that are entitled to receive specified quantities of that material or that piece of equipment. If an enterprise happens not to possess such a certificate, it is extremely difficult to obtain an allocated commodity legally. One applies for these certificates during the process of making up the plan for the following year, based on a guess about what the output targets would be and how much of each type of input would be required during the year to produce that output.

It is evident that, under such a system, the greater the degree of uncertainty about the future, the greater the possibility of having incorrectly forecasts future requirements, and therefore of encountering difficulties in obtaining allocated materials. The system gives strong support to stability of production, and correspondingly strongly discourages innovative change. The wholesale trade reform is designed to ease the problem of obtaining supplies without the possession of an allocation certificate. A number of stores and distribution centres have been established throughout the country that are stocked with allocated supplies that may be purchased by enterprises without having to present official allocation certificates. The notion of wholesale trade, it should be noted, is an extremely radical one in the Soviet context. It brings the middleman back into the economic structure, and conceptually it denies the value of centralized planning of supply for a certain range of commodities, relying instead on a kind of market. Perhaps that is the reason that this reform appears not to have progressed very far. The Tenth Plan calls for the 'continuation' of work on this reform, not for its 'completion'.

With regard to the supply of R & D services, the Plan directs the industrial ministries 'to complete the creation of associations in accordance with the general plans of management . . .' This instruction alludes to a massive merger movement first mandated by the government in 1973.[6] Groups of previously independent enterprises are to be merged into larger corporate organizations called production associations. The typical association is a merger of perhaps a half-dozen to a dozen enterprises in a related line of production. In most cases the merger is a form of vertical integration. The general director of the new association, who is often the former director of the largest of the merged enterprises, has virtually full authority over the constituent units. The broad objective of the movement is to improve the efficiency of the inter-enterprise transactions. These transactions were formerly managed by the ministry and the government planning organs, which dealt with each of the enterprises separately. Now the ministry and the planners deal only with the general director, and the latter bears the responsibility for the individual production and other activities of the merged units. In addition to the general objective of improving efficiency, however, the reform is designed to stimulate technological progress.

To accomplish that, many of the production associations have been given R & D facilities of their own. The most interesting feature of the reform is that many of the largest of the R & D institutes have lost their independent status and have been merged into associations along with a cluster of producing enterprises, experimental plants, and so forth. These mergers are referred to as 'science-production associations'. The general director of a science-production association is usually the head of the merged R & D institute.

The science-production association represents the abandonment of the original notion upon which the organizational structure of Soviet R & D was founded. A substantial portion of all R & D is now to be conducted 'in-house', in the manner of the large high-technology industrial corporations of the capitalist world. Instead of a single all-union R & D institute in each field of technology, which was the original ideal, all the large corporate associations are to be provided with their own R & D facilities of varying sizes. By placing science and production under a single corporate administration, it is hoped that much of the previous resistance to innovation will vanish and technological advance will accelerate. The science-production association is strikingly similar in structure to the capitalist arrangement, the putative wastefulness of which inspired the Soviets to reject it a half-century ago.

These organizational reforms upon which the Tenth Plan is based are by and large in the direction required for an economic structure that will support the new strategy of economic growth. The question is whether they go far enough. It is one thing to mitigate some of the organizational impediments to innovation that characterized the classical economic structure. It is another to adopt a structure sufficiently hospitable to innovation to support the new function that the economy is being called upon to perform – to generate a rate of technological progress equal to that attained by the most progressive capitalist countries. One cannot be dogmatic about such a forecast, but my judgement is that these reforms do not get to the heart of the matter. The central issue is the locus of autonomy in economic decision-making. In the centrally planned economy, autonomy must reside primarily in the agencies of government – the Council of Ministers and the central planning organs.

The producing units correspondingly require relatively little autonomy particularly when the planning system operates well. That distribution of autonomy works reasonably well when an economy is undergoing relatively little technological change. The promotion of change however, appears to require a greater degree of autonomy by the producing units themselves because of the greater uncertainty involved in the process. The central planners can be counted on to perform reasonably well in supplying the enterprise with the inputs required when those inputs consist of familiar commodities with which they have had long experience. But the newer the products involved, the greater the necessity to depend on one's own resources to bring the innovation to successful conclusion. One needs to work directly with one's suppliers, to have sources of supply to which one could turn quickly when required, to be able to drop suppliers who cannot meet the new specifications required and to seek out other suppliers in their stead. One must also have direct contact with one's customers, for unlike standard products, new products require a certain amount of promotion to overcome user resistance which is to be found in any economy. One needs control over the technological process itself, and cannot submit all the many technological choices that have to be made to the ministry for their approval. The greater the autonomy of the producing units over their operations, the less the risk involved in trying something novel, and therefore the greater the willingness to undertake innovation. But to take on the risks of doing something new without a corresponding expansion of the authority to accomplish it is to court trouble.

The organizational reforms discussed above do go some distance in extending the autonomy of the production units beyond that which the typical enterprise director enjoyed in the past. But the associations are still enmeshed in the apparatus of central economic planning. They will have plans to fulfil, and will be evaluated on the basis of the success with which they meet their production quotas. All significant decisions will continue to require the approval of the central government agencies. The general manager of a Soviet production association may preside over a set of operations as large or larger than the modern capitalist giant corporation. But unlike the latter, there is no major decision about which he has the final say. The Soviet organizational structure will continue to manage a certain volume of 'innovation by order' as in the past. But unless the production units are given a much greater degree of autonomy than is contemplated during the next five years, with a corresponding diminution of the scope of authority of the central planners, the organizational structure will continue to bias management generally against change.

PRICE STRUCTURE

Organizational structure is but one of the elements of economic structure that influences the decision to innovate. But it is not the only one. A second is the structure of prices. The organizational structure may be such as to cause the introduction of new products to be very risky to the innovator. But if the price of that product is very high relative to that of an older product, managers may nevertheless be induced to take the risk. The people who manage Soviet industry are not, after all, allergic to risk-taking; they would not have sought out such jobs if they were. But they are sensible men, and when they must choose between a fairly certain alternative like continuing the production of a familiar product, or a risky alternative like undertaking the production of a new one, they must have some assurance that if they succeed in the latter, the reward will be worth the risk they bore. One such reward is the profit that the enterprise earns. The higher the price of a new product relative to that of the older one, the greater the potential profit from product innovation.

In the classical economic structure, however, the people who set the prices of products do not distinguish new products from old. All products are priced by adding a standard profit mark-up to the average cost of production. This principle of determining prices was derived from Marx's labour theory of value, which was interpreted to mean that, in a socialist state, it is proper that a product which contains, say, twice the labour content of another should be assigned a price twice that of the other. Assuming that the average cost of production is a satisfactory approximation of the labour content of a product, the principle of cost-plus-standard-profit became the approved basis of product pricing generally.

When economists began a decade ago to study critically the effect of various elements of economic structure on innovation, it was quickly discovered that that principle of pricing exerted a strong discriminatory effect against product innovation. Suppose an enterprise introduces into production a new model of a tractor that costs the same to produce as an older model but is twice as productive. Since the average cost of production is the same, the new tractor will be assigned the same price as the older one. All the benefit of the technical advance is therefore captured by the purchaser of the new tractor and none by the innovator. The innovator who bore all the risk and who exerted the additional effort required by the innovative process gains nothing. He would have been better off had he simply continued the production of the older model.

This discriminatory effect of the pricing principle on product innovation led to the recommendation that new products be exempted from the general pricing rule. In particular, they should be assigned a price higher than the normal cost-plus-standard-profit, so that the innovator could enjoy a higher profit rate for his pains and thus share in the gains from the technical advance. At first this proposal met with considerable opposition, on ideological grounds. It was thought to imply a denial that labour alone was the source of value, and the introduction of such considerations as utility and productivity into Soviet pricing was regarded as an anti-Marxist deviation. Good sense eventually prevailed over such ideological fundamentalism, and official sanction was eventually given to the inclusion of productivity considerations into the pricing of new products.

The Tenth Plan takes very brief note of the influence of price structure on innovation. With respect to prices the Plan instructs officials 'to increase their role in stimulating the growth of the production of new and progressive items and in improving output quality'. But no new reforms appear to be in the offing. The adoption of 'productivity' in the case of new products, and a variety of other pricing reforms in the last decade, have eliminated some of the cruder discriminatory effects of the classical price structure on the innovation decision. Beyond that, there is a limit to how far pricing policy can be used to encourage innovation.

Prices are important to the Soviet enterprise for many reasons, among them their influence on the volume of profit earned. The earning of large profits is taken to be a sign of successful management and is therefore a good thing. Profits also play a role in determining the incomes of management. But they are not the decisive factor in incomes. The role of incomes introduces the third and last of the elements of economic structure to be discussed, the incentive structure.

INCENTIVE STRUCTURE

A great many personal rewards are available to the successful manager: prestige, promotion, various perquisites of office, and income. The incomes of managerial personnel consist of the salary plus bonuses of various kinds which may amount to a third or more of the total income. The size of the bonuses depends on the enterprise's performance with respect to the specific tasks for which each one is offered.

In the original structure of the economy there was only one bonus. Consistent with the requirements of a centrally planned economy, the bonus was proportional to the enterprise's success in fulfilling its plan. And in line with the classical strategy of economic growth, it was the plan target for total value of output that was the prime basis of the bonus. The bonus proved to be so powerful an incentive, however, that management tended to stress output at the expense of other facets of enterprise performance. Production alternatives would be selected that contributed greatly to the value of output even though they increased production cost unreasonably. To redirect management's attention to these other facets, special bonuses were introduced for various specific tasks, such as reducing average cost of production, reclaiming scrap metal, and so forth. The incentive structure that evolved consisted of the original basic bonus that was tied to the value of output, plus a variety of other smaller bonuses specified for particular tasks.

It is an interesting reflection of the dominance of the classical growth strategy that throughout the classical period no special incentive was introduced for the act of innovation. Bonuses were introduced for conserving fuel, for producing consumer goods from waste products, and so forth, but none for the introduction of technological change. Perhaps it was simply assumed that 'innovation by order' was sufficient; that the innovation decision in the centrally planned economy was the responsibility of the central planners and that the task of the enterprises was simply to carry out instructions regarding the introduction of new products or processes. Or perhaps it was not recognized that the act of innovation competed with the act of production and that the manager who concentrated on the latter would neglect the former.

Whatever the reason, when the demise of the classical growth strategy turned attention to the possibilities of accelerating technological progress, it was quickly realized that the old incentive structure contained a strong bias against innovative activity. The reason is that the changeover to a new product or a new manufacturing process always results in a slowdown in the current rate of output. In all economic systems new products and processes involve a period of time during which various bugs have to be ironed out, labour has to be retrained, spoilage and downtime tend to be higher than normal until the new equipment is shaken down and labour and management skills accumulate. Hence the manager who undertakes innovation must expect a decline in the current rate of output for some period of time. It may indeed take months or even years, depending on the magnitude of the innovation, before the new equipment is brought up to its rated output capacity.

The greater the pressure brought to bear on management to maximize the current rate of output, the stronger the resistance to innovation. Hence, precisely because the old incentive structure was highly successful in motivating managers to concentrate on the fulfilment of their output plans, it proved to be highly discriminatory against change. Managers would, of course, introduce new products or processes when instructed to do so by the ministry.

But Soviet managers are masters of the bureaucratic techniques of finding excuses, procrastinating, and dragging their feet on matters that are defined by the incentive structure to be of lesser importance. We would often read that when the production rate was falling behind the schedule required for fulfilling the output plan, management would pull labour and materials out of the shop that was engaged in introducing a new product insisted upon by the ministry, and reassign them to work on the main production tasks of the enterprise. More important, there was very little incentive for self-initiated innovative activity at the enterprise level, which under appropriate conditions could provide a significant innovative thrust in an economy.

It was not until the mid-1950s that a special bonus was first introduced specifically for the act of innovation (*fond dlia premirovaniia za sozdanie i vnedrenie novoi tekhniki* – the bonus fund for the creation and introduction of new technology.) The size of the bonus depends on the social value of the innovation, which is measured by the reduction in production costs that the innovation entails. The innovating enterprise then receives a bonus equal to a certain percentage of the annual cost savings. An innovation that saves the economy one million roubles a year, for example, will yield a one-time bonus to the enterprise of about 50,000 roubles. That enterprise bonus is then divided among the persons who are credited with the success in having brought the innovation to completion.

The original innovation bonus was followed by a number of other bonuses for various activities related to innovation. The present-day incentive structure is therefore more consistent with the new strategy of economic growth. The question to be asked is, again, whether the transformation of the incentive structure has gone far enough. Are the incentives for innovative activity large enough, relative to the rewards for other activities, to support fully the objectives of the new growth strategy?

Detailed quantitative data on the structure of incentives are not abundant. Some data are available however, on the size of the bonuses earned for various activities in some individual enterprises. It is clear that the major source of managerial bonuses continues to be the basic bonus that is earned primarily for fulfilling the basic enterprise plan targets. Since innovation continues to have a negative effect on the enterprise plan performance, the innovating enterprise earns somewhat smaller basic bonuses than the equally well managed but non-innovative enterprise. But the former receives a certain volume of innovation bonuses that are not available to the latter. It appears, however, that the overall difference is not great. The special innovation bonuses are of such magnitude that they do little more than compensate for the loss of some portion of the basic bonus.[7]

If these tentative quantitative judgements are correct, one must conclude that the current incentive structure does not lend very strong support to the new growth strategy. Consider the manager evaluating a choice between introducing a new product recently announced as completed by the R & D people, or continuing the production of an item that has long been part of the enterprise's standard output. If the enterpise does not innovate, management is highly likely to fulfil its plan assignments and to earn the maximal basic bonuses. If the manager decides to undertake the innovation, he faces the risk that the product will fail to perform as well as its sponsors in the R & D institute claim, that its cost of production will be higher than forecast, that there will be an indefinite period of shakedown and uncertainty until the production process is fully mastered, that new supply problems will arise, that the price set for the product by the price administrators in Moscow will provide for a very small profit, that the basic production plan targets will not be met for some period of time, and that his income will therefore decline during that period. If the innovation is ultimately successful, however, he will receive an innovation bonus. But after all the risk, effort and energy, he ends up with an income that is not much larger than he would have earned had he avoided trouble and stuck to the production of his familiar line of products.

If this is a fair description of the alternatives presented by the incentive structure, then all one can say of the reforms in incentives is that they have removed some measure of the anti-innovation bias of the past. But the incentive structure in its present form must still be regarded as discriminatory against change. What seems to be required is a set of rewards for innovation that is sufficiently larger than the rewards available to the competent but minimally innovative manager to make the innovation decision a highly attractive one.

The Tenth Plan alludes to the structure of incentives for technological change but gives no clues about any major forthcoming reform. The task is 'To enhance the role of economic incentives in increasing production efficiency, improving output quality, accelerating scientific and technical progress and improving the use of labor resoures.' There is no reference to specific measures, however, that are to be taken to accomplish that enhancement of the role of incentives in promoting technological progress.

To summarize the discussion, the Tenth Plan is a milestone in the change in Soviet economic policy from the classical growth strategy based on increases in factor inputs, to the modern growth strategy based on high rates of technological progress. Parallel to this change in the function that the economic system has been called upon to perform is a set of changes in the structure of the economy designed to support this new function. The Plan notes such changes in each of three fundamental elements of economic structure: organization, prices and incentives. By and large, however, the changes noted and endorsed in the Tenth Plan consist largely of the elimination of some of the grosser sources of anti-innovation bias that characterized the classical economic structure. Moreover most of the changes noted have already been introduced. The exception is the production association merger movement, which has been under way for some time but is to be completed during the period of the Tenth Plan. With that exception, the benefits of the cited reforms in economic structure should already have been reaped, and should have been reflected in the rate of technological progress attained in the recent past. The Tenth Plan signals no new initiatives in the reform of economic structure that might be expected to lead to an acceleration of the rate of technological progress. Some benefit may be expected from the policy of importing foreign capital, but that policy cannot substitute for domestically generated technological progress. The conclusion is that the abandonment of the classical growth strategy and the adoption of the new strategy based on the promotion of technological progress was a positive move on the part of the Soviet leadership. The desired outcomes from that change in strategy will not be forthcoming, however, unless the fundamental economic structure continues to change in a direction more consistent with the new function the system is now called upon to perform.

NOTES

1 The Tenth Five Year Plan refers, in this paper, to the 'Basic Guidelines for the Development of the National Economy in 1976–80', in *Pravda*, 7 March 1976, as translated in the *Current Digest of the Soviet Press*, vol. XXVIII, nos. 15, 16 and 17, for 2, 19 and 26 May 1976.
2 Paul R. Gregory and Robert C. Stuart, *Soviet Economic Structure and Performance*, Harper & Row, New York, 1974, p. 389. The percentages reported here were obtained by dividing 'output per unit of combined input' (column 5) by 'output' (column 1).
3 The following analysis of the relationship between economic structure and innovative performance relies heavily on Joseph S. Berliner, *The Innovation Decision in Soviet Industry*, MIT Press, Cambridge, 1976.
4 *Pravda*, 31 March 1971.

5 *Pravda*, 18 January 1967.
6 Alice Gorlin 'Industrial Reorganization: The Associations', in US Congress Joint Economic Committee, *Soviet Economy in a New Perspective*, Washington DC, 1976, pp. 162–88.
7 For the details of the quantitative estimates, see Berliner, op. cit., ch. 16.

PART III

CONCLUSION

12 Continuities in Management from Stalin to Gorbachev 1988

The earlier essays in this volume were based in part on interviews with former Soviet citizens who had occupied management positions in Soviet industry in the last years before the Second World War. Vast changes have occurred in the economy in the succeeding half-century, during which the USSR completed its transformation into a great military and industrial power. It is appropriate to conclude this volume with an inquiry into the extent to which managerial behaviour has also changed since those pre-war years.

To the more durable analysts of the Soviet economy, it is evident that certain features of managerial behaviour have not changed. For example, in his Report to the 27th Party Congress in March 1986, General Secretary Gorbachev analyzed the obstacles to the attainment of his central objective of accelerating the rate of technological progress. 'Unfortunately,' he remarked, 'many scientific discoveries and important inventions lie around for years, and sometimes decades, without being introduced into production.'[1]

Those words had a familiar ring. In my research on management during Stalin's time, a major source was the Report to the 18th Party Conference, delivered by Georgii M. Malenkov in February 1941.[2] Scurrying back to that Report, I found the words, 'highly valuable inventions and product improvements often lie around for years in the scientific research institutes, laboratories and enterprises, and are not introduced into production.' It is remarkable that this item, high on the agenda of the pre-war Party leadership, should appear again on the agenda 45 years later, and in virtually the same words.

A comparison of the two Reports reveals other managerial practices that are criticized by both Party leaders. In all cases, the succession of governments had sought to eradicate them;

269

organizational changes were introduced, incentive arrangements were changed, new pricing methods were tried, new personnel were appointed. The intractability of the objectionable practices to all those efforts suggests that they derive from some fundamental structural properties of the economic system, properties that were untouched by all the remedial measures that had been tried.

The purpose of this concluding essay is to identify the fundamental structural properties of the economic system by examining the practices of management that have proven to be so remarkably persistent. Those properties may serve as a gauge by which to evaluate Gorbachev's new programme of restructuring the economy. No matter how radical his programme may seem to him, unless it alters those properties of the economy, such enduring problems as the reluctance to innovate are likely to survive his tenure of office as they did Malenkov's.

The two Party Reports that span the period provide what may be thought of as the view from on high. A view from below is afforded by the interviews with former Soviet citizens conducted in 1950 as part of the Harvard Refugee Interview Project (Inkeles, 1959)[3]. The informants reported on the last pre-war managerial position they had occupied while still in the USSR, around the same time as Malenkov presented his Report. There was no subsequent extensive emigration from the USSR until the 1970s, when a substantial number of Soviet citizens were permitted to leave. The new wave of emigration led to the organization of the Soviet Interview Project (SIP), one portion of which was devoted to interviews with informants who had occupied positions in enterprise management and in the higher economic bureaucracy [Millar, 1987].[4] The SIP interviews therefore present the view from below of the world of management corresponding to that which Gorbachev reported on from above.[5]

The paper begins with an account of various differences between enterprises of the late 1930s and the late 1970s that reflect the economic and social development of the society over the intervening decades. Part II discusses differences that are the consequence of organizational changes introduced by the leadership in the course of those decades. Part III then identifies features of enterprise management that are very similar in the two periods. The paper concludes with a discussion of the reasons for the stability of managerial behaviour over that long period of time.

I THE MATURE INDUSTRIAL ENTERPRISE

Imagine a managerial official who fell into a deep sleep in 1941 and awoke to find himself in a typical enterprise in 1986. He would surely be overwhelmed by the visible changes from the world that he had known.

Technology

Perhaps the most awesome change would be the technology that lay before his eyes. He would recognize some pieces of equipment as machine tools or motors, though of a size and complexity that he could scarcely fathom. Much of the equipment and the products they produce, however, would be completely incomprehensible, such as computers, automatic controls and plastics.

These are the fruits of the arduous industrialization drive that had begun in the decade before his long sleep. He would surely believe that Stalin's omnipresent slogan, to 'overtake and surpass the West', had come to pass.

He could not comprehend the anxiety that infuses Gorbachev's Report. He had understood Malenkov's concern about inventions that were never introduced into production, but surely that problem must have been solved long since. How else to account for the magnificent technology spread out before his eyes? Yet here is the new Party leader, once again fulminating about inventions that are never introduced into production.

One could not understand the concerns of Gorbachev if one looked only at the progress of the Soviet economy itself between 1941 and 1986. The long-term rate of economic growth has been substantial, although it has been declining for some time. The rate of technological growth must also have been robust to have brought the economy so far since 1941. If the USSR were a world of its own, there would be reason only for celebration.

The trouble with the Soviet economy is not the Soviet economy but all those others – the US and Europe on the West and Japan and the Pacific Rim on the East. In 1941 there was good reason to expect that the West, having experienced the deepest crisis in its history, was no .longer a factor to be reckoned with in the dialectical course of history. Contrary to the expectations of most Marxists, however, the Western economies experienced a resurgence in economic growth and technological advance, joined by the most remarkable newcomer of all, Japan, and various other Asian countries. Hence, rapid as Soviet growth has been, little progress was made in closing the gap.[6] Moreover, while the level of Soviet technology advanced at a highly creditable rate, that of the West

advanced at a comparable rate, signifying that no progress had
been made in narrowing the technological distance behind the
West.[7]

All this would be a very difficult set of ideas for the newly-
wakened manager to absorb. On the one hand he could scarcely
believe that his country's technology had advanced so far in the
45 years of his sleep. On the other, he finds about him an air
of gloom at the prospect that unless something radical is done,
the USSR will enter the next century as a second-rate industrial
and technological country.

The Labour Force

The workers are as much changed as their machines. Most of the
workers of his day were but a few years off the farm. Many of
the older ones had no schooling at all, and that of the younger
was rudimentary. The new machinery, much of it imported from
the West at great cost, suffered at the hands of its inexperienced
operators. One could understand Malenkov's exasperated charge
that ' ... in many of our enterprises ... filth reigns. Workplaces,
equipment, instruments and materials are in slovenly conditions.
Windows and glass roofs of shops are covered with dirt and barely
transmit any light.'

By contrast, the workforce of 1986 are practically 'Germans'.
Most are urban-born children of workers rather than of peasants,
and they have generally had a technical education, often at the
secondary level. They handle the machines with a skill and
familiarity that was rare in the pre-war factory. The workplace
is reasonably clean and orderly.

Visiting a worker's home, it is apparent that they enjoy many
of the fruits of the new economy. Most worker families live in
their own apartments, a rare luxury in the pre-war years when
most apartments were shared, with families often occupying a single
room. Although there are still the familiar shortages and queues,
the diet is better and there is meat to be had several times a week.
Most remarkable is the number and variety of consumer durables
– television, refrigerators, washing machines, even automobiles for
some higher-income workers.

About the worker's spiritual life, things are not so clear. There
are not as many posters, harangues and political meetings as in
Stalin's time, which may strike him as a good thing. On the other
hand communist ideological commitment seems to have been replaced by no other commitment, except perhaps to consumerism.
The pace of work is somewhat sluggish and there is more talk
of excessive drinking. Russian male workers have always been

devoted to the bottle, but there seems to be more drinking now
– at least until the anti-alcohol campaign initiated by Andropov.
Nevertheless it would be the rare worker who would knowingly
prefer the pre-war days to the present.

Management

The visitor from 1941 would be uncomfortable in the presence
of the managers of the 1986 enterprise. As a managerial official
himself before the war, he was probably one of the *praktiki*, able
people with limited education who comprised much of the management corps in those years. The new managers, however, are all
members of the intelligentsia, having had a higher education in
some field of engineering.

They are more self-confident, and there is a reason for it. Most
top officials have held their jobs for a long time, for decades in
some cases. The typical pre-war manager, however, held his job
for about three years, more or less, before being moved up or
down to another. Much of the mobility of management was the
consequence of the great purges; the disappearance or imprisonment
of one official was the occasion for promoting another to his place.
The security of management is one of the striking differences
between the enterprises of the two periods.[8]

Educational attainment and job security have combined to raise
the status of management to a higher level than in the pre-war
period. One can see this in the tone of the two Party Reports.
Malenkov savaged both managers and commissars with vivid and
sarcastic accounts of their stupidity, to the applause and laughter
of the Party delegates to the Conference. In contrast, while Gorbachev intimates that many managers are too conservative and too
unenthusiastic about his plans for restructuring the economy, he
nevertheless treats them with kid gloves and his tone is one of
proper respect.

The material well-being of managers, like that of the workers,
now greatly surpasses that of their pre-war colleagues. It rests partly
on the perquisites of office, such as a large plant-owned apartment
and the use of company cars. Some benefits may be in the form
of monetary gifts, for various degrees of participation in second-
economy activities. Most of it, however, comes from the official
salary and bonuses, as in the pre-war period.

II ORGANIZATIONAL CHANGES

The physical and social transformation of the Soviet enterprise
has been accompanied by a transformation in the organizational

structure and formal rules of procedure. The post-Stalin leadership has been keenly aware of the prevalence of waste and inefficiency and has sought ways of tightening up the operation of the economy. The endless search for better ways of managing the economy accelerated with the beginning of the decline of the growth rate in the 1960s and has now reached a new level of intensity under Gorbachev.

Some of the changes were of massive proportions.[9] On each occasion their sponsors believed that they had found the key to the elimination of the crucial deficiencies of the system. Khrushchev in 1957 sought the key in the abolition of the ministries and their replacement by regional units of economic administration. Brezhnev in 1965 sought it in the elimination of the 'petty tutelage' of enterprise managers by ministry officials. In 1973 he tried another approach – the merger of most of the country's enterprises and R & D establishments into large corporate units called production associations. His last major initiative was a reform of the planning system in 1979 designed to convert operational planning from an annual to a five-year basis, in order to provide longer-term stability to enterprise plan targets. Alongside the major reforms, minor changes of all sorts were constantly introduced, coming with such frequency in the last decade that one analyst described it as a 'treadmill' [Schroeder, 1979].

Some of the reforms and changes were later reversed, and some of their provisions were never fully implemented. Over the years, however, the accretion of changes that endured became quite extensive, so that by 1986 the organization of economic activity was vastly different from that of 1941. The manager of 1941 would still recognize much that was familiar, but he could not step into a managerial position in 1986 without having had a considerable re-education in the ways that things are now done.[10]

The internal structure of the enterprise itself has changed very little. The chief officers and departments largely bear the same names as they did before the war, and they carry out the same functions. However, the organizational world above the enterprise level has changed greatly.

The pre-war enterprise director's 'boss' was usually the Head of a Chief Administration, a line department of the Commissariat responsible for all enterprises in a particular line of production.[11] Most enterprises today are members of production associations, the head of which is the General Director. The latter's boss, in turn, is the Head of the Chief Administration; unless the Chief Administration has been replaced by an Industrial Association, in which case it is to the Head of the latter that the General Director of the production association reports. The main point is that the bureaucracy that stands between enterprise director and his minister is much more complex than in the pre-war period.

New organizations also abound at the state level. Before the war the Commissar of a production commissariat dealt with only a few other organizations: the State Planning Commission on matters of planning, the Commissariat of Finance on taxes and financial accounting, and State Bank on current revenues and expenditures. Now there is a large number of State Committees, the only residue of Khrushchev's reform. They have various functional or coordinating responsibilities indicated by their names: The State Committee on Science and Technology, the State Committee on Wages and Social Problems, the State Committee on Construction. All have been assigned responsibilities requiring communication and negotiation with the production ministries. Formerly the State Planning Commission alone managed all planning operations, including the assignment of output plan targets and allocation of the outputs among the users. Now it handles output targeting and the distribution of some products among users, but the distribution of most products is managed by the State Supply Committee. The work of the ministry, like that of the enterprise, is therefore also more complex than in earlier years.

National planning is more sophisticated than earlier, relying heavily on computers and to some extent on mathematical modelling. The enterprise plan is now a massive document compared to that of the past. It has many more sections, including, for example, a section listing all the technological changes that are to be introduced during the plan period. That and other sections are required in order to justify the requests for supplies that it submits to the State Supply Committee. However, the full content of the plan is used only for the enterprise's own internal schedulling, and for the information of the ministry. Only a small part of it is 'confirmed' by the ministry; this part contains the indicators for which the ministry may lawfully hold the enterprise to account.

A great deal of reform effort has been devoted to the precise specification of the indicators to which the ministry may require the enterprise to conform and by which enterprise performance may be evaluated. The purpose of the 1965 Reform was to greatly expand enterprise autonomy by paring the number of such indicators down to eight; within a few years, however, the effort to hold that particular bridge was defeated and the number of such indicators gradually crawled back to its earlier level.

The choice of the indicators to be used for guiding enterprise decisions and evaluating their performance is of critical importance, for it affects the basic production decisions that have to be made. The longest struggle was waged over one particular indicator – gross value of output, simply referred to as *val*. To the pre-war manager and his commissar, *val* was the paramount indicator. As early as 1939 economists began to point out cautiously that there were certain grave deficiencies in the ways in which that indicator was being used, and by 1941 they had persuaded the government (Berliner, 1957, pp. 35–6, 122–3). Malenkov lashed out against it in his Report and in 1946 *val* was officially dethroned in favour of a different indicator – the so-called 'marketed output'. That indicator also proved to be unsatisfactory and was replaced by two indicators in the 1965 Reform – sales revenue and profit, to which others have subsequently been added. It is therefore startling to read in Gorbachev's Report: 'In other words, the most important thing must not be *val* but the quantity, assortment and quality of output, that which people actually need.' Throughout this long-standing effort to stamp it out, *val* has evidently continued to live a subterranean existence as if by some conspiratorial agreement between ministry and enterprise.

The reason the performance indicator issue is significant for management is that production bonuses, an important component of income, are based on performance as measured by those indicators. The bonus system is much more elaborate than in the simpler pre-war days because over the years, as each new problem came to the fore, one of the ways of dealing with it was to establish a new bonus to motivate management to attend to that matter; there are bonuses, for example for innovation, for exporting, for conserving energy, and so forth. The pre-war manager had a fairly clear idea of the effect a particular choice would have on his bonus and those of his staff. It is doubtful that the present-day manager can actually judge the net effect of a particular choice on the total of all bonuses. It is therefore likely that the bonus system is not as salient as a guide to decision-making as it was in earlier years.

What appears to be common to the organizational changes since the war is the increasing complexity of the system of planning and managing economic activity. Whatever generalizations apply to the effect of increasing complexity on organizations must surely hold for Soviet economy. At the least one would expect the behaviour of the agents to be different in the more complex world than in the simpler.

III   OLD WINE IN NEW BOTTLES

Industrial maturation and organizational change have produced a contemporary enterprise that is very different from its pre-war counterpart. When one delves into the way in which business is actually conducted under these changed conditions, however, one is struck by how little has changed.

The focus of the pre-war manager's concerns was the fulfilment of a monthly output plan target that was generally perceived as 'unrealistic', or excessively 'taut' in the terms of the subsequent Western analysis.[12] It was the pressure to meet such high targets that generated a variety of the operating practices that distressed the leadership, such as hoarding supplies and reducing the quality of output. The major purpose of many of the reforms of the intervening years was to produce more realistic plan targets so that managers would cease to engage in those practices. It is therefore surprising to find that in the testimony of the SIP informants the perception that plans are 'unrealistic' emerges in much the same way as it did in the Harvard interviews.[13]

The persistence of excessive tautness subjects present-day managers to the same pressures as their pre-war colleagues. It does not follow, however, that their responses should be the same. Behaviour is affected not only by pressures of this sort but also by such factors as industrial maturity and organizational structure, both of which have changed a good deal. For example, Linz found that enterprise management regards ministry personnel as more competent and more knowledgeable about enterprise affairs than in the past [Linz, 1986, p. 7]. Hence while SIP informants refer to their efforts to guarantee a 'safety factor'[14] in much the same terms as the Harvard informants, the extent of some of the cruder methods of achieving it has been reduced.

Nevertheless many of the practices of the past have survived virtually unchanged into the present. Portions of the SIP interviews read as if they came right out of the Harvard interviews; there is something eerie about it, like hearing voices from the distant past. Ten such practices are discussed in this section.

1   The Ratchet

The pre-war manager anticipated that if he overfulfilled his current plan target, the authorities would raise his target for the next period to the level that had last been achieved. This practice, dubbed the 'ratchet' principle, was one of the sources of plan tautness.[15]

There was no public mention of the practice in the pre-war years. In the post-war period, however, the authorities were eventually persuaded that the practice had various unfortunate effects such as inducing management to hold back on the overfulfilment of plans.[16] Among the reforms designed to eliminate ratchet-based planning is the principle of 'stable plans'. Under this arrangement the enterprise receives annual plan targets for each of the five years in the forthcoming five year plan period, and those targets are not to be changed in the course of the five years regardless of the degree to which they are overfulfilled. It has proven impossible to hold to the principle of stable plans, however, and the ratchet principle continues to be applied.

The SIP informants describe the practice in virtually the same terms as the Harvard informants: 'The planning conditions in our trust were like this: all planning begins with the figures actually achieved in the preceding years.' The practice is now so institution-alized that there is a term for it in the Soviet economic lexicon: 'planning from the achieved level'.

2   Production Reserves

Since performance is measured against a plan target, every pro-duction unit has an interest in obtaining the lowest possible plan target. Pre-war management did this by understating its production capacity in order to receive a 'reduced plan'. The ministry did it by the method of 'clearance planning'; that is, by assigning to its enterprises a set of production targets the sum of which is greater than the ministry's own aggregate target (Berliner, 1957, pp. 83–5).

The ministry still engages in that practice. The ministry 'reserves a window for itself to fulfil the branch plan' is the way a SIP informant described it. Enterprises still bargain hard for the best plan they can achieve. Linz (1986, pp. 20–1) reports, however, that 'no strong evidence emerges from the interview study to indicate that enterprise managers maintain hidden reserves'. The explanation she offers is that the present-day ministry personnel are more knowledgeable about the enterprise and are therefore better able to control it.

On the other hand the top Party leadership evidently continues to believe that enterprises maintain concealed production reserves. If they did not, it would make no sense to devote such effort to counterplanning, the purpose of which is to induce enterprises to disclose their reserve capacity. The true state of affairs may well lie in-between; concealed production reserves are probably smaller today than in the freer-wheeling past because of better ministry control, but are still sufficiently large to be a source of continued concern by the state.

3 Materials Hoarding

Materials supply continues to be the most frustrating aspect of enterprise management. The discussions of this matter in the SIP interviews are virtually indistinguishable from the Harvard interviews. Even the anecdotes are the same: 'when you need cement, you get pipe, and when you need pipe, you get cement,' said a SIP informant. The Harvard informants did not have a sufficient knowledge of the West to make any comparisons, but many of the SIP informants were working in American industry and volunteered comparative judgements. 'Even today I can't believe how undisciplined it all was,' said one.

In the pre-war period it was common practice to strive for a safety factor in materials supply by ordering larger quantities of materials than one needed. This practice is not often referred to in the SIP interviews and it may have indeed become rarer because of the stronger ministry controls.

Overordering, however, was not the only reason that pre-war enterprises managed to accumulate large excess stocks of supplies. Another was plan changes, which still occur with some frequency. When an enterprise is ordered to accept a new production assignment in place of an earlier one, the materials ordered for the earlier one often continue to be delivered. The confusion in the supply system also results in deliveries of materials that are not required, but they are rarely declined because, under conditions of general shortage, some uses can always be found for them. Hence the stronger control over ordering has not fully defeated management's ability to maintain excess stocks.

The hoarded inventories of supplies help to support many of the other features of the informal supply system that reappear in the SIP interviews. The *tolkachi* (expediters) still scurry about performing the function of middlemen, seeking out supplies needed by the enterprise. A whole range of gift-giving practices are referred to in the interviews, ranging from more-or-less legal high-life dining to direct bribery.[17] Each generation produces its own language for these matters; the expression *Moldavskii privet* (a Moldavian greeting) was not part of the pre-war language.

4 Barter and Resale

Further evidence that hoarding is still fairly widespread is that the practice of barter and resale is, if anything, more extensive than in the past. The Harvard informants reported the practice, but as something that had to be done surreptitiously. The SIP informants, however, give the impression that it had become standard practice, carried out in the normal course of business without having to look over one's shoulder. For example, an enterprise that had ordered a supply of bricks expedited the delivery by providing the brickyard with a supply of pipe that they had in excess. 'The brick enterprise had the bricks, and they didn't care to whom they shipped them,' reported the informant. The practice of exchange appears to be so extensive and is treated so casually that one gets the impression of a significant barter economy operating within the planned economy; 'I won't give to you because what would I get in return?' said one informant.

The expansion of barter and resale is consistent with a change in national policy. The spirit of the pre-war period is captured in the ominous remarks of Malenkov:

The State distributes equipment and materials to enterprises for specified uses, but the managers use them arbitrarily and illegally; they sell them, exchange them and pass them off on the side ... I must state forthrightly, comrades, that this established practice of the sale of so-called out-of-service and surplus equipment and materials amounts to nothing less than the plundering of socialist property.

Forty-five years later, however, the view of the leadership on this matter had changed radically.

In Gorbachev's words:

We must give enterprises and organizations the right to sell, independently, output produced in excess of the plan, and also surplus materials, equipment and so forth. This should also be legalized with respect to sales to the population. Does it make any sense to destroy or to junk things that would be useful to households, in building living quarters, garages or garden sheds?

With the hindsight of history it is striking to recall how much faith the Stalinist leadership had in the potential effectiveness of central economic planning. The system had indeed enabled them to engineer the great transformation of their country from a land of peasants into an industrial power. They therefore saw no reason to doubt that, if only people did their jobs right, the central planners could effectively direct the use of every machine and every ton of pipe in every enterprise. Hence the 'arbitrary' and unplanned redirection of a machine from one enterprise to another had to be viewed as a misallocation of resources.

That naive optimism has long since vanished. Stalin's successors eventually ceased to believe it possible for the Centre to manage the disposition of every machine and every ton of pipe; and in fact the effort to do so actually undermines the ability of the central planners to do well what they can do well. The search for ways of decentralizing local decisions within the framework of central planning is the meaning of Gorbachev's call for 'the union of centralization and the independence of enterprises'.

Hence, while the Soviet enterprise of the SIP informants looks very similar to that of the Harvard informants with respect to the barter and resale of materials and equipment, the greater extent of the practice and the more relaxed conditions under which it takes place reflect the considerable change in the environment of economic policy.

5 Hoarding of Labour

This figured prominently in the Harvard interviews, but it is not as prominent in the testimony of the SIP informants. The explanation cannot be that labour is no longer in short supply, for all the usual evidence of labour shortage does appear in the interviews: a high rate of turnover, problems of labour discipline, and the frequent references to overtime work.[18] The explanation offered by the SIP informants is that controls are too strong. 'You couldn't hire a single worker without an authorization,' is one such statement.

One would be inclined to accept that interpretation except for a major piece of contrary evidence. The authorities continue to hold the view that enterprises retain more workers than they need. 'Some of our managers complain about an inadequate supply of labour,' reported Gorbachev, '...[however] it is well known that some of our design organizations and research institutes have significantly higher employment than equivalent foreign organizations producing the same volume of output.' What then should one believe, the view from above or the view from below?

What appears to be a contradiction, however, may be no more than a difference in perceptions. There are two reasons why this may be so. First, in recent years it has been common practice for local governments to require enterprises to provide labour for such public needs as helping with the harvest, building a public facility, and so forth. The prudent enterprise manager therefore wishes to have excess labour available in order to be able to satisfy these requirements without threatening the rate of enterprise output. He would not regard this labour supply practice as hoarding, but a state inspector would.

Second, there is a difference between the size of the authorized labour force (*shtatnoe raspisanie*) and the size of the actual labour force in the enterprise. In the effort to maintain a comfortable safety factor, management contrives to obtain an authorized labour force well in excess of the normal requirements. However, because of the labour shortage, they are often unable to hire the full number of workers authorized, although actual employment is sufficiently high to provide something of a safety factor. If that is a fairly typical situation, then (a) the authorities, looking at the inflated authorization, will regard the size of the labour force as excessive, while (b) management, unable to fill all the authorized places, will perceive the size of its labour force as inadequate. This state of affairs would explain why the SIP informants did not regard labour hoarding as a significant practice of management, while the state has undertaken a massive campaign of 'workplace certification' to pare down the excessive number of authorized workplaces in enterprises.

I conclude therefore that management continues to hire excess labour as a safety factor, but that the extent of the practice is probably smaller than in the past because of tighter controls.

6 Enterprise Autarky

One of the ways in which the pre-war manager protected his enterprise from the effects of the uncertainty over supply was to resort to self-supply to the extent possible. The pre-war published sources provided accounts of the large volume of machine tools and other equipment that enterprises had accumulated in order to be able to manufacture the components, spare parts, materials, and other inputs required for their own production needs. Enterprise autarky (or 'universalism') was a device for minimizing the risks of dependence on uncertain deliveries from other enterprises.[19]

Self-supply appears again as a prominent theme in the SIP interviews. There are numerous accounts of the construction of auxiliary production shops *khozsposobom*, meaning that they were built not by outside contractors but by enterprise personnel with the enterprise's own resources. Ministries engage in this practice as well – building enterprises that are far from their main line of specialization. Their purpose, like that of their enterprises, is autarky; to assure the supply of resources needed by their own enterprises in order to reduce dependence on deliveries from enterprises of other ministries. The pre-war commissariats very likely engaged in the same practice but it appears to emerge more prominently in the SIP interviews.[20]

One possible reason for the increase in autarky is that, as a consequence of technological advance, products contain many more components manufactured by other enterprises. Ministry and enterprise are therefore more vulnerable to the deficiencies of the supply system and have stronger motivation to produce their own principal components and supplies. A second reason is that state policy has been supportive of vertical integration in other contexts; the motivation for the production association reform, in fact, is that that type of large organization bypasses a portion of the supply system by providing for self-supply. For the same reason, enterprises are now encouraged to organize their own farms to supply food to their labour force.

7 Innovation

The similarity of the remarks by Malenkov and Gorbachev about inventions that 'lie around for years' without being implemented testifies to the persistence of managerial resistance to innovation. In view of the technological transformation that the country experienced over the period, however, it is evident that the economy does have ways of accomplishing innovation [Berliner, 1976, ch. 17]. The problem that exercises the leadership is not that technological progress does not occur, but that it occurs too slowly. Their purpose is to speed it up.

To the pre-war manager the preference for producing established products rather than new ones was a standard form of the safety factor. New products 'present a whole new problem', said a Harvard informant. 'Every new product involves a great deal of waste of labour and money until you get used to producing it.' In the intervening decades a great many reforms were introduced to reduce the resistance to new products and processes, including special bonuses, organizational changes and new pricing methods.[21] The SIP accounts, however, confirm Gorbachev's view that management is still less than enthusiastic about new technology. After describing a case in which a bonus was awarded for a cost-reducing proposal that management never put into use, despite orders from the ministry, a SIP informant concluded, 'And for these "innovations" people get millions of rubles, although they have no practical application.'

8 Quality

At the 18th Party Conference, Malenkov reminded the delegates of the July 1940 Edict that imposed criminal penalties on persons guilty of producing sub-quality output. Despite the new law, he declared:

many economic leaders have a criminally lighthearted attitude regarding the production of poor quality products and the huge quantities of valuable resources wasted by the producers of spoilage ... The Commissariats must demand firm discipline regarding the observance of technological specifications in enterprises, and must forbid enterprises from altering the designs or blueprints of products without permission . . .

Forty-five years later, at a similar forum, Gorbachev reported:

I must particularly underline the problem of the quality of production . . . Because of poor design, deviations from technological specifications, use of low quality materials, and poor finishing, we have to bear large material and moral losses . . . To put an end to this we have to use the full force of material and administrative pressures and to make use of all our laws.

Concern about quality figures prominently in both sets of interviews as well, and many of the reasons are the same. The following statement by a SIP informant is virtually undistinguishable from those in the Harvard interviews:

You often received very low quality materials and you couldn't produce good products from those materials. And the reason for low quality materials was the drive to fulfill the plan, which was too high for the low production capacity of the enterprise.

There does appear to be greater concern now about quality by producers of consumer goods.[22] But, in the case of producer goods, the notion that the buyer 'will take anything' is as prominent today as in the past. A typical formulation, for both periods, is the statement by a SIP informant:

There is a lot of pressure on the buyer also, and if he doesn't take it there is no other place to get it. Therefore he agrees, and then he starts to remake it or to improve it, you understand?

9 Storming

From the earliest days of central planning, the authorities have been exercised about the uneven pace of production. The rate of production is very low during the first part of the plan period (usually the beginning of the month), and is then followed by a rush to fulfil the plan in the last days of the month.[23] Each generation of leaders had its own ideas on how to eradicate this costly nuisance of 'storming'. Malenkov's was singularly naive. He held up as models some commissariats that had achieved good results by requiring every enterprise manager to report to his commissar every morning on the quantity produced the preceding day. 'This kind of reporting', he stated, 'in which only one single figure is required, makes it possible to control the work of the enterprise every day.'

This is an archetypical example of the approach to the control of enterprise activity in Stalin's time. Twenty-five years later it was vigorously denounced as 'petty tutelage'. However Brezhnev was no more successful than Malenkov in stamping out this hardy perennial. In her account of the SIP interviews, Linz writes that storming 'is the strongest source of continuity with past studies' (Linz, 1986, p. 12). That generalization is supported by the view from above. Gorbachev reports:

It is no secret that many enterprises are idle more of the time than they are working at the beginning of the month. Then at the end they begin storming and as a result quality suffers. We have to get rid of this chronic disease.

10 Equality-mongering

Equality-mongering or *uravnilovka*, is the term coined by Stalin in 1931 in derogation of those who regarded equality as the only acceptable wage policy in a socialist society. Under the pre-war wage-incentive system skilled workers' wage rates were set at 3–4 times those of unskilled. The state's efforts to maintain incentive wage differentials, however, were constantly undermined by social pressures within the enterprise. A Harvard informant reported:

We had particular trouble with the women's brigade. They had the easiest jobs, yet they never earned the full amount that was due them. Therefore we had to spend much time in various forms of deceit, writing out different work orders, give them makeshift jobs, in order to increase their pay. (Berliner, 1957, p. 172).

Referring to working in general, Malenkov lashed out at the 'corrupt practice' of artificially raising the wage levels of those workers 'who do not improve their skills, and who do not fulfill output norms.'

In the following decades there was a great deal of lecturing and admonishing, and a certain number of reforms as well, in order to impress upon management the virtue of the principle, 'from each according to his ability, to each according to his work.' Yet in 1986 Gorbachev is obliged to remind the country again of the 'unacceptability of the so-called *vyvodilovki*[24] – the payment of unearned wages, the award of undeserved bonuses, the establishment of a "guaranteed" wage unconnected with the worker's contribution.'

IV   THE FUTURE OF CENTRAL PLANNING

There is a difference in the tone of the 1941 and 1986 Party Reports. Malenkov's is rather upbeat. The deficiencies he criticizes are real and costly, but they can be easily overcome if the laws are tightened and if commissars and managers would simply do their jobs right. Gorbachev's words, however, are filled with foreboding. He is aware that past efforts at reform, bold and fundamental as they seemed at the time, have not got to the heart of the matter, with costly consequences for the Soviet position both at home and abroad.

Malenkov could also believe that time was on his side. Many of the problems he identified are confronted by all newly industrialized economies and could be expected to disappear as the economy matured.[25] Gorbachev can no longer believe that. The problems he confronts have survived both the passage of time and a long stream of efforts of solve them. In order to succeed, Gorbachev's reform will have to strike at whatever it is that accounts for the remarkable continuity of that set of problems over so long a period. Their persistence suggests that they are rooted in some fundamental property of the economic system, a property that has not been touched by even the boldest reforms of the past.[26] It is important to get it right this time; else the agenda of Party Secretaries for years to come will continue to contain the same items as that of Malenkov in 1941 and Gorbachev in 1986.

Shortage

Many of the practices under discussion are the consequence of persistent shortage. They form what may be regarded as a 'shortage syndrome', which includes quality deterioration, hoarding, barter, supply expediters, gifts and bribery, organizational 'autarky' and so forth. The syndrome is no respecter of economic systems but occurs whenever any economy functions under conditions of persistent shortage. They were present in the US and other countries during the Second World War.[27] If the cause of the persistence of shortage can be identified, it may provide the key to the stability of the practices that form the shortage syndrome.

In the Western literature, excessive tautness has long been regarded as the source of the shortage phenomenon in the USSR (Holzman, 1955; Hunter, 1961). Tautness assures that a certain proportion of all plans will not be fulfilled. In a tautly planned economy underfulfilment of the plan by one enterprise is experienced as shortage by the enterprise that was to have received the output that was not produced.[28] Shortage thus percolates through the inter-industry relationships of the system. Under this interpretation, what is required is a policy decision to strive hereafter for optimal, rather than excessive tautness. With adequately provided buffer stocks shortage should then disappear and with it the practices of the shortage syndrome.

An alternative interpretation has recently been offered by Janos Kornai (1980). Kornai argues that the source of shortage is the commitment of the leadership to maintaining production in all enterprises regardless of their efficiency. Knowing that they will always be bailed out by the authorities, enterprises are not firmly constrained by financial budgets to limit the quantities of current and capital resources they seek to obtain. The 'soft budget constraint' acts as an enormous suction pump, drawing resources and products into the warehouses and production lines of enterprises as soon as they become available for delivery. Under this interpretation taut planning may intensify the state of shortage, but as long as the soft budget constraint prevails shortage will persist even with optimal plan tautness. The soft budget constraint is a sufficient condition for persistent shortage. The solution therefore is to create conditions under which an enterprise that is financially insolvent, for more than short-run reasons, will be dissolved and its labour and capital resources redistributed among more productive establishments.

Kornai's argument implies that the reduction of tautness is not a real option for a centrally planned socialist economy. It is not within the power of the central planners to reduce tautness, because the suction generated by the soft budget constraint will continue to sweep all commodities and resources off the shelves, creating shortage even with plans that are optimally taut.

Recent Soviet history provided a test of Kornai's interpretation. In 1975 the government was persuaded that the poor quality of output was the consequence of excess demand generated by taut plans. Determined to strike finally at the root of the quality problem, it took the bold decision to sharply reduce plan tautness, in defiance of longstanding planning tradition. The Tenth Five Year Plan (1976–80) was named the 'Plan of Quality'. In anticipation of the effect of reduced tautness, the planned industrial growth rate for 1976 was reduced to 4.3 per cent, down from the 6.6 per cent achieved in 1975. The growth of planned investment was reduced to 3.5 per cent, less than half that of 1975.

There followed one of the most disastrous periods in recent Soviet economic history. The lower output targets for producers goods reduced the supply of those goods to other producers, whose output fell below the reduced levels planned for them. The decline in new investment slowed additions to capacity and shortages of raw materials increased, affecting steel production which in turn held up investment even further. The industrial growth rate plunged, falling to 1.9 per cent in 1980 (Schroeder, 1985).

This bold attempt to reduce tautness did not in fact do so. On the contrary, 'Enterprise managers probably redoubled their customary efforts to maintain a safety factor ... managers no doubt hoarded materials and kept workers on the payroll almost irrespective of what was happening to production' (Schroeder, 1985, pp. 66–7). That piece of history supports Kornai's view that the regulation of tautness is not the key to the elimination of shortage. Unfortunately, however, like most historical tests, this one is by no means decisive. The details are now known, but there is some reason to believe that the planned reduction in tautness was not carefully implemented.[29] The Tenth Plan therefore provides only a weak test of Kornai's interpretation, but it is a positive test.

It follows from Kornai's analysis that, if the Soviet leadership wishes to eliminate shortage and its consequences, it must find some way of building a hard budget constraint into enterprise decision-making. It is difficult, however, to imagine how such a constraint could operate in a centrally planned socialist economy. The ultimate disciplining force of a hard budget constraint would be the dissolution of the enterprise. Dissolution is a proper action for the central planners to take in a case in which an enterprise is inefficient even when optimally managed; the productivity of the resources would then be greater if they were redistributed among more efficient enterprises. No good purpose would be served, however, by dissolving an enterprise that is inefficient because of poor management. The appropriate recourse in that case is to change the management.[30] That, however, has in fact long been the established Soviet practice; incompetent managers are dismissed, to the extent that that is possible in large bureaucracies of any kind. Yet it has not served in the past to eliminate 'investment hunger' and the other causes of the suction that drives the shortage in Kornai's analysis.[31]

There are many reasons why the threat of dismissal has failed to restrain management's appetite for resources. One major reason is that the primary basis on which performance is evaluated is the fulfilment of the mandatory quantitative output plan target. It is not at all unreasonable for the governors of a centrally planned economy to instruct their managerial agents that their first obligation is to fulfil the output plan targets assigned to them.[32] A commitment to a centralized mechanism for allocating resources implies a commitment by the agents to follow the dictates of the plan.[33] A second reason is that the central planning of the distribution of intermediate products must inevitably be imperfect to some degree, the consequence of which is uncertainty over the supply of inputs to individual enterprises.[34] For these and other reasons, the threat of dismissal motivates management not to economize on resources but, on the contrary, to collect any resources that might be useful someday in fulfilling an output plan.

The conclusion is that neither reduced tautness nor a hard budget constraint are practical policies for eliminating shortage as long as the economic mechanism continues to be based on mandatory quantitative output targets (the 'assortment plan') and centralized distribution of intermediate products ('material–technical supply'). These two planning methods, however, are the core of central economic planning, as that term is usually understood on the basis of Soviet experience. Central economic planning may therefore be regarded as the fundamental property of the economic system that explains the persistence of the shortage syndrome and the practices that accommpany it.

Other Practices

The remainder of the story may now be evident. Central planning accounts not only for the persistence of the practices associated with the shortage syndrome, but it also accounts for the other practices that have endured through the decades. The basis of the argument is implicit in the discussion of these practices presented earlier, but the main points merit a brief review.

The Ratchet   This principle of planning derives from the planners' imperfect knowledge of the true production capacity of enterprises. They cannot refrain from using the revealed past performance of enterprises in their calculation of future plan targets. Some variant of the ratchet must therefore always be part of centralized plan target setting. The use of stable plans as proposed in the Gorbachev reforms is simply a variant of the ratchet, extended over several years.

Production reserves   Central planning requires that enterprises be assigned targets for output and various other aspects of production. The performance of management must be evaluated and rewarded in large part on the basis of the attainment of those targets. There have been heroic periods in the USSR when large numbers of people were selfless enough to provide the correct information required by the planners to set taut but realistic targets. In the normal course, however, it must be expected that managers will contrive, to the extent that they can, to obtain 'easy' plan targets.

Innovation   The introduction of a new product or process always increases uncertainty and generally entails some degree of disruption in the production process. Since central planning requires that the fulfilment of the output plan be the primary responsibility of the enterprise, management must always regard innovation as a secondary and potentially threatening activity.

Storming   Production is a continuous activity but central planning requires the use of discrete time periods like the month or the year. Wherever such critical dates are externally interposed in a continuous activity, there tends to be a bunching of effort as the accounting date approaches.[35]

Equalitarianism   Finally, the more secure an organization, the less the pressure for efficiency and therefore the greater the pressure for equality in income distribution. Since central planning affords each production unit a large measure of security, and since it is all regarded as the state's money anyhow, there will always be a tendency towards keeping peace in the family by taking care of those who are left behind.

Summary and Conclusions

The present-day Soviet economy took form in the 1930s during the first three five-year plans. The leadership under Stalin sought to incorporate the enterprise into the planning system by a set of formal rules designed to govern the productive activity of management. For a variety of reasons, there developed a set of informal practices, sometimes in violation of the formal rules, that management found necessary in order to carry out assignments that often conflicted with each other. Some of those practices became known outside of the USSR from the sharp public criticism to which they were subjected by the Party leadership, such as the Report to the 18th Party Conference by Georgii Malenkov on the eve of the Second World War. A full appreciation of the nature and extent of the informal behaviour of management came later, from the testimony of former Soviet citizens interviewed by the Harvard Refugee Interview Project.

In 1986 the new General Secretary, Mikhail Gorbachev, presented his Report to the 27th Party Congress. Much of his criticism was directed at the same informal practices that Malenkov had announced almost half a century earlier. The persistence of those practices was confirmed by the testimony of a more recent wave of former Soviet citizens interviewed by the Soviet Interview Project.

Some of those practices were thought in the early period to be the consequence of the underdeveloped state of the economy. By 1986, however, a mature industrial economy had long been in place. A high technological level had been attained, the labour force was well educated and technically trained, and the enterprise and higher economic bureaucracy were managed by people with higher education and considerable experience. Moreover, in the intervening decades, the leadership had introduced many organizational reforms expressly designed to eliminate those objectionable practices. Why then have these practices persisted over this long period?

Our interpretation is that the practices of management derive from the fundamental property of the economic system – the direction of the nation's economic activity by the method of central planning, characterized by mandatory quantitative output targets and centralized distribution of intermediate products. The long procession of organizational reforms changed the ways in which central planning is carried out, but always within the framework of central planning. It is the persistence of central economic planning that accounts for the persistence of the informal practices of management.

This interpretation may be in error. It is possible that it is not central planning as such, but some yet undiagnosed deficiency in the way in which planning is carried out that is the source of the problem. In that case, what is required is the discovery of the correct diagnosis, and then an economic reform based on that diagnosis. Our evidence and argument are not sufficiently powerful to rule out that possibility. It would seem, however, that the burden of proof is now upon those who hold that some way may yet be found to eliminate those practices without abandoning central planning.

It does not follow from our interpretation that central planning needs to be abandoned. Every economic system contains some forms of inefficiency and generates some outcomes that are widely held to be objectionable. The persistence of unemployment, fluctuations in economic activity, maldistribution of income, and other such outcomes are the consequence of the market system in capitalist economies. Ways may yet be found to eliminate those outcomes without abandoning the market system, but it is unlikely. There is no great clamour at present, however, to abandon the market system. For one thing, new ways are indeed likely to be found to mitigate, if not to eliminate, those outcomes or their effects. More important however, is that the net performance of the market system, taking all its warts into account, still strikes most of its members as better than any apparent alternative.

Similarly the persistence of objectionable outcomes is insufficient basis for the Soviet leadership to abandon the central planning system. New ways may indeed be found to mitigate them, if not to eliminate them, without abandoning central planning. The judgement should be based on the net performance of the system, warts and all.

In his Report to the 27th Party Congress Gorbachev declared his objective to be 'the union of centralism and the independence of economic organizations'. In declaring for centralism, he appears to have made the judgement that the net performance of the central planning system is still positive. In urging greater independence of economic organizations, he expressed his faith that new ways will yet be found to mitigate the deficiencies of the system. If our interpretation is correct, the commitment to the continuation of central planning signifies that the Reports of future General Secretaries will contain indictments of the same practices as the Reports of Malenkov and Gorbachev, and probably in the same words.

In June 1987, however, in an address to the Central Committee, Gorbachev appears to have changed his mind.[36] He presented a vision of a future economic system in which enterprises would no longer be assigned mandatory plan targets by the higher agencies but would determine their own production programmes on the basis of contracts with other enterprises.[37] Intermediate products would no longer be distributed by the central planners; enterprises would purchase their inputs directly from producers or from wholesale suppliers. If that vision is incorporated into a reform programme that is in fact implemented, then central planning will have effectively been abandoned by the USSR.

It does not follow from our interpretation that in this economic system of the future, resistance to innovation will disappear, quality will rise sharply, and the other informal practices will vanish. The elimination of central planning is a necessary condition for that to occur but it may not be sufficient. The forces that determine such outcomes as the rate of innovation in an economy are exceedingly complex, and no one factor is decisive, not even so weighty a factor as the basic economic mechanism. If central planning should in fact be replaced by another form of socialist economic organization, however, it would provide the first opportunity since the introduction of Stalin's economic system to alter radically not only the formal, but also the informal, organization of the Soviet firm.

NOTES

1 *Ekonomicheskaia gazeta*, no. 10, March 1986.
2 *Izvestiia*, 16 February 1941.
3 Chapter 2 of this volume is based on data gathered by that project. The full monographic study is Berliner, 1957.
4 This article is based on a working paper, 'Soviet Management from Stalin to Gorbachev: A Comparison of the Harvard Project and SIP Interviews', prepared by the author for the Soviet Interview Project. I am indebted to SIP for the support of that research.

   Paul Gregory and Susan Linz are working on the higher economic bureaucracy and the industrial enterprise respectively. I am greatly indebted to them for their cooperation and advice. I also owe a great debt to Holland Hunter for his critical reading of an earlier draft of this paper, and to Abram Bergson and Franz Holzman for their valuable comments.
5 Most of the informants had left the USSR between 1978 and 1981, 5–8 years before Gorbachev's Report. Those were years of government under the ailing Brezhnev and his two brief successors, during which no major economic initiatives were launched. The enterprise they describe is therefore much the same as the subject of Gorbachev's Report.
6 Over the period 1951–79 the USSR annual growth rate was 4.8 per cent per annum, and the US rate was 3.4 per cent. The growth rates of the OECD countries ranged from 2.7 per cent for the UK to 8.3 per cent for Japan [Joint Economic Committee, 1982, p. 20.].
7 In their detailed study of the technological level of the USSR, Amman, Cooper and Davies conclude that there is no evidence of a 'substantial diminution of the technological gap between the USSR and the West in the past 15–20 years', i.e. between 1957 and 1977 [Amman, 1977, p. 66].
8 In the Harvard interviews one could not talk with a former managerial official for half an hour without encountering some reference to imprisonment ('sitting', as the Russians say), sabotage, the secret police, informers and so forth. In the SIP interviews there are occasional references to imprisonment as the possible punishment for a hypothetical serious offence, but I encountered only one account of an actual KGB informer in an enterprise.
9 An account of the major reforms is given in Chapter 5 in this volume.
10 It is interesting to speculate on the question of whether an American managerial official of 1941 would be more or less able than his Soviet counterpart to step into a managerial position in 1986. I would guess that the changes in American industrial organization have not been

as extensive as Soviet, and the American would therefore find it easier to handle the job in 1986 than his Soviet counterpart would. Because of the incomparability of industrial organization, however, one can do little more than speculate.

11 If it was a very large enterprise, the director might report directly to the Commissar himself.

12 The first formal analysis of optimal tautness was published in 1961 by Holland Hunter. See Hunter, 1961.

13 Linz reports that of the 38 SIP respondents who were asked if they received 'impossible' plans, only two said 'no' (Linz 1986, p. 13).

14 Chapter 2 in this volume, pp. 31–2.

15 Chapter 3 in this volume, p. 51. The ratchet principle was first analyzed in Berliner, 1957, pp. 78–90. For a review of the recent literature on the ratchet see Keren, 1983.

16 Some SIP informants recount cases in which the enterprise actually underfulfilled the plan, even at the cost of bonuses, in order to elicit a smaller target for the next period [Linz, 1986, p. 18]. No case of this kind was reported in the Harvard interviews. It implies, not surprisingly, that the techniques of 'gaming' over the ratchet are more sophisticated than in the past. Linz provides a rich collection of descriptions of the ratchet in operation in Appendix A of her paper.

17 The SIP interviews antedate the austere Andropov–Gorbachev anti-alcohol campaign. Today there is certainly less wining and possibly also less dining of officials from supplying enterprises than in the recent past.

18 The demographically-based decline in the growth rate of the labour force was not yet fully felt in the late 1970s, the period to which the SIP interviews referred.

19 This practice was not discussed in *Factory and Manager* (Berliner, 1957). I have a strong recollection, however, of having learned about it from the interviews; perhaps it was reported by some informants but without much attention being given to it. It is discussed in Berliner, 1976, p. 72, however, along with evidence from published sources.

20 The practice extends to territorial units as well. One account describes the construction of a new enterprise by a small republic government in order to reduce dependence on shipments from other republics.

21 Some of these changes are discussed in Chapter 11 in this volume.

22 Linz writes, 'One striking feature emerging from the interview reports is the demand orientation of firms producing goods for consumers' (Linz, 1985, pp. 10–11). The concern for consumer demand is not general, however, but appears to apply to certain kinds of goods in certain places: 'If we can't sell it in Moscow, we can always ship it to the Eastern and Northern regions. They will buy anything,' said a SIP informant. In the Harvard interviews, in contrast, the expression 'they will buy anything' was often used about consumer goods in general.

23 The practice of storming is the subject of Chapter 3 of this volume.

24 Wage supplements unlawfully given to low-income workers in order

to bring their take-home pay up to what is regarded by management (presumably shop-level management) as an acceptable minimal level. This expression was not part of the pre-war economic lexicon.

25 Since he must have studied Volume One of Marx's *Capital*, he may have been aware of the many similarities between the Soviet enterprise as he depicted it and the English enterprise of a century earlier as depicted by Marx on the basis of the reports of English factory inspectors. Some of these similarities are reported in Berliner, 1957, pp. 141–2.

26 Linz questioned the SIP informants on the impact of past reforms on their enterprises. She reports that 'numerous efforts to restructure the Soviet economic bureaucracy in order to improve resource utilization and product quality appear to have had little impact on managerial decision-making at the enterprise level' (Linz, 1987, p. 16).

27 Comparisons with management in other countries are developed in Chapter 4 in this volume.

28 Inventories are too small to serve as buffer stocks. The greater the degree of shortage of a commodity, the smaller the inventory stocks. Hence current output is produced largely with currently produced inputs.

29 Proper implementation would have required an economy-wide revision of the coefficients used to calculate the quantities of each input required per unit of each output. There clearly was insufficient time to carry out so massive a revision. Possibly it was implemented in some haste, simply by a general reduction of output targets. That would have reduced plan tautness relative to the fixed capital stock, but it would also have increased the general shortage of inputs. I am grateful to Susan Linz for calling the problem of implementation to my attention.

30 In a capitalist economy bankruptcy is a sanction applied against the owners, not against the employed managers (directly). In a firm that is intrinsically efficient but badly managed, dismissal is the sanction employed by the owners (directly or through a takeover) against the management. No rational owner would dissolve an efficient enterprise – neither the Soviet government nor a capitalist firm.

31 This discussion deals with the demand for resources that is derived from the directive of fulfilling the enterprise plan. Kornai regards the insatiable demand for inputs as the consequence not merely of plan fulfilment objectives but also of plant patriotism; managers identify with their enterprises and derive utility – prestige and personal satisfaction – from the expansion of their size [Kornai, 1980, pp. 61–4]. They may therefore undertake investment projects that may not be justified by their social benefit. Our analysis here deals only with the motive of plan fulfilment, but the conclusion applies as well to the personal utility motive.

32 It is not unreasonable because, in the absence of markets, the central planners bear the responsibility for the coordination of inter-industry transactions. When machinery output is endangered because of a shortage of steel, the central planners are under intense pressure to find

the steel somehow. Hence their message to the steel producers is 'get the steel out above all'.

33   There are other plan obligations than quantitative targets, of course; quality, size, production cost, spare parts, and so forth. Countless efforts have been made to induce greater managerial emphasis on these obligations, but in the end they have generally been regarded as of lesser importance than the quantitative output target. The persistence of *val* (see above, p. 276) testifies to that fact.

Perhaps some day some economist will invent a way of guiding management to assign appropriate weights to each of the various plan obligations. The long history of unsuccessful efforts to do so, however, gives reason to doubt that it can be done.

34   In the 1960s the development of mathematical modelling and electronic data processing led to a wave of optimism about the possibility of eventually approximating perfect planning. While many improvements have undoubtedly been made, no one anticipates any longer that the imperfections in planning will ever be eliminated. Realistic economic reformers must take imperfect planning as given; the task is to manage the economy as well as possible under that condition.

35   It may be only a tendency and not a necessary outcome. Rostowski and Auerbach have recently found that storming is not practised in the GDR (Rostowski and Auerbach, 1986). They contend that storming can be eliminated even under central planning.

36   *Pravda*, 26 June 1987.

37   A certain proportion of output would be determined by 'state orders', rather than by voluntary contracts. Presumably these would be orders placed by government agencies for such items as military procurement. Fulfilment of those orders would be mandatory.

REFERENCES

Amman, R., Cooper, J. and Davies, R. W. (eds.) (1977), *The Technological Level of Soviet Industry*. New Haven: Yale Univ. Press.

Berliner, Joseph S. (1957), *Factory and Manager in the USSR*, Cambridge: Harvard University Press.

Berliner, Joseph S. (1976), *The Innovation Decision in Soviet Industry*, Cambridge: The MIT Press.

Holzman, Franklyn D. (1955), 'Financing Soviet Economic Development', in Moses Abramovitz (ed.), *Capital Formation and Economic Growth*, Princeton: Princeton University Press, pp. 229–87.

Hunter, Holland (1961), 'Optimal Tautness in Development Planning', *Economic Development and Culture Change*, vol. 9, no. 4, July, pp. 561–72.

Inkeles, Alex and Bauer, Raymond A. (1959), *The Soviet Citizen*, Cambridge: Harvard Univ. Press.

Joint Economic Committee, US Congress (1982), *USSR: Measures of*

Economic Growth and Development, 1950–1980, Washington: GPO, 8 December.

Keren, M., Miller, J. and Thornton, J. R. (1983), 'The Ratchet: A Dynamic Managerial Incentive Model of the Soviet Enterprise', *Journal of Comparative Economics*, vol. 7, no. 4, December, pp. 347–67.

Kornai, Janos (1980), *Economics of Shortage*, Amsterdam: North-Holland.

Linz, Susan, J. (1985), 'Managerial Autonomy in the Soviet Firm', Soviet Interview Project (preliminary draft).

Linz, Susan, J. (1986), 'The Role of Tautness in Soviet Planning', Soviet Interview Project.

Linz, Susan, J. (1987), 'The Treadmill of Soviet Economy Reforms: Management's Perspective', Soviet Interview Project.

Millar, James R. (ed.) (1987), *Politics, Work and Daily Life in the USSR: A Survey of Former Soviet Citizens*. Cambridge, Cambridge Univ. Press.

Rostowski, Jacek and Auerbach, Paul 'Storming Cycles and Economic Systems', *Journal of Comparative Economics*, vol. 10, no. 3, September, pp. 293–312.

Schroeder, Gertrude E. (1979), 'The Soviet Economy on a Treadmill of Reforms', US Congress, Joint Economic Committee, *Soviet Economy in a Time of Change*, Washington: GPO, 10 October, pp 312–40.

Schroeder, Gertrude E. (1985), 'The Slowdown in Soviet Industry, 1976–1982', *Soviet Economy*, vol. I, no. 1, January–March, pp. 42–74.

Acknowledgements

I am grateful to the editors and publishers of the following journals and books for permission to reproduce the articles which appear in this volume: *The American Slavic and East European Review*; John Wiley and Sons, Inc. for material from *The Quarterly Journal of Economics* and *Industrialization in Two Systems: Essays in Honor of Alexander Gerschenkron*; *Administrative Science Quarterly*; Allen and Unwin for material from *The Soviet Economy Toward the Year 2000*; Duke University Press for material from *Frontiers of Development Administration* and *South Atlantic Quarterly*; Cambridge University Press for material from *Economic Welfare and the Economics of Soviet Socialism: Essays in Honor of Abram Bergson*.

JSB

Index